Multi-Cloud Handbook
for Developers

Learn how to design and manage cloud-native applications in
AWS, Azure, GCP, and more

Subash Natarajan

Jeveen Jacob

Multi-Cloud Handbook for Developers

Group Product Manager: Preet Ahuja

Publishing Product Manager: Surbhi Suman

Book Project Manager: Ashwin Kharwa

Senior Editor: Roshan Ravi Kumar

Technical Editor: Arjun Varma

Copy Editor: Safis Editing

Proofreader: Safis Editing

Indexer: Pratik Shirodkar

Production Designer: Gokul Raj S.T

Senior DevRel Marketing Coordinator: Linda Pearlson

DevRel Marketing Coordinator: Rohan Dobhal

First published: February 2024

Production reference: 1160224

Published by
Packt Publishing Ltd.
Grosvenor House
11 St Paul's Square
Birmingham
B3 1RB, UK

ISBN 978-1-80461-870-7

www.packtpub.com

None of my accomplishments would have been possible without my remarkable support system. To my wife, Kavitha, my unwavering pillar of strength, and to my son, Vivan, who selflessly sacrificed our playtimes to help me focus on writing – I owe him a world of thanks. A special note of profound thanks to my mom and dad – your unwavering belief in me and endless encouragement have been the cornerstone of my journey.

To my mentors, colleagues, and friends – thank you for being relentless fountains of inspiration and support.

Additionally, a heartfelt appreciation to the developer and cloud communities for fueling my passion for this book, and to the Packt team for their invaluable assistance and support throughout this process.

– Subash Natarajan

This book is fondly dedicated to my beloved mother, Valsamma, whose love and guidance are my constant light, and to the cherished memory of my father, P O Jacob, whose legacy continues to inspire. To Jeril's family, Sherin and Irene, for their warmth. To my dear wife, Jincy, and our precious daughter, Jenny – your unwavering support and encouragement have been my stronghold throughout this journey. Your sacrifices have not gone unnoticed and have made all of this possible.

Also, I extend my deepest gratitude to my friends, colleagues, the vibrant developer communities, and the dedicated team at the publishing house. Your invaluable support and expert guidance have been pivotal in bringing this work to fruition.

– Jeveen Jacob

Contributors

About the authors

Subash Natarajan is a renowned tech strategist, standing at the forefront of software engineering, advisory, and technical leadership. With a keen focus on system integration, automation, and transformations, he has masterfully steered numerous enterprises through their digital evolution, seamlessly aligning IT frameworks with broad business visions.

Subash's deep insight into digital and emerging tech is reflected in his influential writings, which shed light on digital adoption and the transformative journey of businesses. Celebrated for his innovative tactics in navigating complex tech challenges, Subash's commitment to spreading knowledge and striving for excellence has made him a pivotal figure in the tech landscape.

Jeveen Jacob is a seasoned expert in software and cloud technologies. His career, blossoming from hands-on software development to strategic roles in cloud services, DevSecOps, and site reliability engineering, showcases his adaptability and impact. Jeveen's proficiency lies in tailoring a broad skill set to meet the unique demands of diverse clients, marking him as a versatile and influential professional.

Jeveen's proactive embrace of cloud-native and cutting-edge tech has made him a trailblazer in the field. He is adept at leading organizations to innovative, user-friendly digital solutions, transforming intricate tech into practical tools for business triumph.

About the reviewer

Mario Palma Parra has worked as a cloud architect and in DevOps for over seven years, six years of which were specifically dedicated to working as a cloud trainer. He has performed cloud proposals, architectural designs, documentation, training, migrations, operational definitions, business-specific training, and continuous improvement for cloud and hybrid-related environments for both private companies and government-related entities. He holds several AWS-, Azure-, and DevOps-related certifications. He is currently employed as a senior cloud architect/DevOps engineer for Vodafone Europe.

I'd like to thank my family and friends, especially Arturo Mardones, for believing in me when no one else did. Also, moving from Chile to Portugal was a risk but also something necessary to continue my professional development, and all this would not be possible without the supportive cloud community that has developed over the last several years. Thank you to all the kindred spirits who make this an exciting field to work in each and every day.

Table of Contents

Part 2: Designing and Developing Cloud-Native Applications for Multi-Cloud

3

Designing for Diversity with Multi-Cloud Application Strategies   37

4

Crafting and Deploying in the Multi-Cloud as a Developer   67

Part 3: Managing and Operating Cloud-Native Apps in Multi-Cloud

5

6

7

Troubleshooting Multi-Cloud Applications   139

Part 4: Best Practices, Case Studies, and Future Trends for Multi-Cloud and Cloud-Native

8

9

10

Future-Proofing Your Cloud Computing Skills   213

Preface

Welcome to this comprehensive guide on cloud-native development in multi-cloud environments, a crucial nexus in modern technology. This book is crafted to demystify the complexities and help you leverage the opportunities presented by the multi-cloud and cloud-native paradigms. This book will help cut through the technical jargon and simplify complex concepts, using engaging metaphors to bring clarity to the fast-moving cloud space.

We will start off in understanding the essentials of multi-cloud and cloud-native technologies by breaking them down into simpler terms. From then on, this book will set stage for a deeper dive into the architectural principles of cloud-native applications, highlighting the critical role of microservices, serverless computing, and other foundational concepts. Subsequent chapters guide you through the intricacies of designing, developing, and deploying applications across multiple cloud platforms, emphasizing best practices and modern tooling.

Addressing the core challenges in this domain, the book covers data management, security, compliance, and cost optimization in multi-cloud environments. Furthermore, it equips you with strategies and techniques for troubleshooting, ensuring the resilience and reliability of cloud-native applications.

We will also explore real-life and sample use cases, providing a firsthand perspective on genuine cloud success stories and valuable lessons from diverse industries. The final chapters of the book project into the future, exploring emerging trends and technologies that are set to shape the landscape of cloud computing.

Who this book is for

Targeted at cloud-native developers, platform engineers, and IT specialists, this manual is pivotal for those overseeing cloud-native applications across diverse cloud infrastructures. It's crafted for individuals with foundational cloud knowledge eager to deepen their skills in cloud architecture, development, and operations. The content assumes familiarity with fundamental cloud principles, experience with major cloud services, and proficiency in a programming language, underpinning a practical approach to mastering modern application development within a multi-cloud context.

What this book covers

Chapter 1, Discovering the Multi-Cloud and Cloud-Native Universe, looks into the core concepts of multi-cloud and cloud-native technologies, highlighting their advantages and alerting you to possible hurdles. The chapter will provide a clear overview of how cloud-native and multi-cloud approaches work together, underlining their significance in today's cloud-computing landscape.

Chapter 2, Building the Backbone of Cloud-Native Applications, explores the essential principles and structures that define cloud-native applications. The chapter will also guide you through microservices, serverless frameworks, and the 12-factor app model, ensuring you have a solid foundation for architecting in the cloud.

Chapter 3, Designing for Diversity with Multi-Cloud Application Strategies, helps you tailor your designs for operation across multiple cloud environments. This chapter reveals the secrets behind robust application design that transcends the boundaries of individual clouds.

Chapter 4, Crafting and Deploying in the Multi-Cloud as a Developer, helps you understand the full arc from development to deployment in a multi-cloud context. You'll also gain insights into creating cloud-native applications using infrastructure as code and integrating continuous integration and deployment into your workflow.

Chapter 5, Managing Security, Data, and Compliance on Multi-Cloud, helps you secure your cloud-native applications against the backdrop of varying multi-cloud landscapes. This chapter will empower you with best practices for managing data, enhancing security, and meeting compliance standards.

Chapter 6, Maximizing Value and Minimizing Cost in Multi-Cloud, guides you in understanding the art of cost optimization for cloud-native applications in multi-cloud environments. You will also discover how to apply FinOps principles and right-size your cloud resources without sacrificing efficiency.

Chapter 7, Troubleshooting Multi-Cloud Applications, equips you with strategies and techniques to untangle the complexities of troubleshooting in multi-cloud setups. You will learn how to maintain reliability and resilience with insights into SRE and DevOps best practices.

Chapter 8, Learning from Pioneers and Case Studies, provides lessons from those who've triumphed in the cloud. Through case studies and real-world examples, this chapter shares the successes and strategies of companies that have effectively harnessed the power of multi-cloud and cloud-native technologies. You will gain valuable lessons and proven practices to guide your own cloud journey.

Chapter 9, Bringing Your Cloud-Native Application to Life, dives into the nitty-gritty of cloud-native development with a sample project! You'll learn how to plan, design, implement, and scale a real-world application across different cloud providers. Get ready to roll up your sleeves and put your cloud skills to the test!

Chapter 10, Future-Proofing Your Cloud Computing Skills, explores what's next for multi-cloud and cloud-native applications, including new trends, upcoming technologies, and how AI and other advancements are driving cloud innovation forward.

Starting from a basic-to-intermediate level of understanding, readers can explore and gain insights into the latest and upcoming developments in the world of multi-cloud and cloud-native applications.

To get the most out of this book

You will need to have an understanding of the basic components of a cloud platform and of the IT application development process, administration, support, and monitoring.

Software/hardware covered in the book	Operating system requirements
Node.js v9.8.1	Windows, macOS, or Linux
Docker v24.07	Windows, macOS, or Linux
Terraform v1.6.5	Windows, macOS, or Linux
Jenkins v2.435	Windows, macOS, or Linux
Amazon Web Services (AWS)	Windows, macOS, or Linux
Microsoft Azure	Windows, macOS, or Linux
Google Cloud Platform (GCP)	Windows, macOS, or Linux

Download the example code files

You can download the example code files for this book from GitHub at `https://github.com/PacktPublishing/Multi-Cloud-Handbook-for-Developers`. If there's an update to the code, it will be updated in the GitHub repository.

We also have other code bundles from our rich catalog of books and videos available at `https://github.com/PacktPublishing/`. Check them out!

Conventions used

There are a number of text conventions used throughout this book.

`Code in text`: Indicates code words in text, database table names, folder names, filenames, file extensions, pathnames, dummy URLs, user input, and Twitter handles. Here is an example: "`require('dotenv').config();`: This line loads environment variables from an if `.env` is `process.env`.

A block of code is set as follows:

```
require('dotenv').config();
const port = process.env.PORT || 3000;
```

Bold: Indicates a new term, an important word, or words that you see onscreen. For instance, words in menus or dialog boxes appear in **bold**. Here is an example: "We'll start with **Infrastructure as Code (IaC)**, an approach that allows you to automate the provisioning and management of your cloud resources."

> **Tips or important notes**
> Appear like this.

Get in touch

Feedback from our readers is always welcome.

General feedback: If you have questions about any aspect of this book, email us at `customercare@packtpub.com` and mention the book title in the subject of your message.

Errata: Although we have taken every care to ensure the accuracy of our content, mistakes do happen. If you have found a mistake in this book, we would be grateful if you would report this to us. Please visit `www.packtpub.com/support/errata` and fill in the form.

Piracy: If you come across any illegal copies of our works in any form on the internet, we would be grateful if you would provide us with the location address or website name. Please contact us at `copyright@packt.com` with a link to the material.

If you are interested in becoming an author: If there is a topic that you have expertise in and you are interested in either writing or contributing to a book, please visit `authors.packtpub.com`.

Share Your Thoughts

Once you've read *Multi-Cloud Handbook for Developers*, we'd love to hear your thoughts! Scan the QR code below to go straight to the Amazon review page for this book and share your feedback.

`https://packt.link/r/1-804-61870-5`

Your review is important to us and the tech community and will help us make sure we're delivering excellent quality content.

Download a free PDF copy of this book

Thanks for purchasing this book!

Do you like to read on the go but are unable to carry your print books everywhere?

Is your eBook purchase not compatible with the device of your choice?

Don't worry, now with every Packt book you get a DRM-free PDF version of that book at no cost.

Read anywhere, any place, on any device. Search, copy, and paste code from your favorite technical books directly into your application.

The perks don't stop there, you can get exclusive access to discounts, newsletters, and great free content in your inbox daily

Follow these simple steps to get the benefits:

1. Scan the QR code or visit the link below

https://packt.link/free-ebook/978-1-80461-870-7

2. Submit your proof of purchase

3. That's it! We'll send your free PDF and other benefits to your email directly

Part 1:
Introduction to Multi-Cloud and Cloud-Native

In this foundational part, we explore the essentials of multi-cloud and cloud-native technologies. Here, you'll comprehensively understand the current landscape, including the numerous benefits and challenges these technologies present. This part is designed to provide clarity on what multi-cloud and cloud-native really mean and their significance in today's tech-driven world. Furthermore, it delves into the principles and architecture of cloud-native applications, covering pivotal topics such as microservices, serverless computing, and 12-factor applications. This sets a solid foundation for understanding cloud-native application architecture and design principles, preparing you to harness these technologies effectively.

This part has the following chapters:

- *Chapter 1, Discovering the Multi-Cloud and Cloud-Native Universe*
- *Chapter 2, Building the Backbone of Cloud-Native Applications*

1

Discovering the Multi-Cloud and Cloud-Native Universe

Welcome, fellow developers, to the exciting multi-cloud and cloud-native development world! As you know, the software development landscape is ever-changing, and staying ahead of the curve means embracing the latest trends and technologies. Two significant IT transformations have taken center stage in recent years: multi-cloud and cloud-native development. You must be probably curious about what these buzzwords mean and how they can help you create better, more efficient applications. Well, you're in the right place! As we embark on this journey, we'll stroll down memory lane with the evolution of application development and the pivotal role of cloud computing in ushering in the era of multi-cloud and cloud-native strategies. Then, we'll delve deeper into these concepts, enriching your understanding with real-world examples and addressing common challenges to help you fully grasp their implications on application design and delivery. With this solid foundation, you'll be better equipped to harness the power of multi-cloud and cloud-native technologies to create innovative, efficient, and impactful applications. So, without further ado, let's dive in and uncover the transformative potential of multi-cloud and cloud-native development!

The following topics will be covered in this chapter:

- The evolution of application development
- The rise of cloud computing
- The emergence of multi-cloud and its distinction from hybrid cloud
- The evolution of cloud-native development
- The synergy between cloud-native and multi-cloud
- The cultural shift in development

The evolution of application development

The evolution of application architecture has seen a shift from integrated monolithic structures to the decoupled services of **service-oriented architecture** (**SOA**), leading up to today's microservices and containers. These advancements prioritize flexibility and efficient, independent deployment, reshaping software development in the cloud era. Let's explore each one.

The monolithic era

In the early days of computing, when applications were developed as monolithic architectures, every functionality was bundled together in a single application. The waterfall approach was king, with each development phase (requirements, design, implementation, testing, deployment, and maintenance) occurring sequentially. The advantage of monolithic applications was their simplicity as developers could easily understand the entire application and its dependencies. However, monolithic architectures had significant drawbacks:

- **Limited scalability**: Scaling monolithic applications took time as increasing capacity often required adding hardware or duplicating the entire application stack

- **Rigidity**: Making changes to monolithic applications was time-consuming as any modification required retesting and redeploying the entire application

- **Slow release cycles**: Due to the waterfall approach, it took longer to deliver new features and bug fixes since each development phase had to be completed before the next could begin

To overcome the limitations of monolithic architectures, developers began to adopt SOA in the early 2000s.

The advent of SOA

SOA is an architectural style that structures an application as a collection of loosely coupled, reusable services. These services communicate with each other using standard protocols and can be combined to create composite applications. The key advantages of SOA include the following:

- **Reusability**: Services can be reused across different applications, reducing development time and effort

- **Modularity**: Applications can be broken down into smaller, more manageable components, making it easier to maintain and update individual services

- **Agility**: Changes to one service do not require modifications to other services, allowing for faster release cycles

While SOA helped solve some challenges of Monoliths, it also comes with drawbacks, such as the increased complexity of managing and coordinating multiple services and the overhead introduced by the communication protocols between services.

Microservices and containers

Microservices, an evolution of SOA, are small, independent services that can be developed, deployed, and scaled independently. They communicate with each other via lightweight protocols such as HTTP/REST or message queues. Microservices offer several advantages over monolithic architectures and traditional SOA, including the following:

- **Improved scalability**: Each microservice can be scaled independently, allowing more efficient resource utilization

- **Faster release cycles**: Smaller code bases and independent deployment make delivering new features and bug fixes easier

- **Better fault isolation**: If a microservice fails, it is less likely to impact the entire application, improving overall system resilience

Containers, another key technology in the cloud-native landscape, provide a lightweight, portable way to package and deploy applications and their dependencies. Containers isolate applications from the underlying infrastructure, enabling them to run consistently across different environments. This isolation simplifies deployment and scaling, making containers perfect for microservices-based architectures. We will learn more details about this topic in upcoming chapters.

Figure 1.1 depicts the evolution from **monolithic**, where components are interdependent, to **SOA**, which introduces a service-based structure, and finally to **microservices**, where services are fully independent, embodying cloud-native flexibility and scalability:

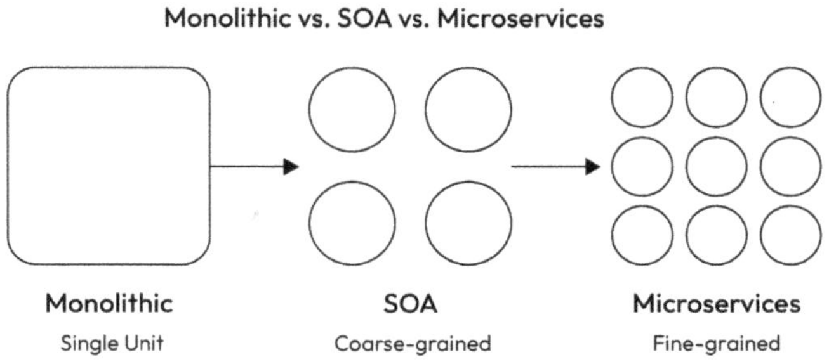

Figure 1.1 – The evolution from monolithic to microservices-based systems

The rise of cloud computing

Lets take a moment to rewind the history of cloud computing, where cloud computing is a narrative of technological progress and conceptual breakthroughs. Time-sharing in the 1960s pioneered the efficient use of computer resources, but the real transformation began with the digital revolution of the 1990s, with the maturity of virtual machines and the early appearance of cloud computing. The internet's proliferation enabled the **application service provider** (**ASP**) model to thrive, offering software solutions remotely. This model matured into **Software-as-a-Service** (**SaaS**), providing software on-demand via the internet, and later in the cloud, erasing the need for local installations. The journey continued with the creation of **Infrastructure-as-a-Service** (**IaaS**) and **Platform-as-a-Service** (**PaaS**), both of which further distanced software developers from the complexities of physical servers.

> **Note**
>
> The ASP model refers to provisioning software solutions via the internet. In this model, software applications are hosted remotely by the provider and made available to customers over a network, typically the internet.

Figure 1.2 represents timeline charts of key milestones in cloud computing's history: from the 1960s' mainframe computing and the 1972 internet emergence to the 1990s' virtual machines by VMware and web services. The 2000s introduced AWS's S3/EC2 services, followed by Google Apps and Microsoft Azure, culminating in the 2010s with the Office 365 SaaS offering and Docker's containerization in 2020:

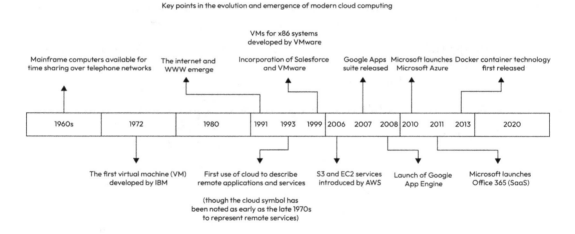

Figure 1.2 – Cloud computing timeline

These cloud-based services provided scalable and elastic infrastructure and development platforms, catalyzing the shift toward more agile, responsive, and cost-effective software development paradigms. This trajectory set the stage for today's cloud-native applications, which are designed from the ground up to harness the distributed, service-oriented nature of the modern cloud.

Cloud computing solutions come tied with new software development practices, paradigms, and cycles. Automated cycles for building, deploying, and testing distributed and modular software have catalyzed the appearance of cloud-based services orbiting each of the software development and deployment phases.

Cloud computing service categories

Upon exploring cloud service models, we find SaaS for software access, PaaS for development platforms, and IaaS for infrastructure. These models form the foundation of cloud computing, addressing diverse digital needs. Let's explore them further:

- **SaaS**: This is a distribution model where applications are hosted by a third-party provider and accessed by customers via the internet. In this model, the service provider takes care of hosting software applications and their corresponding data and ensures optimal execution by providing operating systems and underlying dependencies. Examples include *Salesforce*, *NetSuite*, and *Concur*.

- **PaaS**: This is a model where a third-party provider hosts application development platforms and tools on its infrastructure that can be accessed by customers via the internet. Compared to SaaS models, PaaS providers take less responsibility for software applications but are more committed to serving the operating system and its middleware. Examples include *AWS Elastic Beanstalk*, *Google App Engine*, and *Heroku*.

- **IaaS**: This is a model where a third-party provider hosts servers, storage, and various virtualized computing resources by offering them to customers via the internet. IaaS takes care of less abstract requirements, including networking, data handling, computing power, and ensuring virtualization layers. Examples include *AWS*, *Microsoft Azure*, and *Google Compute Engine*.

Benefits of cloud computing

There are many benefits of cloud computing if it is used right. In general, cloud computing has revolutionized the way we store, access, and process data. It offers a plethora of benefits for individuals and businesses alike, making it a preferred choice for modern computing needs.

The evolution and specialization of cloud computing techniques eventually matured to offer several benefits over traditional on-premises infrastructure, including the following:

- **Scalability**: Cloud services can be easily scaled up or down based on the demand, allowing applications to accommodate fluctuating workloads without overprovisioning resources

- **Cost-effectiveness**: Organizations can pay for only the resources they use, eliminating the need for upfront investments in hardware and software

- **Flexibility**: Cloud providers offer a wide range of services that can be used to build and deploy applications, enabling developers to choose the best tools and platforms for their specific needs

- **Security and Compliance**: Cloud providers often invest heavily in maintaining state-of-the-art security measures and compliance certifications, allowing organizations to leverage these protections for their applications and data

In addition to these advantages, cloud computing has democratized access to cutting-edge technologies such as machine learning, artificial intelligence, and big data analytics. By providing these capabilities as managed services, cloud providers have made it easier for developers to integrate advanced features into their applications, further driving innovation and growth in the software industry.

Consider the case of a start-up who wants to launch a new e-commerce platform. By leveraging cloud computing, the start-up could quickly and cost-effectively build, deploy, and scale its application without significant upfront investments in infrastructure or long-term commitments to a specific technology stack. This ability to rapidly adapt and grow would become invaluable as the business scale and customer needs evolve, demonstrating the power of cloud computing in driving innovation and efficiency in application development.

With such similar cases, cloud computing was bringing undeniable benefits to many businesses, which gave it the momentum to be ever-growing and further specialized to precisely meet evolving business needs. As businesses continued to adopt cloud computing within their operations, new specialized forms of cloud deployment models began to emerge, such as hybrid and multi-cloud deployments. This will be explored in more detail in the next section.

The emergence of multi-cloud and its distinction from hybrid cloud

With businesses increasingly embracing cloud services, they began recognizing the potential benefits of not being tied to a single cloud provider for their diverse application and business needs. This insight led to the emergence of multi-cloud: a strategy that leverages multiple cloud service providers to address the unique requirements of an application or organization. In this section, we'll delve into the factors that inspired developers to adopt multi-cloud strategies, the primary advantages it offers from a developer's standpoint with the support of platform engineers, and the challenges they encounter when implementing a multi-cloud approach. We will also briefly distinguish multi-cloud from the related concept of hybrid cloud.

Multi-cloud versus hybrid cloud

Before diving into multi-cloud details, it is essential to understand the difference between multi-cloud and hybrid cloud since they are related but distinct concepts. Multi-cloud refers to using multiple cloud service providers to fulfill different aspects of an application or organization's needs. In contrast, a hybrid cloud combines different public cloud services with private cloud or on-premises infrastructure. A hybrid cloud enables developers to maintain sensitive data and applications in a private or on-premises environment while leveraging public cloud services' scalability and cost benefits for other workloads.

Though the two concepts differ, some developers may adopt a hybrid multi-cloud strategy for their applications by combining public and private clouds from multiple providers to meet their specific needs and application and business expectations. This approach offers both hybrid and multi-cloud strategy benefits, providing greater flexibility, cost optimization, and risk mitigation.

> **Note**
>
> Throughout this section, we will primarily focus on the multi-cloud concept while ensuring that the information and discussions provided apply to hybrid and multi-cloud cloud models.

- Private cloud (on-premises): A secure, proprietary network or a data center that supplies hosted services to a limited number of people, with certain access and permissions settings
- Public cloud: Computing services offered by third-party providers over the public internet, making them available to anyone who wants to use or purchase them
- Hybrid cloud: An environment that uses a mix of on-premises, private cloud, and public cloud services with orchestration between the two platforms, allowing for greater flexibility and optimization of existing infrastructure
- Multi-cloud: The use of multiple cloud computing services from different providers in a single heterogeneous architecture, to reduce reliance on any single vendor, increase flexibility, and mitigate against disasters

Figure 1.3 delineates the nuances between the following:

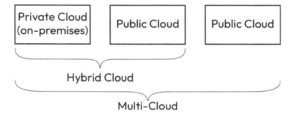

Figure 1.3 – Understanding the different cloud deployment models.

Understanding the significance of multi-cloud

As developers of the different organizations gained experience working with cloud services, they started to see the value of leveraging multiple cloud providers to address their application and business needs. This realization sparked the adoption of multi-cloud strategies, which involve using multiple cloud service providers to achieve a range of objectives.

Several factors contributed to the rise of multi-cloud, including the following:

- **Avoid vendor lock-in**: Developers who rely on a single cloud provider can find it challenging to switch to another provider or adopt new technologies in the future for the application demands. Typically, multi-cloud strategies help developers avoid this lock-in by using a mix of cloud services from different providers, enabling greater flexibility and freedom to innovate.

- **Cost optimization**: Each cloud provider has a pricing model and offers unique services and features. By using multiple cloud providers, developers can optimize costs by choosing the best services for their specific needs and taking advantage of price differences between providers, if this is done correctly.

- **Performance and latency improvements**: Using multiple cloud providers can improve application performance by distributing workloads across data centers and geographical locations, reducing end user latency.

- **Compliance and regulatory requirements**: Developers may need to comply with specific data residency or regulatory requirements that dictate where data can be stored and processed. Multi-cloud strategies enable developers to choose cloud providers that meet these requirements while still benefiting from the advantages of cloud computing.

- **Risk mitigation and business continuity**: Relying on a single cloud provider can pose risks in case of provider-specific outages or service disruptions. Multi-cloud strategies help developers mitigate these risks by distributing workloads across multiple providers, ensuring application resilience.

Challenges of multi-cloud

While implementing a multi-cloud strategy offers numerous advantages, developers, along with platform engineers (who manage the underlying platform for modern applications), must also navigate a unique set of challenges. In this section, we'll discuss some critical hurdles developers may face during multi-cloud implementation and provide insights on overcoming them effectively:

- **Increased complexity**: Managing multiple cloud providers adds complexity to development and operations as developers must deal with different management interfaces, APIs, and service offerings, where still platform engineers play the role of simplifying these complexities.

- **Security and compliance concerns**: Ensuring consistent security and compliance across multiple cloud providers can be challenging as each provider has its security features and configurations.

- **Data management and integration**: Integrating data and applications across multiple cloud providers can be complex, requiring robust data management strategies and tools to ensure data consistency, integrity, and availability.

- **Cost management**: While multi-cloud strategies can optimize costs, they can also make tracking and controlling expenses across different providers and services more difficult. Platform engineers need to implement comprehensive cost management tools and practices to maximize the benefits of their multi-cloud strategy for developers.

As we progress through this book, we'll discuss strategies and best practices from a developer's perspective for overcoming these challenges and successfully implementing a multi-cloud strategy that optimizes cost, performance, and resilience. We'll delve deeper into the principles and architecture of cloud-native applications, explore tools and technologies that facilitate multi-cloud development, and examine real-world examples to help you apply these concepts in your projects.

With a solid multi-cloud and cloud-native development foundation, you'll be well-prepared to tackle the challenges and opportunities of building and deploying modern applications in a multi-cloud world. Stay with us as we explore this exciting new frontier in software development.

Evolution of cloud-native development

The advent of cloud-native technologies marks a paradigm shift in application development and deployment. Embracing cloud-native principles means moving away from monolithic architectures to more dynamic, scalable, and resilient systems. These principles, which are deeply rooted in microservices, containerization, and orchestration, enable applications to leverage the full potential of cloud environments. The automation of development phases is also a central element in cloud-native development. The ability to automate processes in software development, from deployment to testing, is leveraged by modern development teams to increase delivery frequencies. The dynamic management of resource allocation from cloud providers is also essential for establishing a cost-effective cloud-native strategy. Let's have a closer look at these principles.

Figure 1.4 traces the software development evolution: waterfall methods and monolithic structures on physical servers in the 1980s, transitioning to Agile practices with N-tier architectures and virtual servers in the 1990s. The 2000s integrated DevOps with microservices and containers, leading to today's cloud-based infrastructures:

	Development Process	Application Architecture	Deployment & Packaging	Application Infrastructure
-1980 -1990	Waterfall	Monolithic	Physical Server	Data Center
-2000	Agile	N-Tier	Virtual Servers	Hosted
-2010	DevOps	Microservies	Containers	Cloud

Figure 1.4 – The evolution of the application development process

As we discussed earlier, microservices architecture, a cornerstone of cloud-native design, allows for the development of applications as a suite of small, independently deployable services. This approach contrasts sharply with traditional monolithic architectures, where applications are developed as a single, indivisible unit. Microservices offer increased modularity, making applications easier to develop, test, deploy, and scale.

Containerization further revolutionizes deployment. Containers package an application with all its dependencies, ensuring consistency across environments from development to production. This encapsulation aligns perfectly with the cloud-native ethos of building applications that are environment-agnostic.

Orchestration tools such as Kubernetes play a pivotal role in managing these containerized applications and automating deployment, scaling, and operations. This ensures that applications can seamlessly scale to meet demand, maintain high availability, and recover from failures more efficiently.

The shift to cloud-native is not just technical; it also represents a cultural change within organizations. Embracing cloud-native principles often requires adopting new methodologies such as Agile and DevOps, fostering a culture of **continuous integration and continuous delivery** (**CI/CD**), where small, frequent updates are the norm. These principles also lay the groundwork for automating software processes.

Cloud-native would not be a complete strategy if it was not cost-effective. Dynamic management and the ability to allocate resources on the fly are crucial for making cloud-native a profitable solution. Platform engineers should ensure that resources are allocated dynamically in response to fluctuating demand, avoiding unnecessary costs of overprovisioning.

Remember, whatever we have mentioned so far is just the tip of the iceberg to give you a holistic idea and to get you prepared for the journey ahead. So, stay tuned – we will discuss this topic in more detail in upcoming chapters.

The cloud-native advantage

Adopting cloud-native development provides a range of compelling benefits that drive modern developers to embrace this approach. These advantages include the following:

- **Improved agility**: Cloud-native applications can be developed and deployed more quickly, allowing organizations to respond rapidly to changing market demands and continuously deliver value to their customers. This is partly due to CI/CD pipelines, which automate application building, testing, and deployment, ensuring rapid and reliable releases.

- **Enhanced scalability**: Applications designed for the cloud can quickly scale to accommodate fluctuating workloads, ensuring optimal resource utilization and maintaining consistent performance even under heavy loads.

- **Greater resilience**: Cloud-native applications are built to be fault-tolerant, reducing the impact of infrastructure failures on application performance and enabling the system to recover quickly from unexpected events.

Overcoming cloud-native challenges

Despite the undeniable advantages of cloud-native development, developers may encounter challenges as they transition to this new paradigm. Some of the most common challenges include the following:

- **Increased complexity**: Managing distributed systems in a cloud-native environment can be more complex than traditional monolithic or service-oriented architectures, requiring developers to adopt new tools, techniques, and best practices

- **New skills and expertise**: To fully embrace cloud-native development, developers must acquire new skills and expertise in cloud-native technologies, such as container orchestration, microservices patterns, and serverless computing

Let's take a use case. It could be a start-up or enterprise that is planning to transition from a traditional application architecture to a cloud-native approach. By embracing cloud-native development, we can quickly iterate and deploy new features to meet its ever-growing user base's changing needs. Moreover, it can ensure that its infrastructure can scale to handle the demands of millions of users worldwide while maintaining excellent performance and reliability. But to achieve this, they must tackle some complex challenges, as mentioned previously, and have the right skills. Without these, the world of cloud-native technology might feel too complicated

As we move through this journey together, we will share tips, best practices, and hands-on examples to help you build the necessary skills and knowledge to excel in cloud-native development and confidently navigate its challenges.

When cloud-native meets multi-cloud

At this juncture, you should have acquired some basics and gained clarity on why multi-cloud and cloud-native development are two key approaches that, when combined, empower developers to make the most of their strengths. By skillfully merging the benefits of cloud-native technologies with the adaptability of a multi-cloud strategy, developers can create strong, scalable, and innovative applications that effectively meet the ever-changing needs of users and businesses.

The synergy between cloud-native and multi-cloud

It is important to understand that when cloud-native development and multi-cloud strategies are thoughtfully integrated, they complement each other to offer a wide range of benefits. Let's see how:

- **Enhanced adaptability**: A multi-cloud approach allows developers to select and combine services from different cloud providers, enabling them to adapt to changing requirements or embrace emerging technologies. Cloud-native development practices empower developers to rapidly build and deploy new features, further increasing this adaptability.

- **Robustness and high availability**: Merging the inherent fault tolerance of cloud-native applications with the redundancy offered by a multi-cloud strategy results in applications that can recover from failures quickly and maintain high availability across multiple cloud providers.

- **Streamlined performance**: Developers can distribute workloads across various cloud providers and choose the best services for each part of their application, leading to seamless performance and efficient resource utilization.

- **Cost efficiency**: Leveraging a multi-cloud approach allows developers to capitalize on the most cost-effective services from different providers. In conjunction with cloud-native development practices, this can lead to significant cost savings by optimizing resource usage.

- **Independence from vendors**: Adopting a multi-cloud strategy enables developers to minimize dependence on a single cloud provider, allowing them to switch providers or utilize new services without affecting their cloud-native applications.

As illustrated in the following figure, the synergy between cloud-native and multi-cloud emphasizes the importance of integrating these two paradigms in today's application development landscape.

By adopting cloud-native principles, developers can create applications that are inherently scalable and resilient. Simultaneously, utilizing multi-cloud strategies allows them to leverage the best services and features from multiple cloud providers. This approach fosters greater flexibility and innovation, ultimately leading to the development of more efficient, reliable, and adaptable applications.

Figure 1.5 illustrates the progression of multi-cloud and cloud-native applications: starting with cloud adoption through data centers and virtual machines, evolving to cloud automation and culture transformation with DevOps, to accelerating digital projects with cloud-native apps, and finally to achieving enterprise transformation with multi-cloud native apps for optimal efficiency and scale:

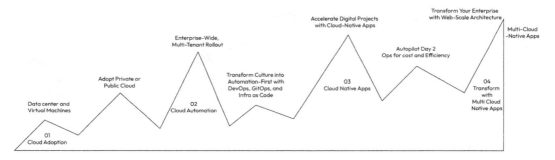

Figure 1.5 – The synergy and journey of multi-cloud and cloud-native applications

Overcoming challenges

While the integration of cloud-native development and multi-cloud strategies offers numerous benefits, it also introduces some challenges. In this section, we'll discuss common challenges developers might face and suggest approaches to overcoming them.

Managing complexity

The nature of cloud-native and multi-cloud strategies combination can organically lead to increased complexity as developers have been tasked to understand handled multiple services, cloud providers, and distributed systems. To overcome this challenge, here are some basic tips to consider:

- Tools such as Kubernetes, Terraform, and Ansible, which can help manage and automate the deployment, scaling, and monitoring of your applications across multiple clouds

- Centralizing logs and metrics from various cloud providers, which can provide better visibility into your applications' performance and simplify troubleshooting

Ensuring security and compliance

Security and compliance are critical aspects of any application, and multi-cloud environments can introduce additional risks. To mitigate these risks, do the following:

- Implement consistent security policies and controls across all cloud providers, ensuring that access controls, encryption, and other security measures are uniformly applied

- Regularly audit your multi-cloud environment to identify potential vulnerabilities and maintain compliance with relevant regulations

Managing costs

While a multi-cloud strategy can lead to cost savings, it may also increase the complexity of cost management. To effectively manage costs, do the following:

- Monitor and analyze resource usage across different cloud providers to identify inefficiencies and optimize resource allocation

- Leverage cost management tools to track spending and set budgets or alerts based on your organization's requirements

Acquiring and developing skills

Mastering cloud-native development and multi-cloud strategies requires developers to acquire new skills and knowledge. To address this challenge, do the following:

- Invest in training and certification programs to help developers acquire the necessary skills to work with cloud providers and cloud-native technologies

- Encourage knowledge sharing and collaboration among team members, fostering a culture of continuous learning and improvement

By addressing these challenges head-on, developers can fully harness the power of cloud-native development and multi-cloud strategies, unlocking their potential to build innovative, efficient, and resilient applications.

Moreover, the advent of cloud computing also fostered the rise of DevOps practices, emphasizing collaboration between development and operations teams to ensure faster, more reliable software delivery. By automating processes such as testing, deployment, and monitoring, cloud platforms enable teams to work more efficiently and reduce the risk of errors, further accelerating the pace of innovation in application development. We will cover the role of DevOps and platform engineering at the end of this chapter, so stay tuned.

The cultural shift in development

As we come to the end of this chapter, It is important to state that the evolution to cloud-native development is a testament to a profound shift in the cultural landscape of software development. For developers, this shift is not just about adopting new technologies; it's about embracing a fundamental transformation in how development teams operate and interact. Historically, development followed a project-based approach, characterized by distinct phases and a hand-off mentality. Teams would work in silos, focusing solely on their part of the project, often in a linear and compartmentalized fashion. This traditional model, while structured, proved inflexible and often misaligned with the dynamic nature of user needs and market demands.

The advent of cloud-native development has ushered in an era of product-centric thinking. In this paradigm, teams are not just builders but also custodians of the product throughout its life cycle. This holistic approach fosters a continuous development cycle, embedding feedback loops that resonate closely with user needs and business objectives. It's a transformative mindset that shifts the focus from merely creating software to nurturing and evolving it in sync with the ever-changing technology landscape and user expectations.

In the traditional waterfall development cycles, rigidity and hierarchy were the norms. Departments with specialized roles operated within strict boundaries, adhering to a linear development trajectory. However, cloud-native development breaks these barriers. It leverages the strengths of cloud providers, not only in terms of robust infrastructure but also through advanced technology stacks and development tools. This synergy gives rise to a novel paradigm, one that demands a reconfiguration of traditional business structures. As companies migrate to the cloud, they encounter structural shifts, necessitating a reorientation of departments and development workflows. This digital transformation calls for readiness at all organizational levels to embrace changes in roles, responsibilities, and methodologies.

In the cloud-native culture, agility and resilience take center stage. Developers, no longer confined to narrow roles, embrace comprehensive practices such as the Agile methodology and DevOps. These approaches enhance collaboration and streamline processes, ensuring that teams can respond swiftly and effectively to changes. Automation and CI/CD pipelines become critical, not just for efficiency but also for the reliability and predictability they bring to application deployment. This culture prioritizes customer-centric design, urging developers to deeply understand user experiences and craft solutions that are not just functional but also intuitive and engaging.

In a nutshell, transitioning to cloud-native is an intricate dance of adopting cutting-edge technologies and nurturing a mindset that champions adaptability, customer focus, and perpetual evolution. This cultural metamorphosis is crucial for organizations aiming to maintain their competitive edge in the fast-paced digital arena. As we delve deeper into the nuances of cloud-native development, particularly the roles of DevOps and platform engineering in multi-cloud environments, it will make these statement clear that this shift is not just a trend but a fundamental redefinition of how software is developed, deployed, and sustained. With that said, let's have a high-level view of how these cultural transformations align with today's internal team hierarchies. This is one example where each individual team fits in the pyramid structure

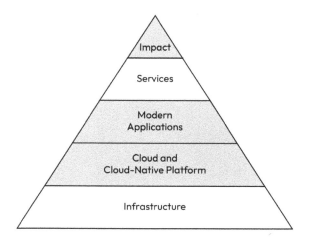

Figure 1.6 – Cloud-Native Value Pyramid

With this, we have come to the end of the chapter.

Summary

In this chapter, we've established a solid foundation for understanding multi-cloud and cloud-native development. To recap, we started with the essentials the evolution of cloud computing and its expansion into hybrid and multi-cloud environments, examining their advantages and challenges. We then learned how cloud-native development synergizes with multi-cloud strategies and the hurdles developers face in adopting these advanced methodologies. Lastly, we emphasized the importance of cultural and mindset shifts in this rapidly changing domain.

As we close this chapter, we have set the stage for a deeper exploration of the principles and architecture of cloud-native applications in *Chapter 2, Building the Backbone of Cloud-Native Applications*. Our journey will take us through the intricacies of designing, developing, and deploying cloud-native applications in multi-cloud environments, enriched by real-world examples, best practices, and practical exercises.

Together, we will navigate the exciting landscape of multi-cloud and cloud-native development, empowering you with the skills and knowledge necessary to confidently create and manage cutting-edge applications in a multi-cloud world. Let's continue this enlightening journey and unlock the full potential of multi-cloud and cloud-native development for developers like you.

2

Building the Backbone of Cloud-Native Applications

Welcome back! Step into the second chapter of our multi-cloud and cloud-native journey. We roll up our sleeves and get our hands on the principles and architectural nuances that underpin cloud-native applications. In this chapter, we will pull back the curtain of cloud-native principles and architecture to the thrilling world of **cloud-native application**. Over this chapter, we are going to use different metaphors to make this journey a fun ride; stay tuned!

The following topics will be covered in this chapter:

- The cloud-native stack
- Principles of cloud-native architecture
- Microservices architecture
- Cloud-native application architecture

The cloud-native stack

Before we get into cloud-native application architecture and practical examples, it is important to understand the cloud-native stack – an architecture that's become essential in the development and operation of modern applications. It's built upon the principles of the cloud, which prioritize flexibility, automation, and scalability. At its base, this stack incorporates the fundamentals – computing resources (compute, storage, and network) – optimized for cloud environments:

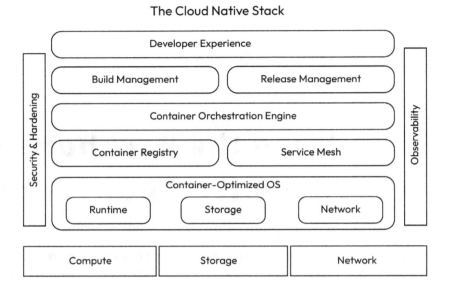

Figure 2.1 – Cloud-native stack

From the preceding diagram, imagine the cloud-native stack as a four-tiered cake, each layer playing a crucial role in crafting resilient applications. Let's peel down from the top of the stack:

1. **Developer experience**: On the top lies the developer experience layer, a smorgasbord of tools designed to accelerate application construction and testing. Here, container registries such as **Docker Hub** house pre-built containerized components, ready to be assembled into your masterpiece. **CI** and **continuous delivery** (**CD**) pipelines automate the build and deployment process, ensuring seamless transitions from code to running application. Container orchestration engines such as **Kubernetes** orchestrate the deployment and management of your containerized troops, taking the burden off your shoulders.

2. **The orchestration engine and runtime**: Now, we descend to the heart of the stack: the container orchestration engine and runtime. Think of it as a skilled conductor, overseeing the performance of your microservices (independent, containerized application components). Typically having a container runtime, the familiar and most preferred orchestrator Kubernetes takes care of scheduling, scaling, and healing your containers, ensuring smooth operation and optimal resource utilization. The orchestration layer is responsible for managing the life cycle of containerized applications, along with security and handling services with the help of a service mesh (for example, Istio).

3. **Infrastructure – compute, storage, and network**: Finally, the foundation of the stack rests on the physical infrastructure: the compute, storage, and network resources. These can be either managed by a cloud provider such as **Amazon Web Services** (**AWS**) or **Google Cloud Platform** (**GCP**) or maintained on-premises, offering flexibility to suit your needs.

Remember – the cloud-native stack is a vibrant ecosystem, constantly evolving with new technologies and best practices emerging on the horizon. Embracing this dynamic paradigm and staying abreast of advancements will empower you to build ever-more agile, scalable, and resilient applications, solidifying your competitive edge in the ever-changing cloud landscape.

Principles of cloud-native architecture

Building a cloud-native application is more than just ticking boxes and moving operations to the cloud. It's about imbibing a new mindset and understanding the unique principles influencing how applications are designed, developed, deployed, and maintained in the cloud environment. Let's take a stroll through these principles.

The Twelve-Factor App – a quick walk-through

The **Twelve-Factor App** is a term you have encountered frequently in cloud-native circles. No – it's not some mysterious secret society but a collection of 12 principles (hence the name) that guide the development of modern and scalable applications. These principles were first laid down by developers at Heroku, who drew on their experiences building applications on the cloud. These days, there are discussions about 15 factors as well, but we will focus on 12 factors in this chapter to keep the standard practice.

> **Note**
>
> You can refer to the following link to learn more about 15-factor applications: `https://developer.ibm.com/articles/15-factor-applications/`.

Figure 2.2 presents the flow of 12 factors in a microservices architecture:

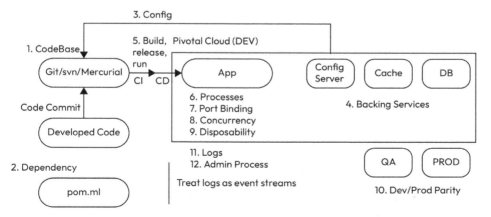

Figure 2.2 – Flow of 12 factors in action

Understanding these principles is akin to having a reliable compass in our cloud-native journey. They ensure we're heading in the right direction as we build our applications. Let's briefly run through these principles with a Node.js application that can be found at `https://github.com/PacktPublishing/Multi-Cloud-Handbook-for-Developers/tree/main/Chapter-2`:

1. **Code base**: The first factor advocates for one code base tracked in revision control, with many deployments. This factor sets the need for applications' code bases to be hosted on a **version control system** (**VCS**) keeping track of deployments and facilitating collaboration between developers. In our case, the Node.js application is facilitated through a GitHub repository, and the first factor is then respected.

2. **Dependencies**: Dependencies explicitly demand that an application never rely on the implicit existence of system-wide packages. It should declare all dependencies, completely and exactly, via a dependency declaration manifest. This is a departure from the days of sprawling code across various environments, leading to the *"it works on my machine"* phenomenon. It's about ensuring that the code base remains singular but deployable across stages, from development to production.

   From the Node.js example, it is evident that the application can load environment variables, which can vary between deployments:

   ```
   require('dotenv').config();
   ```

3. **Configuration**: Pushes for the separation of config from code, arguing that configurations driving different deployments should not be baked into the application. Unlike monolithic architectures that might integrate settings directly into code, cloud-native apps externalize configuration, often through environment variables, enabling seamless transitions between environments without code changes. This factor dictates that external dependencies should also be **application programming interfaces** (**APIs**), databases, and so on.

   In the following Node.js example, the snippet shows code configured and packed to ease software releases, including networking or routing, and communicating with external or third-party servers:

   ```
   require('dotenv').config();

   const port = process.env.PORT || 3000;
   ```

   Here, the following takes place:

   - `require('dotenv').config();`: This line loads environment variables from a `.env` file into `process.env`
   - `const port = process.env.PORT || 3000`: The application port is set from an environment variable, providing flexibility for different environments

4. **Backing services**: These are attached resources needed by software for improved functioning. Backing services are external to the application and can often be provided by a third party. The software might then use dedicated channels to communicate with these services, often requiring credentials or additional parameters, whose configuration should remain external to the application. As a result, software becomes loosely coupled from its backing services, offering modularity and easier deployment.

    A great example is the Node.js application, which treats the backing services as attached resources, meaning they can be attached and detached by the environment. In case of failure, you as developers might need to change the binding to an active backing service, only by modifying an external configuration file or environment variable:

    ```
    const mongoose = require('mongoose');
    const dbUrl = process.env.DATABASE_URL;
    mongoose.connect(dbUrl, { useNewUrlParser: true,
    useUnifiedTopology: true })
    ```

    In this example, we can observe that MongoDB is the backing service and the connection URL is stored in an environment variable. To change the database, you will need to simply modify the environment variable without code intervention.

5. **Build, release, run**: Strictly separates build and run stages, advocating for immutable build releases that transition to the run stage without further modification. This contrasts with traditional approaches where the application may be modified between the build and deploy stages, leading to unpredictable results.

    The three stages of the application life cycle – *build*, *release*, and *run* – are strictly separated. In our Node.js application, this is evident from the use of a dedicated Jenkins file to establish a pipeline for application delivery, which in this case includes three stages: building, testing, and deploying:

    ```
    stages {
        stage('Build') {
            steps {
                sh '''docker build -t my-node-app .
                docker tag my-node-app jeveenj/my-node-app
                docker push jeveenj/my-node-app
                '''
            }
        }
        stage('Test') {
            steps {
                sh 'docker run --rm my-node-app npm test'
            }
        }
        stage('Deploy') {
    ```

```
steps {
    sh 'kubectl apply -f deployment.yaml'
  }
 }
}
```

6. **Processes**: Encourages execution of the app as one or more stateless processes with data persistence managed by a backing service. This is a shift from monolithic apps that might manage state internally, leading to scaling challenges and potential for failures. The Node.js application executes as a stateless process, meaning it maintains no persistent state and can be restarted without affecting data integrity. This is achieved by the use of asynchronous request handling and the process isolation of the `child_process` module that starts a separate admin process:

```
const adminProcess = require('child_process').spawn('node',
['admin.js']);
```

7. **Port binding**: Enables services to be exposed through port binding, which is often managed by the execution environment in cloud-native deployments, as opposed to being embedded within servers.

    The Node.js application is self-contained and does not rely on the runtime injection of a web server. This is demonstrated by the explicit binding of the port using the following lines of code:

```
const port = process.env.PORT || 3000;
app.listen(port, () => {
console.log(`Server listening on port ${port}`);});
```

    In this example, the application is binding to a port number stored in the environment variable or to the default port, 3000. This allows the port to be assigned dynamically by the environment, crucial for deploying applications in a cloud environment, where we usually do not choose which ports to use.

8. **Concurrency**: Scales out via the process model. In a monolithic world, scaling often means running multiple copies of the application on larger hardware. Cloud-native principles advocate for scaling individual components of the app independently. The Node.js application scales out across processes, not threads. This is achieved by the use of multiple instances of the Node.js process running in different containers, as defined by the Dockerfile, which will allow flexible scalability.

9. **Disposability**: Promotes fast startup and graceful shutdown, which is crucial for cloud-native applications that must be resilient and maintainable under the orchestration of platforms such as Kubernetes, contrary to traditional apps, which may not be designed for such rapid cycling.

10. **Dev/Prod parity**: Aim for as close a resemblance as possible between development and production environments, minimizing the time and personnel gaps between code commit and deployment. In the Node.js application, this is achieved by the Dockerfile, which will

represent a packed and portable environment ready to be duplicated. This will ensure that the environment is identical across development phases.

11. **Logs**: Treat logs as event streams; cloud-native applications are often designed to emit logs in a format that can be easily consumed and analyzed by external systems. In the following example, a middleware function logs the HTTP method and URL of each incoming request, demonstrating basic logging functionality:

```
// Basic logging middleware
app.use((req, res, next) => {
  console.log(`Incoming request: ${req.method} ${req.url}`);
  next();
});
```

12. **Admin processes**: Run admin/management tasks as one-off processes, ensuring that these tasks are carried out in an environment similar to the regular long-running application.

    In the Node.js application, the `/restart` admin route sends a request to the admin process to restart the application.

Imagine your application as a concert. In that case, the Twelve-Factor App methodology ensures that every instrument (or factor) plays its part correctly, creating a harmonious symphony pleasing to the ears (or, in our case, the users). Through these principles, the Twelve-Factor methodology lays the groundwork for applications that can leverage the full spectrum of cloud-native capabilities–microservices, APIs, and service discovery–each becoming cogs in a much larger, distributed, and resilient machinery. Microservices architecture breaks down complex applications into smaller, independently deployable services, each scoped around a specific business function. This granularity is the antithesis of monolithic design, reducing interdependencies and improving fault isolation.

Next, we will learn about microservices architecture, another significant principle in cloud-native architecture.

Microservices architecture

Before we dive further, let's take a look at the difference between traditional and cloud-native architecture:

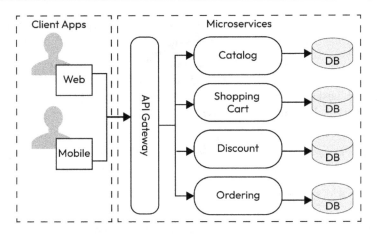

Figure 2.3 – Microservices architecture

Typically, cloud-native architectures help to reduce the amount of non-functional code in our applications. In traditional applications, a lot of code is needed to handle non-functional issues, such as scalability, reliability, and security. In a cloud-native architecture, this code can be stripped out and incorporated into cloud-native infrastructure, products, and technologies. This allows developers to focus more on business code and less on non-functional concerns. As we move further, one term that frequently pops up is **microservices**. It's easy to think of microservices as simply breaking down an extensive application into smaller parts, but it's more than that.

Imagine having a giant, complex Lego structure. It's beautiful and impressive, but it's also delicate. One wrong move could send it crashing down. Imagine having the same structure, but each section is independently built and linked to the others. It's still the same structure, but now it's more resilient and easier to understand, modify, and maintain.

That's what microservices architecture does to your application. It breaks it down into a collection of loosely coupled services, each performing a specific function. These services can be developed, deployed, and scaled independently, providing flexibility and resilience.

But here's where the magic of microservices truly shines. These individual services can communicate and collaborate with each other to perform complex tasks, just like a well-coordinated team. It's like having a group of expert musicians, each playing their own instrument, but together, they create a beautiful symphony.

This architecture is a crucial pillar of cloud-native applications, enabling rapid, frequent updates and facilitating scalability and resilience. But, as you'll see in the following few sections, it works in collaboration. Other principles, such as statelessness, immutability, and service discovery, all work in harmony with microservices to create applications that truly leverage the power of the cloud.

Statelessness and immutability

When building cloud-native applications, two absolute game-changer principles are statelessness and immutability. These two principles, akin to superheroes, ensure that our applications can scale effortlessly, recover from failures rapidly, and provide consistent, reliable service. But what exactly are they?

Statelessness, in the simplest terms, means that your application does not store any client-specific data from one session to the next. Think of it as conversing with someone without memory of your previous interactions. Every interaction is fresh and does not rely on the past. In technical terms, each request to your application should be independent of others.

Why is this so beneficial in a cloud-native world? Well, statelessness makes your application incredibly flexible. Since no session data is stored, any instance of your application can handle any request. This makes it easy to scale your application by simply adding more instances. Also, if an instance fails, others can easily pick up the slack without disruption.

But that's not all. Statelessness also simplifies your application architecture by removing the need for session management, making your application easier to maintain and update.

Let's shift our focus to the second superhero in this narrative – **immutability**. In a world where change is constant, immutability is counterintuitive. It refers to the concept that an entity cannot be changed once it is created.

If statelessness is about not storing data, immutability is not changing data. Once a deployment artifact (such as a Docker container or a compiled Java `.jar` file) is created, it does not change. Instead, new versions of the artifact are created for every change.

Now, why would we want something that does not change? Isn't change a good thing? Yes – change is good, but predictability and reliability are better. Immutable artifacts are predictable because their behavior never changes. They're reliable because you can test them thoroughly before deployment.

Together, statelessness and immutability create an environment where your application can perform consistently and reliably, scale effortlessly, and recover rapidly from failures. But, as powerful as they are, they work with others. They collaborate with other principles such as APIs and service discovery, which we'll explore next.

APIs and service discovery

To make it more interesting, let us go with a metaphor to help understand the topic better. Imagine you're in a large city for the first time, trying to find a specific restaurant. You have the address, but the city is a maze of streets, and you need help. What if you had a local guide who knows the city inside out and can take you directly to the restaurant? Wouldn't that be easier?

That's what APIs and service discovery do in the world of cloud-native applications. With the microservices architecture, your application is a collection of loosely coupled services, each doing its own thing.

APIs act as the interface through which these services communicate with each other and the outside world. They define how other services or users can request information or operations from a service.

Service discovery, on the other hand, is the local guide in our analogy. Keeping track of all services can be daunting in a dynamic environment such as the cloud, where services can be added or removed at any moment. That's where service discovery comes in. It maintains a record of all services, locations, and availability, allowing services to find and communicate with each other. Consider the following example:

```
const express = require('express');
const bodyParser = require('body-parser');
const mongoose = require('mongoose');
const services = require('./models/service');

const app = express();
app.use(bodyParser.json());

// Connect to MongoDB
mongoose.connect('mongodb://localhost/service-registry', {
useNewUrlParser: true });

// Routes for service registration and discovery
app.post('/register', async (req, res) => {
  const service = new services(req.body);
  await service.save();
  res.json({ message: 'Service registered successfully' });
});

app.get('/services', async (req, res) => {
  const services = await services.find();
  res.json(services);
});

// Start the server
app.listen(3000, () => {
  console.log('Service Registry listening on port 3000');
});
```

In this example, we can observe that our application has a library of services; that is, the service discovery. Following this logic, all the services that our application might use are stored in one library. In this case, services are registered with a name, URL, endpoints, and authorization parameters. Only registered services can be used within the application. If a developer needs to add a new service, they can append it to the library without the need to modify the code.

These two aspects are crucial in ensuring your cloud-native applications' smooth operation and scalability. Without them, managing a microservices-based application would be like navigating a bustling city without a map or a guide.

Next, we'll delve into the principles of scalability and elasticity and how cloud-native apps respond to demand. Stick around as we continue our exploration of the underpinnings of cloud-native applications.

Scalability and elasticity

Imagine hosting a party. Initially, only a few guests arrive, and it's manageable. But as the night goes on, more and more people turn up. Suddenly, you find yourself overwhelmed, scrambling to keep up with the demand for food, drinks, and space. What if you could magically increase the size of your house, the amount of food, and the number of servings in response to the increasing number of guests and then scale it all back down once the guests leave? Sounds convenient, right?

Scalability and elasticity in cloud-native applications offer similar convenience. **Scalability** refers to an application's ability to handle an increasing amount of load by adjusting the amount of resources it uses. On the other hand, **elasticity** is the ability to do so quickly and automatically in response to dynamic workload changes.

Why are these concepts crucial in cloud-native environments? In the cloud, traffic patterns can be highly variable. You could have a few users one minute and a few thousand the next. If your application can't scale, it won't be able to handle the load, leading to poor performance or even complete failure.

Cloud-native applications can handle these traffic surges smoothly by being scalable and elastic. When the load increases, they can automatically spin up more instances to handle the load and then spin them down once the surge is over. It's like having a magical house that grows and shrinks based on the number of guests.

However, managing this increase has its challenges. As we scale, we also need to ensure that our application remains resilient and can handle failures gracefully, which brings us to the following principle.

Resilience and fault tolerance

"*Perfection is a myth*," especially in the chaotic world of technology. Yes – servers crash, networks buckle, and glitches surface out of nowhere. It's not about *if* these events occur but rather *when* they strike.

In such an environment, resilience and **fault tolerance** (**FT**) are desirable and essential qualities. A resilient application can cope with failures and continue to function, while a fault-tolerant application is designed to prevent service failures in the case of faults or errors.

But how do we achieve this in a cloud-native application? Well, we weave resilience and FT into the very fabric of our application. We design our application assuming that failures will occur, and we plan for them.

This might mean using redundant components so that others can pick up the slack if one fails. It might mean implementing **circuit breakers** (**CBs**) to prevent a failure in one service from cascading to others. It could also mean designing our application to degrade gracefully in the face of failures, offering limited functionality instead of crashing completely.

One crucial aspect of building resilience and FT is continuous testing. We don't just test our application for happy paths but also for potential failures. We deliberately introduce failures into our system to see how it reacts. This practice, known as **chaos engineering** (**CE**), can uncover hidden issues and help us make our applications more resilient.

Last but not least, the heartbeat of cloud-native apps – CI/CD.

Cloud-native application architecture

The following diagram illustrates the architecture of a cloud-native application. As we can observe, the architecture is composed of different microservices, each serving a specific operation in our application. The microservices can then coordinate with each other thanks to an orchestration layer. On the other hand, requests coming from client apps are routed and sent to the specialized microservice thanks to the API gateway.

Microservices, API gateway, and service mesh are essential practices in the cloud-native arena. In this section, we will explore these concepts from an architectural perspective of cloud-native applications:

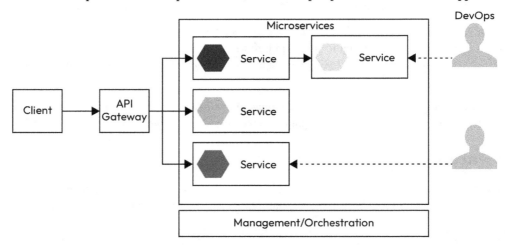

Figure 2.4 – A sample cloud-native architecture

Components of a cloud-native application – the building blocks

First, let's understand the key building blocks of a cloud-native application. Imagine constructing a Lego structure; you wouldn't use one giant piece. Instead, you'd use many smaller blocks, each representing a unique piece of the overall structure. Similarly, cloud-native applications are composed of discrete, modular components. Let us get to understand them one by one.

Microservices, API gateway, and service mesh

The following diagram shows a common architecture for a cloud-native application. In this section, we will take a case study to unveil some essential components of a scalable, flexible, and resilient cloud-native app:

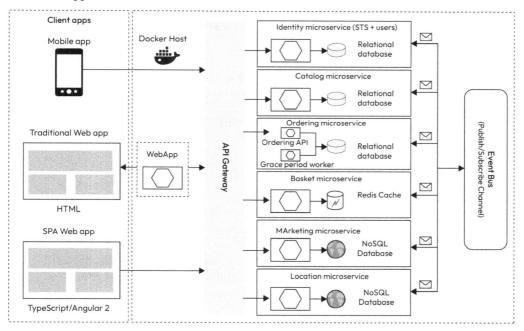

Figure 2.5 – Architecture of a cloud-native application

The three core building blocks of cloud-native applications are *microservices*, *API gateway*, and *service mesh*:

- **Microservices**: This is the equivalent of breaking down your Lego model into individual pieces. Each microservice is a small, independent service that performs a specific functionality. They run in their own process and communicate with lightweight mechanisms, usually an HTTP-based API. This design allows teams to develop, deploy, and scale services independently of one another. This also means that when a part of your application faces an issue, the rest of your services can continue to function without being affected. In the diagram, we can observe that for the e-commerce platform, we will have specialized microservices for each major operation, including managing the catalog, orders, and shopping cart.

- **API gateway:** The API gateway is like the baseplate in a Lego set. It's the foundation that holds all the blocks together. Technically, the API gateway routes requests to the appropriate microservices. It acts as a single entry point into your system, which external clients can access. This pattern can address many concerns such as routing, versioning, rate limiting, access control, and even handling protocol translations. The diagram shows that the API gateway sits between the client applications and the microservices, dispatching requests to the corresponding microservices.

- **Service mesh:** While the API gateway takes care of external requests, the service mesh manages the communication between microservices internally. Imagine it as a communication network between the musicians of our orchestra. A service mesh provides discovery, load balancing, failure recovery, metrics, monitoring, and complex operational requirements such as A/B testing, canary releases, rate limiting, access control, and end-to-end authentication. As illustrated in the diagram, the service mesh allows us to centralize communication between microservices, avoiding direct communication and falling into a classic monolithic architecture.

Event-driven architecture and serverless computing

Two key design patterns that enable cloud-native applications to be responsive, flexible, and scalable are **event-driven architecture (EDA)** and **serverless computing**:

- **EDA:** Think of expanding your Lego model where each piece is designed to respond to specific triggers. Take a Lego car that only begins its journey when you tap a button. This is the spirit of EDA in cloud-native applications. In this framework, services aren't in constant chatter. Rather, they stay on standby, activating only when a certain event signals them to, just like the Lego car that springs to life with a button push. This design ensures that the whole application is more agile and adaptable, offering a clear understanding of its operations at every turn, much like being fully aware of what prompts your Lego car to race ahead.

- **Serverless computing:** Imagine you're ready with a brilliant idea for a Lego set. Instead of manually connecting each piece, envision a scenario where, once your concept is clear, the structure materializes according to your blueprint. This concept mirrors the core of serverless computing in the tech world. Here, developers write their code and deploy it. The cloud provider then steps in, taking over the complex management of infrastructure, paralleling an automated system that assembles your Lego set. This approach allows developers to focus entirely on the creative side of coding their application, reminiscent of concentrating on designing an elaborate Lego masterpiece, while the detailed and labor-intensive construction happens smoothly and invisibly in the background.

Data storage and management in cloud-native applications

Data is the lifeblood of every application, acting as the foundational framework that enables your app to function and deliver value effectively. Similar to how a baseplate in a Lego set secures and aligns every block, data underpins and directs the operations within cloud-native applications. In such environments, applications are typically spread across different settings, necessitating a comprehensive data management strategy to ensure consistency, availability, and durability.

Here are some key data management strategies used in cloud-native applications:

- **Databases**: In the microservices architecture, just as specific Lego blocks are designated for distinct parts of a model, each microservice may have its own database, known as the Database-per-Service pattern. This method allows each microservice to choose a database that best matches its requirements, whether it's a relational database, a NoSQL database, or even a graph database.

- **Data caching**: Consider how certain parts of a Lego set might be the focal points, frequently connected and interacted with. Similarly, applications often need to access specific data repeatedly. Caching is like keeping a Lego piece within easy reach for quick use. By storing copies of frequently accessed data in caches, applications benefit from high-speed data retrieval, enhancing performance and the user experience.

- **Data replication and sharding**: In cloud-native settings, data often spans multiple databases to ensure higher availability and fault tolerance, similar to how a complex Lego structure might extend across several baseplates for added stability and expansiveness. This distribution is managed through techniques such as data replication (involving identical data across multiple databases) and sharding (where different sets of data are distributed across multiple databases). These methods ensure that the data layer remains robust, scalable, and resilient, resembling a well-structured and intricately designed Lego masterpiece.

With this, we have come to the end of the chapter.

Summary

In this chapter, we embarked on an exciting journey through the world of cloud-native applications, using our Lego metaphor to piece together each concept clearly and playfully. We laid the groundwork by introducing key principles such as the Twelve-Factor App methodology, microservices, APIs, and the concept of statelessness, just as you'd start a Lego project by choosing the right base and bricks.

We also navigated through vital features such as scalability, elasticity, resilience, and fault tolerance, understanding how they make cloud-based apps as sturdy and adaptable as a well-designed Lego structure. Our exploration took us deeper into the architecture of cloud-native applications, examining the roles of microservices, API gateways, and service meshes, and appreciating how each part fits together like perfectly interlocking Lego pieces. We didn't shy away from complex topics either, tackling EDA and serverless computing, and adding more unique blocks to our growing Lego masterpiece of cloud-native knowledge.

In our upcoming chapter, we'll dive even deeper into the fascinating world of cloud-native development. We'll explore the intricacies of designing cloud-native applications specifically tailored for multi-cloud environments. So, keep those explorer hats on as we venture further on this captivating journey!

Part 2: Designing and Developing Cloud-Native Applications for Multi-Cloud

This part of the book guides you through the nuanced process of designing and developing cloud-native applications optimized for multi-cloud environments. It starts by introducing you to the core concepts and design principles essential for creating cloud-native applications. You'll learn how to ensure portability and efficiency across different cloud platforms and delve into distributed application design patterns, domain-driven design, and API-first approaches. The chapters also cover practical aspects of development, including using infrastructure as code, continuous integration and deployment, GitOps, and DevOps practices, along with containerization and orchestration techniques using Docker and Kubernetes. By the end of this part, you'll be equipped with a thorough understanding of cloud-native architecture and principles, ready to design and develop applications that thrive in a multi-cloud ecosystem.

This part has the following chapters:

- *Chapter 3, Designing for Diversity with Multi-Cloud Application Strategies*
- *Chapter 4, Crafting and Deploying in the Multi-Cloud as a Developer*

3

Designing for Diversity with Multi-Cloud Application Strategies

Now that we have covered the foundation of cloud-native, let's venture into the heart of designing cloud-native applications for multi-cloud platforms. We commence with the unique considerations and the strategic importance of multi-cloud design. This knowledge forms the basis of understanding **multi-cloud architecture**, an essential pillar for any cloud-native developer. As we navigate through the multi-cloud landscape, we pinpoint the key principles of multi-cloud application design and unravel the art of selecting the right technologies. We emphasize how the right choices can serve as the lifeblood of a successful application. Following this thread, we explore the challenges and strategies in data management across various cloud platforms. By bridging the topic of application deployment and orchestration in multi-cloud, we offer insights into coordinating application components in this complex terrain.

Keeping an eye on our applications, we delve into monitoring and observability, which are vital aspects in maintaining the health of applications in a multi-cloud environment. By shifting our gaze to financial aspects, we shed light on strategies for optimizing costs in multi-cloud, a pivotal consideration for any organization. To reinforce our understanding, we draw from real-world scenarios through insightful case studies and finally distill our learning into a set of practical best practices for multi-cloud application design.

Embark with us on this enlightening journey and harness the potential of multi-cloud environments for your cloud-native applications.

The following topics will be covered in this chapter:

- Cloud-native design patterns
- Designing for multi-cloud

- Role of **Domain-Driven Design** (**DDD**)

- Importance of an API-first approach

- Selecting the right technologies for a cloud-native foundation

- Data management in multi-cloud

- Monitoring and observability in multi-cloud

- Case studies

- Best practices for multi-cloud application design

Cloud-native design patterns

In the architectural tapestry of **cloud-native application development**, design patterns act as the master blueprint. They guide developers through the labyrinth of service interdependencies, data management, and scalability challenges. In this section, we'll delve deep into the realm of cloud-native design patterns, providing you with the requisite understanding and practical insight to create robust and efficient applications. The practical examples used in the explanation can be found in this GitHub repo: `https://github.com/PacktPublishing/Multi-Cloud-Handbook-for-Developers/tree/main/Chapter-3`. Let's understand these design patterns in detail:

- **Microservices architecture**: Let's start with microservices architecture, the linchpin of cloud-native development. Microservices decompose a large application into manageable, independent services, each performing a single business capability, as depicted in *Figure 3.1*. They promote a decentralized approach to software development where teams can work autonomously, selecting the best tools and languages for their specific service. However, remember that with great power comes great responsibility. While the microservices pattern offers flexibility and scalability, it also necessitates intricate service orchestration and demands a robust approach to tackle communication complexities and data consistency challenges.

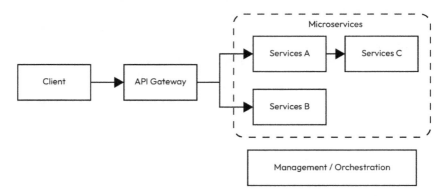

Figure 3.1 – Microservice architecture

Let's consider some of the strengths and weaknesses of microservice architecture:

- **Strengths**:

    - Microservice architecture breaks down applications into smaller, independent components (microservices), each responsible for a specific functionality. This modularity makes it easier to understand, develop, and maintain applications. Teams can focus on building and maintaining the smaller, well-defined parts of the application, leading to increased productivity and faster development cycles. Isolating functionalities within separate microservices also improves code reusability and makes it easier to refactor and improve specific parts without affecting the entire application. Microservices can be deployed independently of each other. This enables **continuous integration and continuous delivery (CI/CD)** practices. Developers can release updates to individual microservices without affecting the entire application, reducing the risk of downtime and allowing for faster release cycles. Independent deployment also enhances fault isolation. If a particular microservice fails, it doesn't necessarily lead to the failure of the entire application.

    - Microservices encourage the use of different technologies, languages, and frameworks within different services. This flexibility allows development teams to choose the best tools for their specific microservices based on their requirements and expertise. It fosters innovation and adaptation, as teams can adopt new technologies without affecting the entire architecture.

- **Weaknesses**:

    - Microservices introduce a distributed architecture where components communicate over networks, leading to increased complexity compared to monolithic architectures. Distributed systems are susceptible to issues such as network latency, communication failures, and partial failures. This complexity can make debugging and troubleshooting more challenging. Ensuring data consistency and maintaining a cohesive user experience across multiple services can be complex and require careful design.

    - As services operate independently, ensuring proper co-ordination between them is crucial to maintaining overall application functionality. Challenges arise when services need to collaborate on complex operations that span multiple microservices. Implementing proper choreography or orchestration can be complex. Achieving data consistency across services becomes more difficult, especially in scenarios where multiple services need to update related data. Techniques such as distributed transactions or eventual consistency must be carefully considered.

- **Example**: An e-commerce application can be broken down into microservices, such as user management, product catalog, shopping cart, and payment processing. In the following example, the **Node.js** service handles user data. It's an example of a microservice responsible for a specific functionality (user management):

```
const express = require('express');
const app = express();
const port = 3000;

app.get('/user/:id', (req, res) => {
  res.json({ userId: req.params.id, name: 'John Doe' });
});

app.listen(port, () => {
  console.log(`User service running on port ${port}`);
});
```

- **Containerization**: Moving on, we find ourselves amidst the containerization pattern. Containers are the lifeboats of the cloud-native sea, providing a consistent and isolated environment for your application to thrive. They encapsulate your application and its dependencies into a standalone executable unit, ensuring the application behaves consistently across various computing environments, as depicted in *Figure 3.2*. However, the caveat lies in managing these containers. Without proper orchestration and monitoring tools, handling a myriad of containers can quickly become a Herculean task.

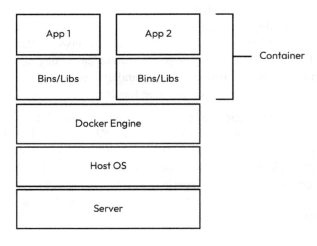

Figure 3.2 – Container architecture

Let's consider some of the strengths and weaknesses of containerization:

- **Strengths**:

  - Containerization ensures that applications run consistently across different environments, ensuring uniformity across teams and environments. Developers can package everything needed to run an application into a container image. Containers encapsulate the application along with its dependencies, libraries, and configurations, ensuring the same behavior from development to testing to production. This consistency improves collaboration between developers, testers, and operations teams, leading to fewer deployment-related surprises.

  - Containers are an ideal match for a microservices architecture, as each microservice can be packaged as an independent container. Teams can develop, test, and deploy microservices independently, enabling faster development cycles and allowing teams to focus on specific functionalities. Containers facilitate distribution development by providing a unified packaging format that can be shared across teams and easily moved between different environments. Containers are lightweight and share the host OS's kernel, reducing overhead compared to virtual machines. Containers start quickly and consume few resources, enabling rapid scaling based on demand. This is especially valuable for applications with varying workloads. The ability to quickly provision and scale containers makes them well-suited for modern, dynamic infrastructures.

- **Weaknesses**:

  - While containers offer numerous benefits, managing them at scale can be complex, especially without proper orchestration tools. Learning and implementing orchestration platforms, such as **Kubernetes**, requires expertise and can be overwhelming for small teams or those new to containerization.

  - While containers provide isolation, they share the host OS kernel. Vulnerabilities in the kernel could potentially affect multiple containers. Proper security practices must be followed, such as regularly updating base images, scanning images for vulnerabilities, and configuring container security settings.

- **Example**: Docker containers running the different services of a microservices-based application orchestrated by Kubernetes. In the example that follows, a Docker file is used for containerizing a Node.js application. This demonstrates how to package a Node.js app with its dependencies in a container:

```
FROM node:14
WORKDIR /app
COPY package.json .
RUN npm install
COPY . .
CMD ["node", "app.js"]
```

- **Event-driven architecture**: This paradigm originates from handling software application events. **Events** are software signals that indicate, for example, the completion of a bank transfer. Events usually finish with a notification given to the end user to inform them that a task was completed or that its processing has started. This makes event-driven architecture asynchronous in nature, and software execution doesn't wait for a task to finish and can perform intermediary tasks (send notification) while the initial task (bank transfer) continues to be executed. This makes event-driven architecture ideal and suitable for distributed cloud-native designs.

In the following diagram, we can observe a classic event-driven architecture, where a producer sends events to consumers who acknowledge the event after processing the corresponding task. Communication between the parties is centralized and dynamically dispatched through an event manager, which forwards events/acknowledgments in either direction:

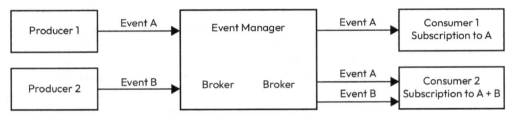

Figure 3.3 – High-level event-driven architecture

Let's consider some of the strengths and weaknesses of event-driven architecture:

- **Strengths**:

  - High responsiveness and flexibility, as services can react to events in real time

  - Supports asynchronous, non-blocking communication

  - Promotes decoupling, as services don't need to be aware of the existence of others

- **Weaknesses**:

  - Event choreography can be complex to handle, especially in larger systems

  - Debugging can be challenging as there is no direct invocation of services

- **Example**: In a banking application, an event can be triggered when a customer makes a transaction. This event can trigger services such as a balance update and a transaction history update. In the example that follows, a simple Node.js application to connect to a RabbitMQ server illustrates how microservices can communicate asynchronously via a message queue:

```
const amqp = require('amqplib/callback_api');

amqp.connect('amqp://localhost', (error0, connection) => {
```

```
  if (error0) throw error0;
  connection.createChannel((error1, channel) => {
    const queue = 'hello';
    channel.assertQueue(queue, { durable: false });
    channel.consume(queue, (msg) => {
      console.log(`Received: ${msg.content.toString()}`);
    }, { noAck: true });
  });
});
```

- **API gateway**: No discussion of cloud-native design patterns would be complete without mentioning the API gateway. By acting as the grand concierge, the API gateway simplifies client interactions by providing a single entry point to your system. While an API gateway can do wonders for request routing and protocol translation, it can quickly become a bottleneck if not managed correctly. *Figure 3.4* illustrates the high-level architecture of an API gateway pattern. It depicts how a client, or a web app interacts with backend services through a centralized API gateway:

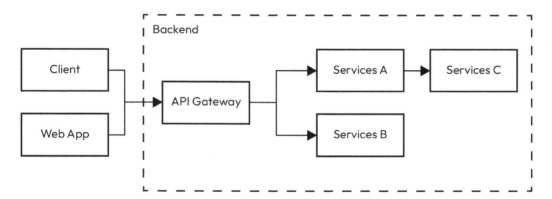

Figure 3.4 – High-level architecture of an API gateway pattern

Let's consider some of the strengths and weaknesses of an API gateway architecture pattern:

- **Strengths**:
  - Simplifies the client interface by aggregating requests to multiple services
  - Centralized management of cross-cutting concerns
  - Enables developers to manage APIs across the life cycle, from creation to deprecation

- **Weaknesses**:
  - It can become a bottleneck if not properly designed and managed
  - Adds an extra network hop, which might slightly affect latency

- **Example**: The Amazon API gateway provides developers with a simple, flexible, fully managed pay-as-you-go service that handles all aspects of creating, deploying, maintaining, monitoring, and securing APIs at any scale. In the following example, a Node.js application acts as an API gateway, routing requests to different microservice endpoints (**/users** and **/orders**), demonstrating the central point of processing API requests:

```
const amqp = require('amqplib/callback_api');

const express = require('express');
const app = express();
const userRouter = require('./userRouter');
const orderRouter = require('./orderRouter');
app.use('/users', userRouter);
app.use('/orders', orderRouter);
app.listen(3000);
```

- **Circuit breaker**: Among the arsenal of design patterns, the circuit breaker pattern stands out for its resilience. The circuit breaker pattern serves to identify failures and contains the logic to avoid repetitive failures during maintenance, temporary external system outages, or unexpected system challenges. It acts as a protective mechanism to handle potential disruptions and ensures smooth operation in the face of adversity.

The circuit breaker will open a failure circuit after a defined threshold of failed attempts has been exceeded. Take a look at the following diagram:

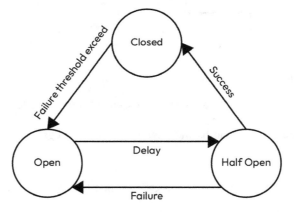

Figure 3.5 – High-level architecture of a circuit breaker pattern

Let's consider some of the strengths and weaknesses of the circuit breaker architecture pattern:

- **Strengths**:

  - Prevents resource overload by excessively trying to connect to a failing service

  - Prevents cascading of failures to other services by isolating the failing service

  - Enables automated recovery of services by gradually checking if a service has recovered

- **Weaknesses**:

  - Designing a successful circuit breaker can be increasingly complex

  - Synchronizing the state of the circuit breaker across different instances of an application can be challenging

- **Example**: If your application relies on third-party APIs, circuit breakers can be extremely helpful in managing API failure. In the example that follows, the circuit breaker pattern is implemented by using the **Opossum** package in Node.js, showcasing a strategy for handling failures in distributed systems:

```
const circuitBreaker = require('opossum');

function asyncFunctionThatCouldFail() {
  return new Promise((resolve, reject) => {
    // simulated function logic
    if (Math.random() > 0.5) resolve('Success!');
    else reject('Failed!');
  });
}

const options = { timeout: 3000, errorThresholdPercentage: 50,
resetTimeout: 30000 };
const breaker = new circuitBreaker(asyncFunctionThatCouldFail,
options);

breaker.fallBack(() => 'Fallback response');
breaker.on('success', (result) => console.log(result));
breaker.fire().catch(console.error);
```

- **Sidecar pattern**: The sidecar pattern stands out for its versatility. In the sidecar pattern, each service instance is paired with a sidecar container that takes over the networking features. It provides platform-agnostic features such as service discovery, dynamic routing, and circuit breaking. *Figure 3.6* depicts the sidecar pattern in containerized applications, where a main container running the primary application is paired with a sidecar container:

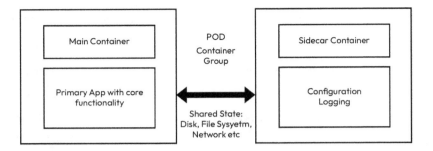

Figure 3.6 – High-level architecture of a sidecar pattern

Let's consider some of the strengths and weaknesses of the sidecar architecture pattern:

- **Strengths**:

  - Enables the separation of responsibilities between application logic and network communication

  - Makes the services portable, as they remain decoupled from the network details

- **Weaknesses**:

  - It can increase complexity as the number of instances increases

  - The sidecar's life cycle needs to be managed alongside the service

- **Example**: Istio's **Envoy** sidecar proxies handle the inbound and outbound network traffic of the service in a Kubernetes Pod.

- **Strangler fig pattern**: The strangler fig pattern, named after the fig tree, which gradually envelops and replaces its host tree, provides a blueprint for incremental system rewriting. In the context of software architecture, the strangler fig pattern works by creating a new system that gradually takes over the functionality of the legacy system. The new system is initially small and simple. However, it gradually expands to replace more and more of the legacy system's functionality. The following figure shows the architecture of the strangler fig pattern:

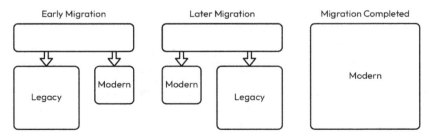

Figure 3.7 – High-level architecture of a strangler fig pattern

Let's consider some of the strengths and weaknesses of the strangler fig architecture pattern:

* **Strengths**:

    * Allows incremental updates and rewrites, minimizing risk

    * Old and new parts can coexist, enabling gradual replacement

* **Weaknesses**:

    * This may lead to a temporary increase in complexity as the old and new parts coexist

    * Requires careful planning to avoid tight coupling between the old and new parts

* **Example**: An e-commerce site transitioning from a monolithic application to microservices could use the strangler fig pattern to gradually replace its inventory management system. While the old system is still in operation, a new service has been built to handle some of the requests. Over time, more and more requests are handled by the new service until the old system can be decommissioned.

* **Saga pattern**: The saga pattern is a sequence of local transactions where each transaction updates the data within a single service. It is used in microservices architectures to ensure data consistency across services. In the event of a failure in one transaction, the saga executes a series of compensating transactions to undo the impact of the preceding transactions. *Figure 3.8* illustrates the saga pattern, which manages transactions across microservices. It ensures that either all parts of a transaction are completed successfully or compensates for those transactions that are triggered to revert each step in the case of failure:

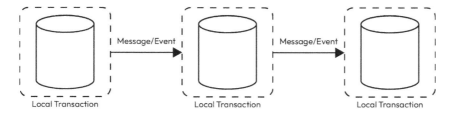

Figure 3.8 – High-level architecture of the saga pattern

Let's consider some of the strengths and weaknesses of the saga architecture pattern:

* Strengths:

    * It helps maintain data consistency across multiple services in a microservices architecture

    * It provides a mechanism to handle business transactions spanning multiple services by coordinating distributed transactions

- Weaknesses:

  - It adds complexity to the system design, as developers need to design compensatory transactions for every transaction that could potentially fail

  - It can lead to increased latency due to the asynchronous nature of communication

- Example: An e-commerce application that manages distributed transactions across an inventory service, payment service, and shipping service by using the saga pattern to ensure data consistency.

- **Backend for frontend** (**BFF**): In the BFF pattern, the backend for each user experience is developed separately. This enables the backend to be closely aligned with the needs of the specific frontend, allowing it to provide exactly the data needed in the optimal form for that frontend. *Figure 3.9* illustrates the BFF pattern, which involves setting up a backend layer that specifically caters to the needs of a frontend client, such as a browser. This BFF layer acts as an intermediary, handling and aggregating requests to various services (services A, B, and C) and ensuring that the browser receives data in the most optimal format for UI rendering:

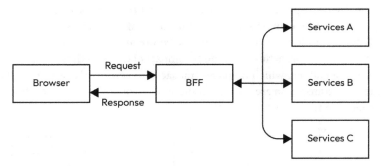

Figure 3.9 – High-level architecture of the BFF pattern

Let's consider some of the strengths and weaknesses of the BFF architecture pattern:

- Strengths:

  - It allows better user experience by aligning the backend requirements closely with the frontend requirements

  - It simplifies microservices for the frontend developers, as they only need to communicate with one backend (the BFF) instead of many

- Weaknesses:

  - It could lead to code duplication if not handled carefully, as similar logic might be implemented in multiple BFFs

- It increases the number of deployable units

- Example: A media streaming application, such as Netflix, could have separate BFFs for TV, mobile, and web users, each catering to the unique requirements of that platform

- **Command query responsibility segregation (CQRS)**: The CQRS pattern is an architectural pattern where the model responsible for updating the data (command) is separated from the model used to read the data (query). This allows each model to be optimized for its specific purpose. *Figure 3.10* illustrates the CQRS pattern (separating the operations that modify data (command) from the operations that read data (query)). This architectural pattern enhances performance, scalability, and security by allowing the read and write workloads to scale independently and to be optimized according to their specific needs. The UI interacts with distinct command and query services, which communicate with a common storage mechanism that has separate models for handling write and read operations:

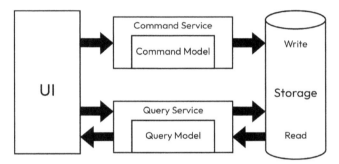

Figure 3.10 – High-level architecture of the CQRS pattern

Let's consider some of the strengths and weaknesses of the CQRS architecture pattern:

- Strengths:

  - It allows the read and write workloads to be scaled independently

  - It enables the optimization of read and write models for their respective operations

- Weaknesses:

  - It can lead to increased complexity in system design, as maintaining two separate models requires careful co-ordination

  - It may cause data synchronization issues between the read and write models

- Example: An e-commerce application could use the CQRS pattern to separate the read operations (such as browsing products or checking order status) from the write operations (such as placing orders or adding products to carts), allowing better performance optimization

- **Sharding pattern**: In the era of big data, applications often have to deal with an enormous amount of data. Sharding is a technique where data are partitioned and spread across multiple databases, which handle a portion of the data load in parallel. This pattern is exceptionally useful in a cloud-native environment where horizontal scalability is a fundamental requirement. The ability to add more databases (shards) as the data grows ensures that the application can scale out effectively. *Figure 3.11* illustrates the sharding pattern in database architecture, which is a method for achieving horizontal scalability. By dividing data into distinct partitions or "shards," each database shard manages a subset of the data. This division allows parallel processing and can enhance the performance and manageability of large datasets, making it an effective strategy for scaling cloud-native applications:

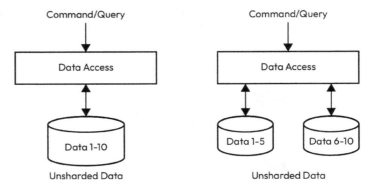

Figure 3.11 – High-level architecture of the sharding pattern

Let's consider some of the strengths and weaknesses of the sharding architecture pattern:

- Strengths:

  - Improves scalability and data management efficiency

  - Enables parallel processing, accelerating query responses

  - Allows for geographical data distribution, aligning with user locality

- Weaknesses:

  - It can lead to data hotspots if the sharding keys are not chosen carefully

  - Increases complexity, especially around data distribution and query performance optimization

- Example: A global e-commerce platform could use the sharding pattern to manage its extensive product data. They could distribute their vast product catalog across different databases (shards) based on regional popularity, hence improving application performance and enabling region-specific optimizations.

In conclusion, understanding and applying these cloud-native design patterns can provide significant benefits when building and maintaining applications in a multi-cloud environment. These patterns, with their specific strengths and weaknesses, offer solutions to common challenges faced by developers. However, selecting the right pattern is a matter of evaluating the needs and constraints of your particular application and organizational context.

Having examined the cloud-native design patterns and their applicability in the multi-cloud context, we are now well-equipped to take a deeper dive into designing specifically for multi-cloud environments.

Designing for multi-cloud

Alright, to make this topic more interesting, we will be using metaphors. So, let's get started. Imagine you're a globe-trotter setting out on a worldwide journey. You've got a map, a backpack filled with essentials, and an adventurous spirit. However, instead of just one map to guide you, you've got maps for different regions that have unique terrains, climates, and cultures. Navigating through this diverse landscape requires a keen understanding of these differences and a strategy to effectively use your resources across multiple regions.

Designing applications for multi-cloud environments presents a similar challenge. With a plethora of cloud providers that each offer unique capabilities and features, designing applications for a multi-cloud environment can feel like navigating through multiple maps at once. It's an expedition into an intricate landscape of platforms and services that each have their own set of rules, strengths, and constraints.

Why would you want to undertake such a complex journey? The benefits of a multi-cloud approach are plentiful. It offers improved reliability by eliminating single points of failure, increased flexibility by providing a wide choice of services, and optimized costs by allowing you to use the most cost-effective services from multiple providers. It can also help prevent vendor lock-in to a certain extent, which can be a significant advantage in the ever-evolving cloud landscape.

However, while the rewards can be substantial, so too are the challenges. Managing resources across different cloud providers that have their own set of APIs, data storage solutions, and security measures is no easy task. It requires a strategic approach to architecture and design, the careful selection of technologies, and a deep understanding of the key principles of multi-cloud application design.

This chapter aims to equip you with the compass and the map for your multi-cloud journey. We'll delve into the architecture and principles of multi-cloud application design, explore the role of key technologies, discuss data management strategies, and touch upon cost optimization, among other topics.

Fasten your seat belts; it's time to embark on the multi-cloud expedition!

Understanding multi-cloud architecture

At its core, a multi-cloud architecture involves the use of two or more cloud computing services from any number of distinct cloud vendors. It can be a blend of public, private, and hybrid clouds based on the specific needs of an organization. This design allows businesses to diversify their cloud strategy by spreading workloads across multiple platforms, effectively eliminating a single point of failure and reducing the risks associated with relying on a single provider.

Gaining a comprehensive understanding of the distinct architectural models that inform how organizations utilize diverse cloud service providers is paramount to optimize resource utilization, mitigate vendor lock-in, enhance performance, manage risks, and ensure business continuity in a dynamic and diverse cloud environment. There are primarily three types of multi-cloud architecture:

- **Homogeneous cloud architecture**: This architecture involves the use of the same cloud service provider across multiple regions. It's like setting up parallel universes where each universe operates independently, but all universes are governed by the same laws or, in our case, the same cloud provider's technologies and infrastructure. This type of architecture is often adopted when organizations want to ensure higher availability, disaster recovery, or data redundancy. Compliance with data sovereignty laws, where data must reside in the same country where it's created or used, also prompts companies to go for this approach. Although this setup has the advantage of familiarity with a single provider's technology stack, it doesn't necessarily provide the benefits of using different services from different providers, which may be superior in certain areas.

- **Heterogeneous cloud architecture**: As the name suggests, this architecture is a medley of different cloud service providers, where each provider is chosen based on their strengths and the specific needs of the application. This is like playing to the strengths of each player on a team; for example, you might use Amazon S3 for its superior storage capabilities, Google Cloud for its cutting-edge machine learning services, and Microsoft Azure for its extensive enterprise application services. The heterogeneous model delivers high degrees of flexibility and access to unique features from different providers. But remember, with this flexibility comes increased complexity. Developers need to become adept at using different cloud providers' interfaces, and the organization must deal with multiple vendor relationships, which can complicate administration and billing.

- **Hybrid multi-cloud architecture**: This architecture blends the use of private and public clouds, marrying the benefits of both worlds. This approach provides a secure environment for sensitive data on a private cloud or an on-premise data center while leveraging public cloud resources for high-compute tasks, large volumes of non-sensitive data, or rapid scalability. This approach offers flexibility, cost-effectiveness, and heightened security. However, it also introduces challenges, such as the need for secure, seamless integration between public and private environments and the complexity of managing and governing diverse cloud resources.

In a nutshell, a solid understanding of multi-cloud architecture is crucial for effectively designing and managing cloud-native applications across multiple cloud platforms. This knowledge will guide you in choosing the right strategies and tools to build resilient, scalable, and cost-effective applications in a multi-cloud environment.

Key principles of multi-cloud application design

In our metaphorical journey, the principles of multi-cloud application design are akin to the essential survival skills required to navigate the diverse landscapes and weather patterns we encounter. Just as a seasoned traveler needs to be adaptable, resourceful, and prepared for unexpected challenges, so too does an application in a multi-cloud environment. Let's understand some of the key principles of multi-cloud application design:

- **Scalability**: Designing applications to handle variable workloads:

    Scalability is the ability of an application to efficiently handle increases in workload. In the context of our journey, it's like being able to walk, bike, or even climb when the terrain demands it. An application that is scalable can serve a handful of users just as effectively as it can serve millions. In a multi-cloud environment, the challenge lies in maintaining this adaptability across different platforms.

    Achieving scalability involves designing applications in a way that their components can be easily replicated or distributed. Microservices and serverless architectures, which we touched upon in previous sections, play a significant role in enabling scalability. These architectures allow the individual components of an application to scale independently according to demand, a practice known as horizontal scaling.

- **Availability**: Ensuring continuous service even in the case of failures:

    Availability is the degree to which an application is accessible and functional when needed. It's akin to having a reliable GPS or compass during our journey, one that continues to work even when the weather is harsh, or visibility is low.

    In a multi-cloud setup, high availability is achieved through redundancy and fault tolerance. Redundancy is like carrying an extra pair of batteries for your compass, ensuring that you have a backup if one fails. In application terms, this involves deploying multiple instances of an application component across different cloud environments so that if one fails, others can take over.

- **Portability**: Allowing applications to run on different cloud platforms:

    Portability, in our travel metaphor, is akin to a traveler's ability to easily move and adapt from one country to another. In a multi-cloud context, it is the ability of an application to be moved seamlessly from one cloud environment to another.

    Containers are a key enabler of portability in a multi-cloud environment. They encapsulate an application and its dependencies into a single, self-contained unit, allowing it to run consistently across different cloud environments.

- **Resilience**: Making applications capable of dealing with problems without major disruptions:

  Resilience equates to our ability to withstand storms and other unforeseen events. For an application, resilience means its capacity to cope with failures without suffering significant downtime or data loss.

  In a multi-cloud environment, resilience can be achieved through a combination of high availability, robust error handling, and a strong disaster recovery plan. Techniques such as automatic retries, circuit breakers, and rate limiting can be used to build fault-tolerant systems.

- **Security**: Addressing security concerns in a multi-cloud environment:

  Security is a crucial aspect that must not be overlooked. It's like ensuring we're safe from threats in the regions we travel to.

  Security involves protecting data, applications, and infrastructures from threats. This could mean implementing encryption, managing user access, ensuring compliance, and more. Given the distributed nature of multi-cloud environments, a centralized approach to security, such as using unified threat management platforms or cloud access security brokers, can be effective.

Now that we've mastered the survival skills for our journey let's turn our attention to selecting the right gear. In the next section, we'll delve into the technologies that will aid us on this adventure.

Role of domain-driven design

Domain-driven design (DDD) is like our native language, allowing us to communicate effectively with the local inhabitants of each cloud environment. DDD is an approach to software development that focuses on understanding the business domain, its problems, and its complexities. It emphasizes creating a model of the domain, implementing it as code, and constantly refining it based on feedback from domain experts.

In the context of a multi-cloud environment, DDD helps break down a complex system into more manageable parts called **bounded contexts**. These bounded contexts can be seen as individual territories on our map, each with its unique culture (domain logic) and language (APIs).

Figure 3.12 represents a DDD for an e-commerce website. The main domain is e-commerce, which is responsible for managing product information, orders, and customer data. Payment, offer, customer, and shipping are subdomains. Each subdomain is further divided into services, which are self-contained units of functionality responsible for specific tasks within the domain:

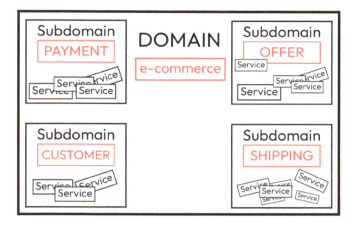

Figure 3.12 – DDD for an e-commerce website

DDD also introduces the concept of **Ubiquitous Language** which is a common language between developers and domain experts. In our journey, it's like a universal translator, enabling clear communication and understanding between the team members, irrespective of the cloud environment they are working with.

In the next section, we will understand the API-first approach, which represents a significant part of modern software development.

Importance of an API-first approach

Embracing an API-first approach in our multi-cloud journey is like a global adventurer having a universal translator device. This device helps the adventurer seamlessly communicate and interact with the locals, regardless of the language they speak.

With the API-first design, APIs are developed upfront and serve as the universal translators for our applications. They are not just an addition or an afterthought but are the foundational stones that set the course for the development journey. In the multi-cloud environment, where our applications are scattered across various landscapes that have their own dialects, the API-first approach becomes our universal translator. It ensures our applications (no matter where they are hosted) can understand and interact with each other effortlessly.

These well-crafted APIs are also like handy travel guides, allowing our applications to grow and adapt independently. They facilitate continuous exploration and adaptation to new experiences in our multi-cloud journey, much like a resourceful adventurer who learns to thrive in changing landscapes.

In essence, just as a universal translator is indispensable to a global adventurer, the API-first approach is fundamental to navigating the complex terrains of multi-cloud environments. So, gear up, and make sure you pack this vital tool, and let's venture further into our multi-cloud journey!

Selecting the right technologies for a cloud-native foundation

Continuing on our metaphorical multi-cloud journey, we now understand the importance of having a map (cloud-native design patterns) and establishing a common language (API-first approach). Now, it's time to assemble the right equipment. Selecting the right technologies for our expedition is akin to choosing the best gear and equipment. It's about finding tools that will help us navigate the terrain more efficiently, keep us safe, and allow us to overcome any obstacles that we might encounter. Let's touch on a few key tools and technologies that are truly shaping the cloud-native transformation:

- Cloud-native technologies that facilitate multi-cloud application design (Kubernetes, Istio, etc.):

  To navigate through different cloud environments, we need versatile tools that are recognized and can function well in all of them. In the cloud world, such universal tools are **cloud-native technologies**. These technologies are designed to leverage the full benefits of the cloud computing model, making them an essential part of our multi-cloud journey.

  Consider Kubernetes, for example. It's like our multi-purpose Swiss army knife. Kubernetes is an open-source platform designed to automate the deployment, scaling, and management of containerized applications. With its impressive array of features, such as service discovery, load balancing, and automated rollouts and rollbacks, Kubernetes aids in maintaining and managing our applications across different cloud platforms. *With recent developments Kubernetes (k8s) is becoming the operating system for Multi-cloud environments.*

  Another powerful tool in our multi-cloud gear is **Istio**. Imagine it as our compass guiding us through the intricate network pathways of our applications. Istio is a service mesh that provides a way to connect, secure, control, and observe services. In a multi-cloud environment, Istio provides consistent visibility and network control, helping to manage complex communication across multiple cloud platforms.

- **Function-as-a-Service (FaaS)** and its role in multi-cloud:

  As we journey through multiple cloud environments, we need to travel light, carrying only what's necessary for each phase of the journey. This is where FaaS comes into the picture.

  FaaS is like our pack of dehydrated meals, ready to be used as needed. FaaS allows developers to execute chunks of code (or functions) in response to events without the complexity of building and maintaining the infrastructure.

  In a multi-cloud environment, FaaS enables developers to focus on writing the code while the cloud provider manages the underlying infrastructure. It supports the development of scalable, event-driven applications and allows you to pay only for the computing time consumed—a perfect addition to our lightweight travel gear.

- **Service mesh** and its benefits:

  As we traverse the terrain of multiple cloud environments, it becomes challenging to manage the intricate pathways that our applications take. This is where a service mesh comes in handy. It's like our GPS system, managing the communication between services, ensuring they find the quickest and safest routes.

  A service mesh creates a special infrastructure layer for managing communication between services. It makes sure that requests are delivered reliably through the complicated network of services making up a modern cloud-based application. In a multi-cloud scenario, a service mesh ensures that this communication is seamlessly maintained across different cloud platforms.

Remember, when selecting technologies or tools, consider your specific use cases, what problems are you trying to solve, your team's skillset, and the trade-offs associated with each technology. The goal is to choose the technologies that best align with your business needs and enhance your multi-cloud strategy.

Data management in multi-cloud

As we venture deeper into our multi-cloud journey, it's time to explore the cave systems that span different regions: **data management** in multi-cloud environments. Just as the careful mapping and understanding of caves is crucial to avoid getting lost, effective data management strategies are pivotal for ensuring the seamless operation of our multi-cloud expedition. Here are some of the major topics:

- **Data storage** and **migration strategies**:

  The first step is to understand how we're going to store our precious data artifacts and how we can move them around. In the world of multi-cloud, this translates to data storage and migration strategies.

  Selecting the right data storage for each cloud provider is akin to choosing the right type of gear for each segment of our journey. We need to consider the nature of the data, the frequency of access, any latency requirements, and the cost when choosing a storage solution. We might choose different types of storage solutions, such as block storage for databases or object storage for multimedia, based on the specific requirements of each application.

  In multi-cloud environments, we might need to transfer data between different cloud providers or from on-premise data centers to the cloud. Various tools and services can assist with this, such as **AWS's Database Migration Service (DMS)** or **Google Cloud's Transfer Service**. Remember, when migrating data, it's crucial to plan carefully, considering factors such as data integrity, migration speed, downtime, and cost.

- Ensuring **data consistency** and managing **data replication**:

  Ensuring data consistency in a multi-cloud environment can feel like trying to synchronize watches across different time zones when you are traveling to different countries. When data is replicated across different cloud environments to improve availability and durability, it's essential to ensure that all replicas remain consistent.

  This is a non-trivial task, given the potential for network partitions and other failure scenarios. Techniques such as eventual consistency, strong consistency, or transactional consistency can be employed depending on the nature of the application and the trade-offs between consistency, availability, and partition tolerance that the application can tolerate.

  Data replication, on the other hand, can be thought of as having multiple copies of our map. If one gets lost or damaged, we have others as a backup in multi-cloud environments; data is often replicated across different regions and cloud providers to improve resilience and reduce latency for users. The strategy for data replication depends on the nature of the data and the specific requirements of the application.

- Implementing effective **data backup** and **disaster recovery plans**:

  As every seasoned explorer knows, you always need a contingency plan. For our multi-cloud journey, this translates to effective data backup and disaster recovery plans. Just as we might carry a first-aid kit for medical emergencies, we need to have plans in place for data emergencies, such as data corruption, data breaches, or catastrophic system failures.

  Backup strategies in multi-cloud environments can leverage the unique strengths of different cloud providers. For instance, we might choose to use Amazon S3's object life cycle management for the long-term archiving of data or Google Cloud Storage for frequently accessed data due to its lower cost.

  Disaster recovery in a multi-cloud environment could mean having a failover system in a different cloud provider. If a disaster occurs and our primary cloud provider becomes unavailable, we can switch to the failover system in the second cloud provider, minimizing downtime and service disruption.

  For instance, consider an e-commerce application that uses AWS for user management and order processing, Google Cloud for inventory management, and Azure for analytics. To ensure data consistency across these services, the application could use a distributed database, such as Google's **Cloud Spanner**. To backup data, it could regularly export data to a separate storage service. In case of a disaster, the application could switch to a standby replica in a different region or cloud.

Remember, successful data management in multi-cloud requires a clear understanding of the nature of the data, the regulatory requirements, the capabilities of different cloud providers, and a well-defined data life cycle management strategy.

Monitoring and observability in multi-cloud

Designing cloud-native applications for multi-cloud environments necessitates a solid strategy for **monitoring and observability**. It is instrumental in maintaining the operational health of your application while improving its performance across various platforms. In the following list, we will see a few points to get started with (a detailed explanation is mentioned in *Chapter 7, Troubleshooting Multi-Cloud Applications*):

- The significance of comprehensive monitoring and observability: Monitoring and observability are central to understanding your application's behavior, predicting and mitigating issues, and ensuring seamless performance. Comprehensive monitoring gives you a panoramic view of your application's performance across different cloud environments, offering actionable insights to enhance reliability and user experience. Observability, an evolution of monitoring, allows you to infer the internal state of your system from its outputs, which is essential in a distributed and complex multi-cloud environment.

- Multi-cloud monitoring and observability tools: Several tools cater to the need for monitoring and observability across multi-cloud platforms. These tools provide crucial metrics for diagnosing problems and optimizing performance. For instance, **Datadog** provides an extensive platform for monitoring and analytics, ensuring observability across multi-cloud environments. **Prometheus** (with **Grafana**) is a popular open source tool for monitoring applications in Kubernetes environments. Tools such as **New Relic**, **Splunk**, and others provide similar capabilities.

Imagine deploying your application across AWS, Google Cloud, and Azure. With the use of an effective monitoring and observability tool, you'll have a comprehensive view of your application's performance across all these platforms. Suppose there's a sudden increase in latency or error rates in a specific service; in that case, these tools will enable swift identification and resolution, thereby maintaining the application's high availability and reliability.

In essence, monitoring and observability aren't optional extras but integral components of successful multi-cloud application design. Choosing the right tools and building a robust monitoring strategy paves the way for reliable and high-performing applications across multiple cloud platforms.

In the next section, let's understand how cost can be optimized in multi-cloud.

Optimizing costs in multi-cloud

Wisely budgeting your resources is a critical part of a globetrotter's adventure. Just like carefully rationing food and water supplies on a trek, effectively managing costs is crucial when traversing the multi-cloud terrain. As organizations scale and expand their applications across multiple cloud platforms, **managing and optimizing costs** becomes a crucial aspect of their multi-cloud strategy. More details are provided in the following list:

- Understanding and managing costs across multiple cloud platforms

Every cloud service provider has a unique cost structure, which is analogous to different currencies across countries. Juggling these costs can feel much like a globetrotter dealing with fluctuating exchange rates. To navigate this complexity, a thorough understanding of each provider's pricing model, the diligent analysis of usage reports, and accurate forecasting of future costs are fundamental.

- Strategies for cost optimization

  The strategies for cost optimization in a multi-cloud environment are as varied as the techniques a traveler might employ to stretch their budget. Selecting the appropriate services, leveraging off-peak hours, and turning off idle resources can significantly impact your financial footprint.

  Automation can also be a powerful tool for cost management, much like an experienced guide who knows the lie of the land. Lastly, negotiation can lead to more favorable pricing, much like bargaining can help a traveler get the best deals.

As an example, consider an e-commerce company that hosts its application on AWS, Google Cloud, and Azure. By using cost optimization strategies, they can match their resource usage with the varying demand during peak shopping seasons, optimizing costs while ensuring that their application performance doesn't dip. With effective monitoring, they can identify underutilized resources and decommission them, resulting in substantial savings.

Thus, *cost optimization in a multi-cloud environment is not just about reducing costs. It's about making strategic decisions that allow you to make the most of your cloud investments, ensuring you're getting maximum value from each dollar spent.*

In the next section, let's delve into a few case studies to sharpen our understanding of multi-cloud application design.

Case studies

In this section, we will delve into some compelling case studies that encapsulate the process and benefits of successful multi-cloud application design.

Case Study 1: E-commerce platform using microservices and sharding

An e-commerce company faced scalability issues with its monolithic architecture as the user base grew. They needed a solution that could handle the increasing demand while ensuring reliability, scalability, and efficient resource utilization. Additionally, they faced challenges in managing the large volume of data generated by their operations, requiring a scalable data management approach:

- **Approach**:

  - **Microservices**: Decomposed the monolithic application into smaller, independent microservices to enable independent development, deployment, and scalability

- **Scaling**: The microservices architecture allowed the scaling of specific components based on demand, optimizing resource allocation and reducing costs

- **Sharding**: Distributed data across multiple databases to handle large data volumes

- **Resolution**:

  - **Scalability**: The microservices architecture enabled the independent scaling of components to handle increasing user demand efficiently

  - **Reliability**: The microservices architecture enhanced reliability and fault tolerance by isolating failures within specific components

  - **Resource utilization**: The scaling of specific microservices based on demand optimized resource allocation and reduced costs

  - **Effective data management**: Sharding improved data management by distributing the data load across multiple databases, improving performance and scalability

- **Key takeaways**:

  - The microservices architecture enables independent scalability and fault isolation, improving reliability and resource utilization

  - Sharding is an effective approach for managing large volumes of data, allowing for horizontal scalability and improved performance

  - Careful planning and management are essential during the transition from a monolithic architecture to microservices and for implementing data sharding

  - The monitoring, testing, and proper management of distributed microservices and data shards are critical for system performance and availability

  - Cloud-native technologies and platforms enhance the scalability, resilience, and management of distributed systems

Case Study 2: Financial services firm leveraging circuit breaker and replication

A financial services firm operating across multiple cloud platforms required high availability and data durability. They needed a solution to ensure continuous access to critical data and mitigate the risk of system failures:

- **Approach**:

  - **Replication**: Implemented the replication pattern to create multiple copies of data across different cloud providers, ensuring high data availability and an additional layer of data protection.

- **Circuit breaker**: Implemented the circuit breaker pattern to handle potential failures in the distributed system. If a service in one cloud provider experienced an outage, the circuit breaker prevented any continuous attempts to access the failing service, preventing system-wide outages.

- **Resolution**:

  - **High availability**: The replication of data across multiple cloud providers ensured continuous access to critical data, even in the event of a failure in one provider

  - **Data durability**: The replication pattern provided an additional layer of data protection, reducing the risk of data loss and enhancing data durability

  - **Resilience and reliability**: The circuit breaker pattern improved system resilience by preventing cascading failures and system-wide outages, resulting in reduced downtime and improved customer satisfaction

- **Key takeaways**:

  - The replication pattern provides high data availability and an additional layer of data protection by creating multiple copies across different cloud providers

  - The circuit breaker pattern helps handle potential failures in a distributed system, preventing system-wide outages and improving resilience

  - Implementing data replication and circuit breakers requires careful consideration regarding data consistency, synchronization, and failover strategies

  - Regular testing and monitoring are crucial for ensuring the effectiveness and reliability of the replication and circuit breaker mechanisms

  - Leveraging multiple cloud providers can enhance system availability, durability, and resilience by mitigating the risk of a single provider failing

Case Study 3: Media streaming company adopting eventual consistency and API gateway

A global media streaming company faced challenges in managing high levels of traffic across different geographical regions. They needed a solution that could ensure high availability, consistency, and performance while effectively managing their microservices architecture:

- **Approach**:

  - **Eventual consistency**: Adopted the eventual consistency pattern, which allows temporary inconsistencies in data but ensures their eventual convergence to a consistent state. This approach provided high availability and improved the overall user experience, especially in distributed systems.

- **API gateway**: Implemented the API gateway pattern to manage the multiple microservices within their application effectively. The API gateway served as a single entry point for clients, enabling better security, rate limiting, request handling, and overall service manageability and performance.

- **Resolution**:

  - **High availability**: The eventual consistency pattern allowed the media streaming company to handle high traffic levels across different geographical regions, ensuring that users could access the service even during peak usage periods

  - **Improved user experience**: While temporary inconsistencies may occur, the eventual consistency pattern ensured that all users would eventually receive consistent and up-to-date data, enhancing the overall user experience

  - **Efficient microservices management**: The API gateway pattern streamlined the management of multiple microservices by providing a centralized entry point. It enhanced security, allowed effective rate limiting, and facilitated easier request handling, leading to improved manageability and performance

- **Key takeaways**:

  - The eventual consistency pattern provides high availability and a better user experience by allowing temporary inconsistencies while ensuring eventual convergence regarding consistent data

  - The API gateway pattern simplifies the management of microservices by serving as a centralized entry point, improving security, rate limiting, and request handling

  - Implementing eventual consistency requires careful consideration of data replication, synchronization, conflict resolution, and recovery mechanisms

  - Proper load balancing, caching, and monitoring are crucial for ensuring the scalability, performance, and reliability of the API gateway

  - The global distribution of services, along with eventual consistency and an API gateway, enables media streaming companies to effectively handle high traffic levels, provide a seamless user experience, and manage their microservices architecture

Through these case studies, it's evident that designing applications for multi-cloud environments can bring about substantial improvements in resilience, scalability, operational efficiency, and cost optimization. However, the journey towards successful multi-cloud implementation necessitates a comprehensive understanding of multi-cloud architecture and the appropriate use of cloud-native design and practices.

Best practices for multi-cloud application design

After an in-depth exploration of designing cloud-native applications for multi-cloud platforms, it's crucial to distill this knowledge into a series of best practices. By following these guidelines, cloud-native developers can effectively navigate the complexities of multi-cloud environments and build robust, scalable, and efficient applications. More details can be seen in the following list:

- **Embrace cloud-native principles**: It's vital to adopt cloud-native principles, such as microservices, containerization, and automation, to ensure your applications are portable, scalable, and resilient across different cloud environments.

- **Invest in interoperability**: The success of a multi-cloud strategy depends heavily on interoperability between various cloud platforms. Prioritize open standards and interfaces that ensure smooth interplay between technologies across diverse platforms.

- **Leverage service meshes and orchestration tools**: Tools (such as Kubernetes) and service meshes (such as Istio) can be instrumental in managing deployments and facilitating efficient communication between services in multi-cloud environments.

- **Incorporate comprehensive observability**: Invest in comprehensive observability using monitoring, tracing, and logging tools that provide insights into your applications' performance across various cloud platforms.

- **Focus on data management**: Implement robust data management strategies that address data storage, migration, replication, and backup across multiple cloud platforms. This ensures data consistency and aids in disaster recovery.

- **Plan for cost optimization**: Understanding and managing costs across multiple cloud platforms is vital. Leverage cost management tools and strategies, such as auto-scaling and right-sizing, to keep costs in check.

- **Prioritize security**: Multi-cloud environments can add complexity to security management. Embrace a security-first approach, employ robust security practices, and leverage cloud-native security tools to ensure the integrity of your applications.

- **Continuous learning and adaptation**: The cloud technology landscape is continually evolving. Stay updated with the latest trends, learn from real-world case studies, and be ready to adapt your strategies as needed.

By adhering to these best practices, developers can effectively confront the challenges of multi-cloud environments, harnessing their advantages to deliver highly performant, resilient, and cost-efficient applications. This chapter's content serves as a roadmap in your journey towards designing successful multi-cloud applications. If you continue on this learning path you'll be well-equipped to create cloud-native applications that are truly platform-agnostic.

Summary

As we draw a line under our multi-cloud expedition chapter, let's pause and take a breath, enjoying the spectacular panorama from this vista. The obstacles we've negotiated, the enlightenment we've acquired, and the best practices we've unearthed—they all contribute to making this journey enriching.

Let's reflect on the rich insights we've gleaned regarding the design of cloud-native applications for multi-cloud platforms. We have delved into the unique aspects of multi-cloud environments and understood the nuances of multi-cloud architecture, as well as the instrumental role played by cloud-native technologies, containers, and microservices in such settings. We have explored essential principles for designing applications in this landscape and navigated the labyrinth of data management in multi-cloud.

We have also underscored the vital role of monitoring and observability, identified the significance of cost optimization, and illustrated these principles with real-world case studies. Finally, we consolidated our understanding into a set of best practices for effective multi-cloud application design.

However, as any seasoned adventurer will tell you, the trek is far from over. Our compass points towards our next challenge: managing data in multi-cloud landscapes. As we wrap up this chapter and gear up for the next leg of our journey, we anticipate encountering new hurdles and gaining fresh insights. Until then, mull over the landscapes we've traversed, the wisdom we've accrued, and the expertise we've garnered. Remember, on this multi-cloud exploration journey, every step taken is a step forward. See you in the next chapter.

4

Crafting and Deploying in the Multi-Cloud as a Developer

As we continue our expedition into the multi-cloud landscape, we've reached the stage of setting up our base camp. This base camp is the heart of our operations – the place where we plan our routes, store our supplies, and prepare for the journey ahead. In our technological journey, this translates to developing and deploying cloud-native applications in a multi-cloud environment.

To fully exploit the benefits of the multi-cloud environment, you, as a developer, along with platform engineers, need to embrace new practices and methodologies. You have to think in terms of cloud-native platform which consists of **Infrastructure as Code (IaC)**, **continuous integration/continuous deployment (CI/CD)**, GitOps and DevOps, and container orchestration.

In earlier chapters, we focused more on the cloud-native application side of topics with practical hands-on exercises. In this chapter, we will learn how to employ the strategies, tools, and practices that are fundamental to developing and deploying cloud-native applications across multiple cloud environments, so, as a developer, you will be stepping into understanding the platform and continuing the journey of setting up the cloud-native platform for your cloud-native applications. We'll start with IaC, an approach that allows you to automate the provisioning and management of your cloud resources. Then, we'll explore CI/CD practices that enable rapid, reliable, and consistent application delivery. Next, we'll delve into GitOps and DevOps methodologies that empower teams to achieve efficient, automated, and predictable deployment processes. Finally, we'll cap it off with a thorough exploration of containerization and orchestration using Docker and Kubernetes.

Just as every mountaineer needs the right gear and a solid plan to tackle the peaks, in this chapter, we'll equip you with the essential strategies and tools for scaling the heights of cloud-native development in a multi-cloud world.

With each topic, we'll delve into case studies that demonstrate the practical application of these practices. These real-life examples will illuminate the value of these approaches, providing you with concrete evidence of their effectiveness.

The following topics will be covered in this chapter:

- IaC
- CI/CD
- GitOps and DevOps practices
- Service meshes in multi-cloud environments
- Containerization and orchestration
- Multi-cloud networking and security

Fasten your seatbelt as we take off on this journey through the world of developing and deploying cloud-native applications on multi-cloud environments. Let's begin!

IaC

Before we start this journey, let's say you need to set up a base camp. You need to choose the right location, set up tents, arrange supplies, and ensure everything is ready for the expedition team. Now, imagine doing this for multiple base camps across different mountains. It's a daunting task, isn't it?

IaC is like your detailed base camp setup plan. It's a documented, repeatable process that ensures you can set up the base camp efficiently each time, without manually arranging the supplies over and over again. With IaC, you describe and automate the process of creating and managing your cloud resources. Instead of manually setting up each base camp, you write a plan. This plan, when executed, automatically sets up your base camp exactly as you've specified. Need to replicate it? Simply re-run the plan. If a base camp gets destroyed, rebuild it instantly with the same plan.

Picture yourself as a developer in a time before cloud computing was a common phrase. Your task is to set up a server. You are given a piece of hardware, and you go about setting it up manually – installing the operating system, configuring it to specifications, installing the necessary software, and ensuring it works perfectly. It's a tedious and time-consuming process, and it's also prone to human error. If a server fails or needs to be replicated, you need to do the entire process again. It's almost like baking a cake from scratch each time someone requests a piece.

Enter the cloud era, and we start baking cakes in bulk! We're no longer dealing with one or two servers; instead, we're managing hundreds – sometimes thousands – of servers. In a multi-cloud environment, this complexity only magnifies. Would you still bake each cake from scratch? This is where IaC steps in, transforming the way we manage our cloud resources.

IaC is like your favorite cake recipe. It's a documented, repeatable process that ensures you can produce the same delicious cake each time without manually mixing the ingredients over and over again. With IaC, you describe and automate the process of creating and managing your cloud resources and your target environments (development, production, and so on). Instead of manually clicking through the UI of your cloud provider, you write code. This code, when executed, automatically sets up your cloud resources exactly as you've specified. Need to replicate it? Simply rerun the code. If a server fails, rebuild it instantly with the same code.

IaC has revolutionized the way infrastructure is managed and provisioned. It allows teams to define infrastructure configurations through code, providing numerous benefits in terms of consistency, scalability, and efficiency. However, just as every base camp setup plan has its strengths and weaknesses, so does IaC. Let's explore them.

Strengths of IaC

IaC offers several strengths that contribute to more efficient, consistent, and reliable management of IT infrastructure. Here are some of the key strengths of IaC:

- **Consistency and reproducibility**: IaC ensures that every base camp (infrastructure) is set up in a consistent and reproducible manner. It's like having a detailed checklist for setting up each base camp, ensuring that nothing is missed, and everything is set up correctly.

  IaC enables the provisioning of infrastructure in a consistent and reproducible manner. Infrastructure configurations are defined as code, eliminating manual configuration drift and ensuring consistent environments across development, staging, and production.

- **Agility and speed**: With IaC, you can set up and modify your base camps (infrastructure) rapidly. It's like having a team of experienced mountaineers who can quickly set up the base camp based on the plan, allowing you to focus on the expedition (developing applications).

  With IaC, infrastructure changes can be managed and deployed rapidly. Infrastructure code can be version-controlled, allowing for easy tracking of changes, rollbacks, and collaboration among team members. This agility leads to faster time-to-market for applications and enables teams to respond quickly to evolving business requirements.

- **Scalability and elasticity**: IaC allows you to easily scale your base camps (infrastructure) to meet the needs of your expedition team. Need more tents or supplies? Simply adjust the plan and execute it. By defining scalable patterns in code, infrastructure can be automatically provisioned, scaled up, or scaled down based on workload patterns or defined policies. This ensures efficient resource utilization and cost optimization.

- **Automation and efficiency**: IaC automates the provisioning and configuration of infrastructure, reducing manual effort and human errors. Infrastructure changes can be validated and tested through continuous integration and deployment pipelines, ensuring reliable and efficient deployments.

Weaknesses of IaC

Some of them are as follows:

- **Learning curve and complexity**: Adopting IaC requires a learning curve as team members need to acquire knowledge of infrastructure provisioning tools and programming concepts. Teams may require training and upskilling to utilize IaC frameworks and understand the underlying infrastructure components effectively.

- **Initial investment and setup**: Implementing IaC may require an initial investment in tooling, infrastructure, and resources. Configuration management tools, infrastructure orchestration platforms, and cloud provider-specific integrations may be necessary, adding complexity to the setup process.

- **Limited portability**: IaC solutions are often tied to specific cloud providers or infrastructure platforms. While some tools offer multi-cloud support, there may be limitations in porting infrastructure code across different providers. Care should be taken to abstract provider-specific configurations and maintain portability whenever possible.

- **Version control and collaboration**: Effective utilization of IaC requires disciplined version control practices and collaboration among team members. Managing conflicts, ensuring proper branching and merging strategies, and establishing code review processes become important to maintain code quality and minimize errors.

Tools to implement IaC

By understanding the strengths and weaknesses of IaC, organizations can make informed decisions about adopting and implementing this practice. It's like choosing the right mountaineering equipment for your expedition. You need to consider the terrain, the weather, and the specific needs of your team. Leveraging the consistency, agility, scalability, and automation provided by IaC while addressing the learning curve, setup complexity, portability, and collaboration challenges will empower teams to build and manage robust, scalable, and efficient infrastructure in a modern software delivery pipeline.

There are numerous tools out there to implement IaC. **Terraform**, developed by HashiCorp, stands out for its cloud-agnostic approach. It allows you to write code in a high-level configuration language that describes the resources you need. This code is then translated into the appropriate service calls for the cloud providers of your choice. **Ansible**, another popular open source tool, uses a simple language called **YAML** to define automation jobs in a way that is straightforward to read.

> **Note**
> There are other tools as well, such as Chef, Puppet, Pulumi, AWS CloudFormation, Azure Resource Manager, Google Cloud Deployment Manager, and more, available to use for the IaC approach.

Let's delve into a practical scenario where IaC was game-changing. Picture a fintech start-up that operates in a multi-cloud environment, for reasons of resilience, redundancy, and avoiding vendor lock-in. Initially, their small team of developers had to manually configure resources on AWS and Google Cloud, which consumed significant time and often led to inconsistent configurations across the platforms.

Upon adopting Terraform as their IaC tool, they managed to drastically cut down the time spent on resource configuration. By writing Terraform code once, they were able to use the same configurations across both AWS and Google Cloud, ensuring consistency. The developers were now able to focus more on delivering features and less on tedious configuration tasks. Whenever they needed to scale their infrastructure, they simply adjusted a few parameters in their Terraform code and let the tool do the heavy lifting. This case shows how IaC can significantly streamline resource management in a multi-cloud environment.

Here's an example of a Terraform script snippet that creates a **virtual private cloud** (**VPC**) in AWS and a VPC network in Google Cloud:

```
# Configure the AWS Provider
provider "aws" {
  region = "us-west-1"
}
# Create a VPC in AWS
resource "aws_vpc" "aws_vpc" {
  cidr_block = "10.0.0.0/16"
  tags = {
    Name = "my-aws-vpc"
  }
}
# Configure the Google Cloud Provider
provider "google" {
  project    = "volksdevenv"
  region     = "us-central1"
}
# Create a VPC network in Google Cloud
resource "google_compute_network" "gcp_vpc" {
  name                   = "my-gcp-vpc"
  auto_create_subnetworks = "false"
}
# Outputs to display the created resource IDs
output "aws_vpc_id" {
  value = aws_vpc.aws_vpc.id
}
output "gcp_vpc_name" {
  value = google_compute_network.gcp_vpc.name
}
```

Let's take a look at what this Terraform script does:

- It sets up providers for both AWS and Google Cloud
- It creates a VPC in AWS with a specified CIDR block
- It creates a VPC network in Google Cloud with auto-created subnetworks disabled
- It outputs the IDs of the created resources

The following diagram illustrates two main steps for deploying IaC to multiple cloud providers, which are plan and apply. When changes are made to the infrastructure code, the developer needs to double-check and stage the new code before actually applying the changes to a production environment:

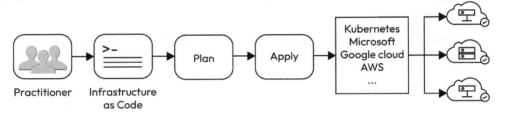

Figure 4.1 – Terraform flow

> **Note**
> Terraform provides handy commands to plan and apply changes to our infrastructure code. The **plan** command stages the changes for review and can later be committed thanks to the **apply** command.

As a cloud-native developer working in a multi-cloud environment, mastering IaC is an essential skill. It helps you automate and streamline resource management, enforce consistency, quickly recover from failures, replicate infrastructure, and ultimately focus more on building great applications.

In the next section, we will explore CI/CD, an important aspect of software engineering, and its best practices.

CI/CD

Continuous Integration (CI) encourages developers to merge their code changes into a central repository frequently, preferably several times a day. This frequent integration can help prevent the dreaded "merge hell." It allows teams to catch bugs and conflicts early and rectify them when they're still fresh and relatively easy to fix.

When CI is combined with **continuous deployment** (**CD**), we have a robust system that takes the freshly integrated code and automatically tests, builds, and deploys it. This can mean deploying to a staging environment for further testing, or it could mean deploying straight to production if the automated tests provide enough confidence in the quality of the build. This continuous process ensures rapid feedback on the software and quicker delivery of features to the end users.

There are various tools available to implement CI/CD. **Jenkins**, an open source automation server, provides numerous plugins for building, deploying, and automating any project. **CircleCI**, another popular tool, offers a cloud-based solution that's easy to set up and highly customizable.

CI/CD involves planning, coding, building, testing, releasing, and delivering software in a streamlined process for efficient development and deployment. All these stages are depicted in the following flow diagram:

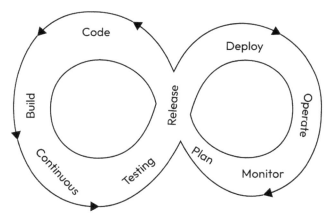

Figure 4.2 – CI/CD flow diagram

Consider the story of a software company that embraced the multi-cloud approach for its cloud-native application. Despite enjoying the benefits of multi-cloud, such as preventing vendor lock-in and improved reliability, the company faced challenges in managing deployments across different cloud platforms. Deployment processes varied, leading to inconsistencies, increased error rates, and slower time-to-market.

The adoption of Jenkins for CI/CD changed the game for them. Jenkins, with its flexibility and vast array of plugins, allowed the company to standardize its build, test, and deployment processes across multiple clouds. When a developer pushes a change, Jenkins automatically triggers the build process, runs tests, and, if all tests pass, deploys the application to the respective cloud platforms. This consistent and automated process reduced errors and accelerated the company's ability to deliver updates and new features.

For any cloud-native developer in a multi-cloud environment, CI/CD is not just a nice-to-have – it's essential. It streamlines the process from code commit to deployment, ensuring quicker feedback and faster delivery of value to users. Moreover, it supports the consistency that's required when working with multiple cloud platforms.

Let's look at the following diagram and draw the scope of each phase in the software development life cycle. CI relies on the frequent commits of new code, unit tested, to centralized repositories. In this phase, it is important to guarantee consistent and tested environments. CD relies heavily on automated functional and performance tests before a release approval. CD comes at the end of the life cycle to automatically deploy the release. The deployments are frequently fully automated and don't require human intervention. User and system feedback is collected and gracefully taken into account in a new iteration of the CI/CD cycle:

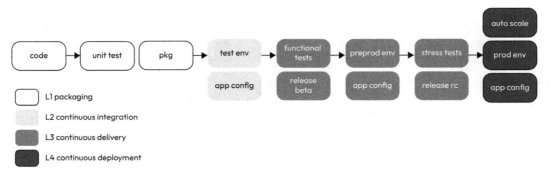

Figure 4.3 – Phases in the software development life cycle

Let's consider a sample CI/CD Jenkins pipeline that demonstrates automated testing, building, and deployment in the Kubernetes environment:

```
pipeline {
    agent any
    stages {
        stage('Build') {
            steps {
                sh '''docker build -t python-hello-world .
                docker tag python-hello-world jeveenj/python-hello-
world
                docker push jeveenj/python-hello-world
                '''
            }
        }
        stage('Test') {
            steps {
                sh 'docker run --rm python-hello-world:latest python
-m unittest'
            }
        }
        stage('Deploy') {
            steps {
                sh 'kubectl apply -f deployment.yaml'
```

```
                }
            }
        }
    }
}
```

The preceding Jenkins pipeline can be divided into two parts: CI and CD. Let's discuss them in detail:

- **CI**:

    - **Build stage**: This stage, `stage('Build')`, automates the process of building the application's Docker image. This ensures that the code can be compiled and packaged successfully, catching potential build issues early.

    - **Test stage**: This stage, `stage('Test')`, runs automated tests within a container to verify the application's functionality and identify any bugs or regressions. This helps maintain code quality and prevent problems from reaching production.

- **CD**:

    - **Deploy stage**: This stage, `stage('Deploy')`, automates the deployment of the application to a Kubernetes cluster using `kubectl apply`. This streamlines the delivery process and enables frequent releases with minimal manual intervention.

CI/CD best practices

In today's fast-paced software development landscape, implementing effective CI/CD practices is crucial for delivering high-quality software rapidly. CI/CD enables development teams to automate various stages of the software delivery pipeline, ensuring faster feedback loops, improved collaboration, and accelerated time to market. Here are some best practices to consider when implementing CI/CD:

- **Automation is key**:

    - Automate the build, test, and deployment processes to eliminate manual and error-prone tasks. Use build automation tools such as Jenkins, Travis CI, or GitLab CI/CD to automate the build process.

    - Implement CI by configuring triggers to automatically build and test code whenever changes are pushed to the repository.

- **Leverage version control**:

    - Integrate version control systems comprehensively into your CI/CD process. Utilize branching strategies such as Git Flow to manage features, fixes, and releases efficiently. This approach helps in tracking and merging changes effectively, ensuring that the code base is always in a deployable state.

    - Leverage version control systems such as Git to automate code integration.

- **Adopt a microservices architecture**:

  - Design your applications using a microservices architecture, where complex applications are decomposed into smaller, loosely coupled services.

  - Implement CI/CD pipelines for each microservice, enabling independent development, testing, and deployment of individual services. This allows for faster iterations and deployment of new features.

- **Maintain a single source of truth**:

  - Establish a central repository for your CI/CD configurations, scripts, and IaC templates. This ensures consistency and provides a single source of truth for your CI/CD pipeline.

  - Version control these artifacts to track changes and rollbacks, and also maintain a history of your pipeline configuration.

> Tip
> Jenkins provides tools to reuse IaC templates thanks to Jenkins Shared Libraries.

- **Implement CI**:

  - Practice CI by frequently integrating code changes into a shared repository. This ensures early detection of integration issues and reduces the risk of conflicts during code merges.

  - Automate unit tests, code quality checks, and static analysis tools such as SonarQube or ESLint to catch bugs, vulnerabilities, and code quality issues as early as possible.

- **Automated testing at all levels**:

  - Implement a comprehensive testing strategy that includes unit tests, integration tests, and end-to-end tests. Each test level serves a specific purpose and provides confidence in the stability and correctness of your application.

  - Use test automation frameworks and tools such as JUnit, Selenium, or Cypress to enable fast and reliable test execution within the CI/CD pipeline. Execute tests in parallel to speed up the feedback loop.

- **CD with canary releases**:

  - Implement CD by automating the deployment process to staging and production environments. Use deployment automation tools such as Kubernetes, Docker, or AWS Elastic Beanstalk.

  - Implement canary releases to gradually roll out new features or changes to a subset of users. Monitor key metrics and user feedback during canary deployments to ensure stability before proceeding with full deployment.

- **IaC:**

  - As we explored in detail in the previous section, IaC allows you to define your infrastructure using code and employ tools such as Terraform or AWS CloudFormation to provision and manage your infrastructure resources. This approach allows infrastructure changes to be versioned, tested, and deployed alongside application code.

  - Treat your infrastructure code as part of your application code, applying the same CI/CD practices for infrastructure changes. Infrastructure changes should go through the same testing and deployment pipelines as application code changes.

- **Monitor and collect feedback:**

  - Implement robust monitoring and observability practices to gain insights into the performance and behavior of your applications in production. Use tools such as Prometheus, Grafana, or Datadog to monitor key metrics, track errors, and identify performance bottlenecks. Set up alerts and notifications to proactively detect and respond to any issues or anomalies in your application's behavior.

  - Collect feedback from users through various channels, such as surveys, user interviews, or feedback forms. Leverage analytics tools such as Google Analytics or Mixpanel to understand user behavior, preferences, and pain points.

  - Use the feedback and analytics data to drive continuous improvements in your software, prioritize feature enhancements, and optimize user experiences.

  - Establish a feedback loop with your development team, product managers, and stakeholders to incorporate user feedback into the development process and align your roadmap with customer needs.

By adopting these CI/CD best practices, development teams can streamline their software delivery pipeline, reduce manual errors, increase productivity, and ultimately deliver high-quality software faster. Embracing automation, test-driven development, and IaC principles enables teams to iterate rapidly, respond to customer needs, and stay ahead in today's competitive software landscape.

Just as the mountaineers continuously refine their strategies based on feedback, weather conditions, and the terrain, development teams should continuously refine their CI/CD practices. The mountain is ever-changing, and the strategies that worked yesterday may not work today. And so is the software landscape ever-evolving. By staying agile and adaptable, both the mountaineers and the development teams can overcome any challenges they face and reach their respective peaks.

In the next section, we will explore DevOps and GitOps practices, which are like the compass and map for our mountaineers, guiding them through their journey and ensuring they stay on the right path.

Scaling mountainous success – a tale of DevOps and GitOps

Alright, let's once again wear our globe-trotter hat and imagine that there is a team of mountaineers embarking on a challenging ascent to the summit of a towering mountain. The climbers, representing the developers, are responsible for pushing forward and establishing progress, while the support team at the base camp, analogous to the operations team, plays a crucial role in providing critical support and ensuring the overall stability of the journey.

In the traditional approach, the climbers would operate independently, with the base camp responding to their progress. This siloed approach often leads to communication gaps, delays, and potential risks. This is where DevOps comes in, bridging the gap between the climbers and the base camp, transforming them into a cohesive unit sharing a common goal.

DevOps acts as an advanced communication system, enabling seamless connectivity between the climbers and the base camp. Updates are exchanged in real time, collective decisions are made collaboratively, and everyone remains aligned with the overall plan. This cultural shift fosters collaboration, transparency, and shared responsibility, ensuring that everyone contributes effectively, rather than operating in isolation.

GitOps, on the other hand, serves as the detailed map and compass that guides the team's ascent. It establishes a single source of truth, a repository where all infrastructure configurations and application manifests are meticulously documented. Every change, every decision, every deviation from the established plan is meticulously recorded, providing a clear historical record of the team's journey. This transparency facilitates rollbacks in case of unforeseen challenges and enables proactive error detection.

In essence, DevOps represents the foundation of effective teamwork, fostering collaboration and communication, while GitOps provides the foundational tools to ensure that everyone is on the same page and that the software journey is conducted in a controlled and efficient manner. Together, these practices empower teams to scale the mountains of software development and operations with unwavering resilience. The following table gives you the key differences between DevOps and GitOps:

Factors	DevOps	GitOps
Principles	DevOps enables practices to break the silo between development and operations.	GitOps involves implementing intelligent and automated operations
CI/CD	DevOps enables CI/CD with the usual push.	GitOps powers CD by introducing pull
Deployment	DevOps covers the imperative and declarative approaches.	GitOps has declarative IaC.
Monitoring	DevOps provides monitoring at all layers.	GitOps monitors the states of desired versus current user-used operators.

Factors	DevOps	GitOps
Automatization	DevOps automates development and operations and closely binds them.	GitOps closely binds the monitoring and deployment processes.
Scope	DevOps encompasses a broad range of practices, encompassing collaboration, CI/CD, automation, and tools.	GitOps focuses specifically on using Git as the single source of truth for infrastructure and applications.
Focus	DevOps emphasizes cultural transformation, breaking down silos between development and operations teams.	GitOps focuses on automating infrastructure, environments, and application deployments, ensuring consistency with the desired state defined in Git repositories.
Tools	DevOps utilizes a wide range of tools, from source code management systems to CI/CD pipelines and configuration management tools.	GitOps primarily relies on Git, containerization, and orchestration tools such as Kubernetes.
Applications	DevOps applies to a wide range of applications, from traditional monolithic applications to cloud-native microservices architectures.	GitOps is primarily used for containerized applications, leveraging their flexibility and scalability.

Table 4.1 – Key differences between DevOps and GitOps

As we have seen, DevOps and GitOps are complementary approaches that aim to streamline and optimize software delivery processes. DevOps provides the overarching framework for collaboration and communication, while GitOps acts as the orchestrator, ensuring that infrastructure and applications are aligned with the desired state defined in Git repositories. By adopting these practices effectively, organizations can achieve greater agility, reliability, and efficiency in their software development and operations endeavors.

The following diagram shows a classic GitOps pipeline. A developer pushes code to the Git repository, which automatically triggers the build and registry of a container image. The new infrastructure configuration is staged for the developer, who performs a pull request to obtain the latest update. The developer needs to validate the changes before merging and deploying the changes to production:

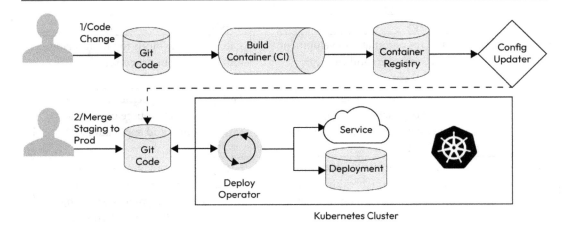

Figure 4.4 – GitOps pipeline

Challenges

However, as with any journey, adopting DevOps and GitOps practices can present certain challenges. Let's explore some common challenges and strategies for overcoming them:

- **Challenge – cultural transformation**:

  - **Silos and resistance to change**: Organizations often have separate teams with different priorities and processes. Breaking down these silos and fostering a culture of collaboration requires strong leadership, open communication, and creating shared goals and responsibilities. Encourage cross-functional teams, promote knowledge sharing, and incentivize collaboration to overcome resistance to change.

  - **Lack of a DevOps mindset**: Embracing a DevOps mindset requires a shift in mindset and a focus on continuous improvement, collaboration, and accountability. Foster a culture of experimentation, learning from failures, and embracing automation and feedback loops. Provide training, mentorship, and resources to help team members understand and adopt the DevOps principles and practices.

- **Challenge – tooling and automation**:

  - **Tool selection and integration**: The DevOps landscape is filled with a variety of tools and technologies. Evaluate and select tools that align with your organization's needs and goals. Focus on tool integration to create a seamless toolchain and automate processes. Establish clear guidelines and standards for tool adoption to maintain consistency and avoid tool proliferation.

  - **Automation challenges**: Implementing automation requires upfront investment and ongoing maintenance. Start small by identifying manual, repetitive tasks that can be automated and gradually expand automation efforts. Involve cross-functional teams in the automation process to gain buy-in and ensure the automation solutions meet their needs. Regularly review and update automation scripts and processes to adapt to changing requirements.

- **Challenge – security and compliance**:

  - **Security as code**: Incorporate security practices into the entire software delivery life cycle by treating security as code. Implement automated security testing, vulnerability scanning, and code analysis as part of the CI/CD pipeline. Integrate security practices into the development process and ensure that security considerations are addressed early and continuously.

  - **Compliance requirements**: Identify and understand compliance requirements specific to your industry and organization. Implement controls and processes to ensure compliance with regulations and standards. Leverage IaC and configuration management tools to establish auditable and repeatable processes that meet compliance requirements.

- **Challenge – GitOps adoption**:

  - **GitOps principles and workflows**: Educate teams on the principles and workflows of GitOps, emphasizing the importance of version control, declarative infrastructure, and the use of Git as a single source of truth. Provide training and resources to help teams understand the benefits of GitOps and how to implement them effectively.

  - **Infrastructure automation**: Ensure that infrastructure and configuration changes are managed through version control, enabling traceability, reproducibility, and rollback capabilities. Leverage IaC tools such as Terraform or AWS CloudFormation to codify infrastructure changes. Automate the deployment and synchronization of infrastructure changes using GitOps practices.

By understanding and addressing these challenges, organizations can successfully adopt DevOps and GitOps practices, as well as cultivate a culture of collaboration, invest in the right tools and automation, prioritize security and compliance, and educate teams on the principles and workflows of GitOps. With these strategies, organizations can overcome barriers and fully realize the benefits of DevOps and GitOps in their software delivery pipeline.

Consider, for instance, the story of a cloud-native software company juggling operations across multiple cloud platforms. Managing these operations became a major headache. Changes needed to be tracked across each platform, leading to inconsistencies, misconfigurations, and slower recovery from outages.

The introduction of DevOps and GitOps practices brought about a revolution. The company began using tools such as Jenkins for CI/CD, Kubernetes for orchestration, and Terraform for infrastructure management. But the most transformative tool was Git. With Git at the center of its operations, the company could now handle infrastructure changes in the same way it managed code changes. A simple pull request could update a Kubernetes deployment configuration, which would then be automatically applied to the clusters on all cloud platforms. This reduced human error, simplified rollback processes, and improved recovery times.

The adoption of DevOps and GitOps is essential for any cloud-native developer operating in a multi-cloud environment. It provides consistency, speeds up recovery times, and eases the management of complex systems. The practices of CI/CD, IaC, and container orchestration all contribute to an effective DevOps strategy. Having explored DevOps and GitOps, let's delve into the service mesh, a crucial orchestra layer for modern microservice choreography.

Service meshes in multi-cloud environments

As our mountaineering team traverses the challenging terrain of multiple cloud environments, managing the intricate pathways our applications take becomes increasingly challenging. This is where a **service mesh** comes in handy. It's like our GPS, managing the communication between services, ensuring they find the quickest and safest routes.

As mentioned in *Chapter 3, Designing for Diversity with Multi-Cloud Application Strategies*, a service mesh acts as a control tower for service communication in complex applications, ensuring reliable connections even across multiple cloud platforms. It's like a hidden network conductor, orchestrating smooth data flow between services regardless of their location.

Consider **Istio**, for example. It's like the compass guiding our mountaineers through the intricate network pathways of our applications. Istio is a service mesh that provides a way to connect, secure, control, and observe services. It provides traffic management capabilities, allowing intelligent routing and load balancing of traffic. It also offers robust security features, including identity and credential management and enforcement of network policies. Moreover, it provides insights into your applications through telemetry, logging, and tracing capabilities.

However, implementing a service mesh in a multi-cloud environment can be complex. It requires careful planning and configuration to ensure seamless communication across different cloud platforms. It also requires monitoring and management to ensure its reliable operation.

Despite these challenges, a service mesh is a powerful tool in the multi-cloud toolkit. Let's have a look at some of the essential features that a service mesh provides to a cloud-native application deployed in a multi-cloud environment:

- **Service discovery**: This feature allows developers to register and keep track of all services used within the application. Moreover, an agnostic service mesh can enable service discovery across multiple cloud environments.

- **Load balancing**: A service mesh can allow traffic control, such as load balancing, across multiple instances of a service:

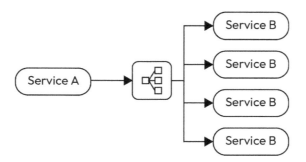

Figure 4.5 – Service mesh as a load balancer

- **External traffic control**: In addition to managing the traffic within the network, a service mesh can also facilitate access to services by external parties. Some service mesh tools have integrated API gateways to help manage both internal and external traffic.

Service mesh provides the visibility, control, and security needed to manage complex, microservices-based applications across multiple cloud platforms. By leveraging a service mesh, developers can focus on building and deploying applications, while the service mesh handles the complexities of inter-service communication.

The following diagram shows the architecture of a service mesh, which in this case uses a proxy instance called a sidecar. This sidecar is linked to each microservice and is responsible for security and monitoring. The services, attached sidecars, and their interaction are usually referred to as the data plane. In a separate layer, the control panel ensures tasks such as instance creation, monitoring, and managing network security:

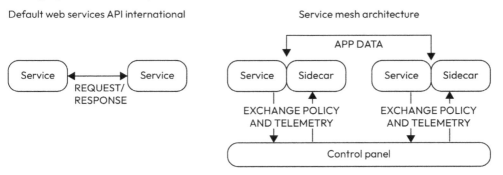

Figure 4.6 – Architecture of a service mesh

Let's discuss the strengths and challenges of service mesh.

Strengths

Here are its strengths:

- **Improved communication and visibility**: A service mesh acts as a centralized control plane for service-to-service communication, providing features such as service discovery, load balancing, and traffic routing. This improves overall network visibility and makes troubleshooting easier.

- **Resilience and fault tolerance**: Service meshes implement features such as circuit breaking, retries, and timeouts to handle service failures gracefully without cascading downtime. This increases the overall resilience and availability of applications.

- **Security and authentication**: Service meshes can enforce strong authentication and authorization policies for service communication, preventing unauthorized access and malicious attacks. They also enable features such as mutual TLS encryption to secure data in transit.

- **Observability and monitoring**: Service meshes provide comprehensive metrics and tracing data for service interactions, enabling deep insights into application performance and behavior. This helps with identifying bottlenecks, optimizing resource utilization, and improving overall service quality.

- **Microservices architecture support**: Service meshes are well-suited for microservices architectures, allowing independent development and deployment of services while ensuring reliable and secure communication.

Challenges

Here are some of the challenges:

- **Complexity**: Implementing and managing a service mesh can introduce additional complexity, especially for large and complex deployments. Choosing the right tools and practices is crucial for effective management.

- **Performance overhead**: Service mesh components such as sidecars can introduce some performance overhead, especially in resource-constrained environments. Optimizing configurations and choosing efficient implementations can mitigate this impact.

- **Vendor lock-in**: Choosing a specific service mesh solution can lead to vendor lock-in, making it difficult to switch to other technologies or platforms in the future. Opting for open source solutions and focusing on interoperability can help with avoiding this.

- **Operational overhead**: Managing and monitoring a service mesh requires additional operational effort. Automation tools and skilled personnel are needed to handle this overhead effectively.

- **Security considerations**: While service meshes improve security, they also introduce new attack surfaces. Implementing proper security practices and securing sidecar configurations are essential.

Overall, the benefits of service mesh often outweigh the challenges for applications with complex microservice architectures and strict requirements for security, reliability, and observability. However, it's important to carefully consider the potential drawbacks and choose the right tools and practices for your specific needs.

In the next section, we will learn about containerization and orchestration, as well as their strengths and challenges.

Containerization and orchestration

This section dives deeper into the dynamic duo (containerization and orchestration), exploring the strengths and challenges of containerizing and orchestrating your applications to achieve agile, efficient, and resilient deployments. Get ready to witness the magic of containerized applications taking center stage!

Containerization

Traditionally, Docker has been the dominant containerization platform. **Containerization** stands out as a promising option, offering lightweight and efficient container runtime capabilities while maintaining the core functionalities of Docker Engine. Its streamlined architecture enhances performance and security, making it an attractive choice.

Another notable alternative is CRI-O, an open source container runtime built on containers. It excels in lightweightness and flexibility, further reducing overhead and improving overall efficiency. Additionally, CRI-O enjoys strong support from the Kubernetes community, making it a suitable choice for Kubernetes deployments.

Beyond container runtimes, additional containerization tools provide higher-level abstractions, simplifying container management and orchestration. Popular alternatives include *Podman*, *Buildah*, and *Skopeo*. Podman mimics Docker's functionalities, while Buildah focuses on image creation and manipulation. Skopeo facilitates image sharing and replication across different registries.

> Note
>
> Kubernetes is deprecating Docker as a container runtime after v1.20. However, this doesn't mean that Kubernetes can't run applications that are packaged as Docker containers. Rather, it signifies a shift in the underlying container runtime being used by Kubernetes.

Selecting the right containerization solution

The ideal containerization solution depends on specific project requirements. For Kubernetes users, CRI-O is a natural choice due to its native support within the platform. Lightweight and flexible options such as *containerd* or CRI-O are suitable for applications seeking minimal overhead and efficient resource utilization. For higher-level abstractions, Podman, Buildah, and Skopeo offer comprehensive management and orchestration capabilities.

The containerization landscape is evolving rapidly, with new technologies constantly emerging. While Docker has left an indelible mark, lightweight, efficient, and secure solutions such as *containerd* and CRI-O are paving the way for a more streamlined and secure containerization experience. Cloud-native developers should stay abreast of these advancements to effectively leverage these tools and build resilient, agile, and scalable cloud-native applications.

The following table provides a comparative analysis of two lightweight container runtimes: containerd and CRI-O. Both alternatives are necessary in the container ecosystem as they provide a runtime environment for executing containers and managing images. The table compares the two alternatives across different features, such as runtime type, container format, orchestration platforms support, image registry support, security, network, and performance features. As discussed, choosing the right containerization solution will depend on your project requirements, and a table similar to the following can help you make a wise decision:

Feature	containerd	CRI-O
Runtime type	Lightweight container runtime	Lightweight container runtime
Container format	OCI	OCI
Orchestration platform support	Kubernetes, Docker Swarm, Mesosphere DC/OS	Kubernetes
Image registry support	Docker Hub, Quay.io, Google Container Registry	Docker Hub, Quay.io, Google Container Registry
Security features	Sandboxing, seccomp, user namespaces	Sandboxing, seccomp, user namespaces
Networking	CNI	CNI
Performance	Faster than Docker Engine	Faster than containerd

Table 4.2 – Comparison between containerd and CRI-O

> **Note**
>
> **Virtual machines (VMs)** virtualize the hardware to run many different operating systems on a single host. Containers virtualize the operating system, allowing multiple tasks to run on a single operating system instance.

Let's discuss the strengths and challenges of containerization.

Strengths

Here are its strengths:

- **Isolation**: Each container runs in an isolated environment with its own filesystem, network, and resources. This improves security and stability by preventing conflicts between applications and resource exhaustion.

- **Portability**: Containers are packaged with all their dependencies, making them independent of the underlying infrastructure. They can be easily moved between different environments (physical or virtual machines, cloud platforms, and so on) without modifications.

- **Scalability**: Containers are lightweight and start up quickly, enabling you to easily scale your applications by adding or removing containers on demand. This improves resource utilization and responsiveness.

- **DevOps efficiency**: Containers streamline the development and deployment process. Developers can build and test their applications in isolated environments, and operations teams can easily deploy and manage applications across different environments.

- **Microservices architecture**: Containerization facilitates the development and deployment of microservices architectures, where applications are broken down into small, independent services that can be easily scaled and updated.

Challenges

Here are its challenges:

- **Complexity**: Managing a large number of containers can be complex. Tools and processes are needed to manage container life cycles, security, and networking.

- **Security**: While containers provide isolation, they still require proper security measures to prevent vulnerabilities and attacks. Shared kernel and runtime environments can introduce additional security risks.

- **Storage**: Container images can consume significant storage space, especially when dealing with large applications or numerous microservices. Efficient storage and image management strategies are necessary.

- **Networking**: Configuring and managing network connectivity between containers and with external services can be a challenge, especially in complex deployments.

Despite these challenges, the benefits of containerization often outweigh the drawbacks. With the right tools and processes, containerization can significantly improve the agility, efficiency, and scalability of your applications.

Kubernetes

Now, imagine if our team of climbers was quite large, each with a backpack, and they needed to work together to reach the summit. This is where *Kubernetes* comes in. **Kubernetes** is like the expedition leader, who coordinates the climbers, ensuring they work together effectively. It manages the climbers (containers), ensuring they have the resources they need, are properly balanced, and can recover quickly in case of any mishaps.

Kubernetes architecture

Kubernetes is a container orchestration system that automates the deployment, scaling, and management of containerized applications. Kubernetes is composed of several different components (listed here), each of which plays a specific role in the overall architecture:

- **etcd**: etcd is a distributed key-value store that stores the state of Kubernetes. This includes information about all of the Pods, Services, and other resources that are running in the cluster.

- **Controller manager**: The controller manager is responsible for maintaining the state of Kubernetes. This includes tasks such as creating and deleting pods, scaling pods, and ensuring that pods are running on the correct nodes.

- **Scheduler**: The scheduler is responsible for assigning pods to nodes. This is done based on several factors, such as the availability of resources, the load on the nodes, and the affinity and anti-affinity rules for the pods.

- **API server**: The API server is the main entry point for interacting with Kubernetes. It exposes a RESTful API that can be used to create, delete, and manage resources.

- **Kubelet**: Kubelet is a process that runs on each node in the cluster. It is responsible for running pods and ensuring that they are healthy.

- **Kube-proxy**: Kube-proxy is a process that runs on each node in the cluster. It is responsible for routing traffic to the pods that are running on the node.

- **Container runtime**: The container runtime is the software that is responsible for running containers. Kubernetes supports several different container runtimes, such as Docker and CRI-O.

As discussed previously, *Figure 4.6* presents different components of the Kubernetes architecture:

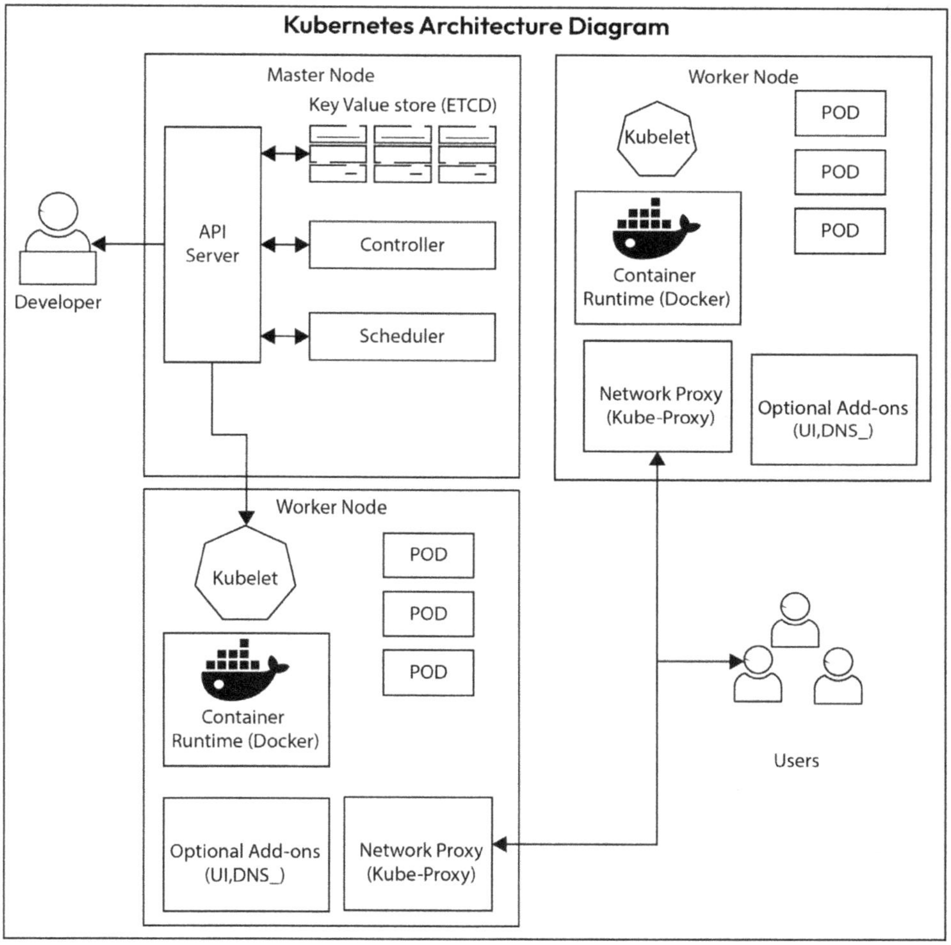

Figure 4.7 – Kubernetes architecture

Kubernetes provides features such as load balancing, network traffic distribution, scaling, and automated rollouts and rollbacks, making it the go-to tool for container orchestration. Let's explore the strengths and weaknesses of Kubernetes.

In this section, we will provide a Kubernetes deployment file. This deployment is designed to manage and scale a collection of Pods, each running an instance of the Docker image. This step effectively demonstrates how a containerized application, defined in a Dockerfile, can be orchestrated and managed at scale in a Kubernetes environment. The deployment configuration ensures consistent, automated deployment of our application, maintaining the desired number of replicas for high availability and load balancing.

Assuming the Docker image created from your Dockerfile is named `python-hello-world` and is available in a Docker registry (such as Docker Hub), the Kubernetes `Deployment` file will look something like this:

```
apiVersion: apps/v1
kind: Deployment
metadata:
  name: python-hello-world-deployment
  labels:
    app: python-hello-world
spec:
  replicas: 3
  selector:
    matchLabels:
      app: python-hello-world
  template:
    metadata:
      labels:
        app: python-hello-world
    spec:
      containers:
      - name: python-hello-world
        image: <your-docker-username>/python-hello-world:latest
        ports:
        - containerPort: 80
```

This file tells Kubernetes to create a deployment that will ensure three replicas of the `python-hello-world` container are running at all times. `containerPort` is set to `80`, which is the port we exposed in the Dockerfile.

> **Note**
>
> The preceding code snippet can be found in this book's GitHub repository: `https://github.com/PacktPublishing/Multi-Cloud-Handbook-for-Developers/tree/main/Chapter-4`.

Strengths

Kubernetes excels in several key areas that make it a popular choice for organizations of all sizes:

- **Powerful orchestration**: Kubernetes automates many of the tasks involved in managing containerized applications, such as scaling, load balancing, service discovery, and self-healing. This frees up developers to focus on building applications, while Kubernetes handles the underlying infrastructure.

- **High scalability and availability**: Kubernetes is designed to handle large-scale applications, seamlessly scaling them up or down based on demand. It distributes containers across multiple nodes, ensuring that applications remain available, even if one node fails. This high availability ensures that users can always access your applications, even in the event of hardware issues.

- **Declarative configuration and rolling updates**: Kubernetes utilizes declarative configuration files (YAML or JSON) to define the desired state of your applications. This means you specify the desired state, and Kubernetes works to ensure that the application always matches that state. This approach simplifies deployment, versioning, and rolling updates, allowing you to update applications gradually without disrupting service.

- **Vibrant ecosystem and community support**: Kubernetes has a thriving ecosystem of tools and plugins, as well as a strong community that provides support and solutions to common challenges. This ecosystem makes it easier to find the resources you need to develop, deploy, and manage your containerized applications.

Challenges

Despite its strengths, Kubernetes also presents some challenges that you should be prepared for:

- **Steep learning curve**: Kubernetes has a complex architecture and an extensive set of features, which can make it challenging to learn and master. This learning curve may be particularly steep for teams new to container orchestration.

- **Infrastructure complexity**: Kubernetes operates at a lower level of the infrastructure stack, requiring the setup and management of additional components, such as etcd, kube-proxy, and kube-dns. This can add complexity and overhead to managing Kubernetes clusters.

Addressing challenges

To mitigate these challenges, organizations can consider using managed Kubernetes services or cloud-based Kubernetes platforms. Managed Kubernetes services provide a hands-off approach to cluster management, while cloud-based Kubernetes platforms offer built-in features and integrations to simplify deployment and management. Consider a cloud-native software company developing an application with a microservices architecture. They decide to deploy their microservices as Docker containers, ensuring that each service runs in isolation with all its dependencies. However, they quickly realized that managing each container manually across multiple cloud platforms is not feasible. That's when Kubernetes entered the picture. With Kubernetes, they can manage their containers across all platforms from a single control plane. This improved their deployment speed, reliability, and resource utilization.

From this narrative, it's clear how crucial Docker and Kubernetes are to any cloud-native developer working in a multi-cloud environment. Containerization with Docker provides a consistent and reliable environment for your applications to run, while Kubernetes allows seamless orchestration of your containerized applications across multiple cloud platforms.

Multi-cloud networking and security

In the context of our mountaineering expedition, effective communication and safety are paramount. The climbers use radios for communication and adhere to safety protocols to mitigate risks. This is analogous to the networking and security aspects in a multi-cloud environment.

In single-cloud or multi-cloud deployments, networking ensures seamless communication between applications hosted on different cloud platforms. It involves setting up load balancers, configuring network policies, establishing private connections, and more. Each cloud provider offers its own set of networking services, and understanding how to use them for optimal communication between services is a key skill for a cloud-native developer.

Security, on the other hand, is about protecting your applications and data from threats. In a multi-cloud environment, security becomes even more complex due to the distributed nature of applications and data. Security must be implemented at all levels – application, data, network, and access control. This includes configuring firewalls, managing access controls, encrypting data at rest and in transit, and regularly auditing the systems for potential vulnerabilities.

Let's consider our software company embarking on a multi-cloud strategy. They have applications deployed on *AWS*, *Azure*, and *Google Cloud*. These applications need to communicate with each other to provide a unified service to the end users. The company uses **virtual private networks** (**VPNs**) and load balancers to establish secure and efficient communication between the applications across the different cloud platforms.

However, networking is just one part of the puzzle. The company also needs to ensure that their applications and data are secure. They implement firewalls to protect against unauthorized access, use **identity and access management** (**IAM**) to control who can access what resources, encrypt their data to protect it from being compromised, and regularly conduct security audits to identify and fix potential vulnerabilities.

In this scenario, the company is like a group of climbers communicating via radio and following safety protocols to ensure a successful expedition. Just as the climbers need to adapt their communication and safety protocols based on the terrain and weather conditions, the company needs to adapt its networking and security strategies based on the specific requirements and features of each cloud platform.

As a cloud-native developer, understanding multi-cloud networking and security is crucial. It allows you to design and implement robust, secure, and efficient applications that can leverage the benefits of multi-cloud environments. It's like being the climber who knows how to use the radio effectively and follows the safety protocols diligently – a valuable asset in any mountaineering expedition.

Summary

By embarking on a mountaineering expedition metaphor, we ventured through the landscape of cloud-native application development in a multi-cloud realm. We began with the essentials of automation, containerization, and orchestration, drawing parallels between Docker as the climber's backpack and Kubernetes as the expedition leader coordinating the journey.

While navigating intricate multi-cloud networking and security, we likened this to climbers adhering to communication and safety protocols. We explored the significance of robust networking for application interaction and security measures to safeguard data and applications across diverse cloud platforms.

In the next chapter, we'll shift our focus to the secure and compliant handling of data within the intricate multi-cloud environment. Comparable to a skilled navigator ensuring safe passage through unpredictable terrain, cloud-native developers must master strategies for managing data, ensuring security, and complying with regulations across various cloud platforms.

Part 3: Managing and Operating Cloud-Native Apps in Multi-Cloud

This part takes you through the essentials of managing data, security, and the compliance of cloud-native applications in multi-cloud environments, emphasizing best practices in these areas. You'll explore how to effectively handle data privacy and DevSecOps and align with CIS/CSA benchmarks. Additionally, it focuses on optimizing costs for cloud-native applications, including implementing shift-left cost strategies and FinOps practices. Moreover, it delves into troubleshooting strategies for cloud-native applications, covering the roles, tools, and best practices for SRE and DevOps, including chaos engineering. This comprehensive approach ensures you have the insights and techniques to maintain the reliability and resilience of cloud-native applications across multiple cloud platforms.

This part has the following chapters:

- *Chapter 5, Managing Security, Data, and Compliance on Multi-Cloud*
- *Chapter 6, Maximizing Value and Minimizing Cost of Multi-Cloud*
- *Chapter 7, Troubleshooting Multi-Cloud Applications*

5

Managing Security, Data, and Compliance on Multi-Cloud

We now arrive at a critical juncture that demands our utmost attention: the intersection of data management, security protocols, and compliance regulations. This chapter is not merely a guide but a technical manual, designed to equip cloud-native developers with the concrete skills and knowledge required to navigate this complex multi-cloud terrain.

In a multi-cloud architecture, data doesn't reside in a monolithic storage system but is often distributed across various cloud services. This distribution poses unique challenges for data integrity, security, and compliance with legal regulations such as the **General Data Protection Regulation (GDPR)** and industry-specific standards such as the **Health Insurance Portability and Accountability Act (HIPAA)** for healthcare or the **Payment Card Industry Data Security Standard (PCI DSS)** for finance.

Within the chapters, we will explore five main topics, which are as follows:

- Managing data and security in multi-cloud environments
- Introduction to security in cloud-native multi-cloud environments
- DevSecOps best practices for cloud-native apps in multi-cloud environments
- Managing compliance across multiple clouds environments
- **Identity and access management (IAM)** across multiple clouds environments
- Data privacy and protection

By the end of this chapter, you'll have an understanding of the technical intricacies involved in managing data, implementing security measures, and ensuring compliance in a multi-cloud environment.

Managing data and security in multi-cloud environments

In this section, we will explore the profound significance of data security and privacy in the dynamic multi-cloud environment. We will look into best practices for securing data across multiple cloud platforms, address data residency and sovereignty requirements, and navigate the intricate web of data privacy and compliance considerations.

Understanding data security and privacy in multi-cloud

It is evident that data plays a central role in the functioning and vitality of cloud-native applications. In this context, data serves as the lifeblood, fueling the operation and functionality of these applications. Data encompasses a wide range of information, from user data and application state to configurations and logs. It holds immense value, but its exposure to threats (such as data breaches, data loss, data tampering, **denial-of-service (DoS)** attacks, and so on) can be catastrophic. In the multi-cloud environment, where data traverses different platforms and boundaries, safeguarding its integrity and privacy becomes paramount. Let's delve into the details of data security and privacy within the multi-cloud landscape and explore best practices that are pivotal in protecting our digital assets against ever-evolving threats.

Data security and privacy in multi-cloud

It is important that navigating the multi-cloud landscape requires a robust defense strategy to protect data security and privacy. **Encryption** serves as the first line of defense, transforming data into unreadable formats that can only be decrypted with the correct key. But encryption is just the tip of the iceberg. Data access controls act as additional layers of fortification, ensuring that only authorized personnel can access specific datasets. These controls are implemented through IAM policies, which can be fine-tuned to grant permissions at granular levels.

Best practices for data security

In a multi-cloud environment, securing data requires a multi-faceted approach that goes beyond mere encryption. Various encryption techniques, such as the **Advanced Encryption Standard (AES)** and **Rivest-Shamir-Adleman (RSA)**, are essential for protecting data at rest and in transit. But the security measures don't stop there. Data access controls are implemented through IAM policies, which can be configured to provide granular permissions. These policies ensure that only authorized users can access specific datasets, thereby enhancing security. Additionally, data integrity is maintained through cryptographic hash functions, which ensure that the data has not been tampered with during storage or transit. Next are some best practices for data security in a multi-cloud environment:

- Use IAM to enforce the **principle of least privilege (PoLP)**
- Utilize AES for data at rest and **Transport Layer Security (TLS)** for data in transit
- Conduct periodic reviews of security policies and access rights

- Adhere to local laws regarding data storage and transfer

- Standardize security measures across all cloud platforms

- Prepare and practice responses to potential data breaches

- Ensure that APIs have strong authentication and are accessed over secure connections

- Implement automated backup solutions and a **disaster recovery** (**DR**) strategy

- Monitor all environments for unusual activities indicative of a breach

- Protect data life cycle stages from creation, through usage, to deletion

- Use tools that can manage security across multiple clouds

- Regularly train staff on new threats and best security practices

Data residency and sovereignty

When it comes to data residency and sovereignty present another layer of complexity. Different jurisdictions have varying regulations about where data can be stored and processed. For example, the European Union's GDPR imposes stringent rules about data storage and transfer. Understanding these regulations is crucial for compliance. Developers can manage this through data localization strategies and by leveraging regional cloud services that comply with local laws.

Automated compliance checks and data portability

Given the complexity of adhering to multiple compliance frameworks, automated compliance checks are invaluable. Tools that can scan your configurations and compare them against compliance benchmarks can save time and reduce the risk of human error. These tools can be integrated into the CI/CD pipeline to ensure continuous compliance as code is developed and deployed. Furthermore, data portability is essential for both operational flexibility and contingency planning, such as DR. Developers should be familiar with each cloud provider's data export tools and APIs and should design data models that are easily portable.

By delving into these nuanced aspects of data security and privacy, developers arm themselves with the knowledge and tools to navigate the complex terrains of multi-cloud environments. Just as a seasoned traveler would not embark on a journey without a well-stocked kit and a detailed map, a prudent developer should not venture into multi-cloud computing without a comprehensive understanding of its security and privacy implications.

Implementing best practices for data protection

It is important to remember that safeguarding data is not merely a matter of good intentions or theoretical understanding; it demands the meticulous implementation of practical strategies and tools. Just as a seasoned traveler wouldn't rely solely on a compass but would also carry a map, GPS, and survival gear, a cloud-native developer must employ a comprehensive toolkit for data protection. This toolkit should include encryption, data access controls, and methodologies for maintaining data integrity and confidentiality. The following are toolkits for data protection:

- **Encryption techniques**: Encryption is the cornerstone of data protection. While encryption algorithms such as AES and RSA are widely used, it's crucial to understand their appropriate use cases. AES is generally faster and suitable for encrypting large datasets, while RSA is often used for secure key exchanges. Implementing encryption at both the data-at-rest and data-in-transit stages is essential. For data at rest, disk-level or database-level encryption can be used. For data in transit, **Secure Sockets Layer (SSL)**/TLS protocols are the industry standards.

  The following example uses Node.js's `crypto` module to demonstrate basic encryption and decryption functions using the *AES-256-CBC* algorithm. It generates a random key and **initialization vector (IV)**, encrypts a text string, and then decrypts it, showcasing a method to secure sensitive data:

```
const crypto = require('crypto');


const algorithm = 'aes-256-cbc';
const key = crypto.randomBytes(32); // Store this key securely
for later decryption
const iv = crypto.randomBytes(16);


function encrypt(text) {
  let cipher = crypto.createCipheriv(algorithm, Buffer.
from(key), iv);
  let encrypted = cipher.update(text, 'utf8', 'hex');
  encrypted += cipher.final('hex');
  return { iv: iv.toString('hex'), encryptedData: encrypted };
}
```

> **Note**
>
> Code snippet resources used in this chapter can be found in the GitHub repo for this chapter (`https://github.com/PacktPublishing/Multi-Cloud-Handbook-for-Developers/tree/main/Chapter-5`).

- **Data access controls and confidentiality**: Data access controls are the sentinels that guard the gates to your data repositories. These controls are implemented through IAM policies, which can be as granular as needed to restrict access to specific data fields. **Role-based access control (RBAC)** can be used to assign permissions based on job functions, ensuring that users have just enough access to perform their roles but not more. **Attribute-based access control (ABAC)** can further refine these permissions based on other attributes such as location, time, or the type of data being accessed. Confidentiality ensures that data is not disclosed to unauthorized individuals, and it often goes hand in hand with encryption and access controls. Techniques such as data masking can be employed to display only a portion of the data, thereby maintaining confidentiality.

- **Data integrity**: Maintaining data integrity is about ensuring that once data is written, it remains accurate and unaltered unless changed by authorized personnel. Cryptographic hash functions such as *SHA-256* can be used to verify data integrity.

- **Data backup and recovery**: Data protection is incomplete without a robust backup and recovery strategy. In a multi-cloud environment, this involves not just regular backups but also ensuring that these backups are secure and compliant with regulatory requirements. Versioning can be used to keep track of changes and roll back to previous states if needed. Recovery objectives should be clearly defined and tested regularly to ensure they meet **business continuity** (**BC**) requirements.

- **Monitoring and auditing**: Continuous monitoring and auditing are essential for maintaining a secure data environment. Logging all access and changes to data can provide a trail for audit purposes and for investigating any security incidents. Tools such as **security information and event management** (**SIEM**) systems can be integrated to provide real-time analysis of security alerts generated by applications and infrastructure.

By implementing these best practices for data protection, developers equip themselves with a robust toolkit that not only safeguards data but also ensures compliance with regulatory standards. This comprehensive approach to data protection is akin to a traveler who prepares for all contingencies, ensuring not just a successful journey but also a safe return.

Data privacy and compliance considerations

Navigating the multi-cloud environment is akin to traversing a labyrinth of laws, regulations, and ethical considerations. Just as a responsible traveler respects the local customs and laws of the lands they visit, cloud-native developers must adhere to a complex web of data privacy regulations and compliance standards. We will now look into the intricacies of data privacy and compliance, providing actionable insights for developers:

- **Understanding data privacy regulations**: The first step in ensuring data privacy and compliance is understanding the regulations that apply to your data. Prominent regulations such as GDPR in the European Union and CCPA in the United States have far-reaching implications. These regulations dictate how personal data should be collected, processed, stored, and shared. Non-compliance can result in hefty fines and reputational damage. Therefore, a thorough understanding of these laws is essential for any cloud-native application that handles sensitive data.

- **Strategies for compliance**: Compliance is not a one-time task but an ongoing process. It involves implementing strategies that align with data privacy requirements. Techniques such as data anonymization, masking, and tokenization can be effectively applied to meet regulatory requirements. For example, data anonymization can be used to remove all **personally identifiable**

information (PII), where identification of data cannot occur without additional information that is held separately.

- **Compliance auditing and reporting**: Regular audits are crucial for maintaining compliance. These audits should be comprehensive, covering all aspects of data storage, access, and processing. Automated auditing tools can help in continuously monitoring compliance metrics and generating reports. These reports can be invaluable during internal reviews or in the case of a regulatory audit.

- **Data retention policies**: Data should not be retained indefinitely. Regulations such as GDPR require that data be kept only for as long as it serves the purpose for which it was collected. Implementing automated data retention policies can help in the timely deletion of data, thereby reducing the risk of non-compliance.

- **Incident response plan (IRP) for data breaches**: Despite best efforts, data breaches can occur. Having an IRP is not just good practice but often a regulatory requirement. The plan should outline the steps to be taken in the event of a breach, including notifying affected parties and regulatory bodies as required by law.

- **Vendor and third-party compliance**: In a multi-cloud environment, data often traverses networks and systems controlled by different vendors. Ensuring that these third parties are also compliant with relevant regulations is crucial. Vendor compliance should be assessed regularly, and any non-compliance should be addressed immediately.

By meticulously addressing these aspects of data privacy and compliance, cloud-native developers can build applications that are not just secure but also ethically and legally sound. This is akin to a traveler who respects both the written laws and the unwritten customs of the lands they visit, ensuring a journey that is enriching and free from legal entanglements. In the next section, we will now explore foundational elements of security in cloud-native multi-cloud environments.

Introduction to security in cloud-native multi-cloud environments

Before digging deeper into the security of cloud-native applications in a multi-cloud environment, let's explore the classic approach of the *4Cs of cloud-native security*. The 4Cs approach (as presented in *Figure 5.1*) is a layered approach to ensuring the security of cloud-native applications:

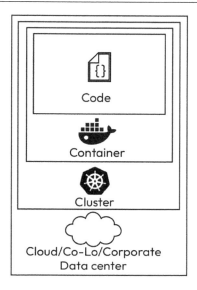

Figure 5.1 – 4Cs of cloud security

Each layer in this approach is dependent on the security of the layer outside it. For example, secure code will be dependent on the security of the container where it's deployed. Let's have a closer look at each one of the components of the 4Cs approach:

- **Cloud**: This is the infrastructure layer that hosts and executes your application. At this layer, you should ensure data and configuration security and follow the best security practices recommended by your cloud provider.

- **Cluster**: As we have explored in previous chapters, this layer will coincide with the Kubernetes components that will hold the aforementioned containers. In this layer, security should focus on securing communication between Kubernetes components by using certificates to authorize incoming traffic and ensuring security and network standards are met.

- **Container**: This layer involves containerized applications. Security in this layer involves scanning for container vulnerabilities, updating containers regularly, and creating users with the fewest privileges.

- **Code**: This is the application and innermost layer. This layer focuses on secure coding practices, including dynamic and static code analysis, and ensuring the same compliance for third-party providers.

Security is a paramount concern when developing cloud-native applications across multiple cloud providers. Organizations need to ensure that their applications are resilient to various security threats. To achieve this, they can leverage industry benchmarks and best practices such as those provided by the **Center for Internet Security (CIS)** and the **Cloud Security Alliance (CSA)**.

CIS benchmarks

CIS is a renowned organization that provides comprehensive security benchmarks, guidelines, and best practices for various technology domains, including cloud-native applications. These benchmarks offer a valuable resource for securing your applications in multi-cloud environments. Key aspects covered by CIS benchmarks for cloud-native applications include the following:

- **IAM**: Implementing stringent access controls and ensuring proper user authentication
- **Network security**: Configuring **network security groups** (**NSGs**), firewalls, and security policies to safeguard communication between cloud-native components
- **Data protection**: Encrypting data both at rest and in transit and managing encryption keys securely
- **Logging and monitoring**: Setting up robust logging and monitoring solutions to detect and respond to security incidents promptly
- **Container security**: Ensuring container security by following best practices for securing Docker containers and Kubernetes clusters

CSA framework

CSA is an organization dedicated to promoting cloud security best practices. Its **Cloud Controls Matrix** (**CCM**) and **Security, Trust, Assurance, and Risk** (**STAR**) program provide valuable insights into securing cloud-native applications in multi-cloud environments:

- **CCM**: CCM offers a framework for assessing cloud security risks across multiple cloud platforms. It provides a set of security controls and guidelines for cloud-native applications.
- **STAR program**: The STAR program helps organizations assess the security posture of **cloud service providers** (**CSPs**). It provides a framework for evaluating the security capabilities of different cloud providers in a multi-cloud environment.

Implementing CIS and CSA benchmarks involves the following steps:

1. **Assessment**: Evaluate your cloud-native application against the security controls and best practices outlined in CIS and CSA benchmarks.
2. **Remediation**: Address any identified security gaps or vulnerabilities by implementing recommended controls.
3. **Continuous monitoring**: Set up continuous monitoring and auditing processes to ensure ongoing compliance with benchmarks.
4. **Security automation**: Leverage automation tools to enforce security policies and controls across multiple cloud providers consistently.

By adhering to CIS and CSA benchmarks, organizations can bolster the security of their cloud-native applications in multi-cloud environments, mitigating risks and ensuring robust protection against threats. The next section will cover DevSecOps and its best practices.

DevSecOps best practices for cloud-native apps in multi-cloud environments

Since we have discussed data and security, we now encounter a critical juncture where DevOps and security intersect. This section serves as a comprehensive guide for embedding security into the DevOps life cycle, following the principles of DevSecOps.

Integrating security into the DevOps workflow

At the very heart of the DevSecOps fortress lies the core understanding of its significance—an agile and seamless integration of security practices into the very fabric of the DevOps workflow. In multi-cloud environments, where agility, speed, and security converge to create a formidable alliance, DevSecOps stands as a guardian, ensuring that cloud-native apps flourish under an umbrella of protection. Key aspects of DevSecOps principles are the following:

- **The imperative of DevSecOps**: In any well-coordinated expedition, each team member must be well equipped and informed. The same holds true for cloud-native app development in a multi-cloud setting. DevSecOps is not an optional add-on but a necessity. It ensures the safety and reliability of cloud-native applications by embedding security checks and controls directly into the DevOps pipeline. This ensures a multi-layered security approach where security becomes a concern of all departments of an organization. For proper implementation of this principle, organizations should consider dedicated security training to ensure a seamless cultural shift.

Figure 5.2 represents security as the responsibility of each stakeholder:

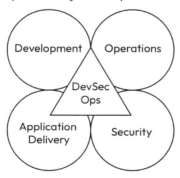

Figure 5.2 – DevSecOps

Beyond tools and processes, DevSecOps is fundamentally a cultural shift. It propagates the idea that every stakeholder, from developers to operations specialists, is responsible for security. It's a mindset where security is an omnipresent concern, not just a checkpoint.

- **Security throughout the software development life cycle (SDLC)**: Security is not a phase but a continuous requirement that must be integrated throughout the SDLC. Starting from the design phase, threat modeling can identify potential security risks. During the coding phase, static and dynamic code analysis tools such as **Checkmarx** or **Fortify** can be used to scan the code for vulnerabilities.

- **Automated security testing**: The CI/CD pipeline should include automated security tests to ensure that security checks are performed at every stage of development. Tools such as OWASP ZAP for dynamic analysis or SonarQube for static code analysis can be integrated into the pipeline. These tools automatically scan the code base and dependencies for vulnerabilities, providing immediate feedback to developers.

Automation and configuration management for secure deployments

In this topic, we will understand the art of automation, leveraging **infrastructure-as-code (IaC)** and configuration management tools to fortify our cloud-native bastions:

- **IaC**: IaC is a cornerstone for the multi-cloud deployments. Utilizing tools such as Terraform or Ansible, developers can codify their infrastructure, ensuring that it is consistent, repeatable, and secure across diverse cloud platforms. This code-based approach to infrastructure allows for version control, making it easier to roll back changes and track security configurations.

- **Automating security controls**: Automation is a key enabler of security in a DevSecOps environment. Tools such as Chef or Puppet can be employed to automate the enforcement of security configurations, patch management, and compliance checks. These tools can be integrated into the CI/CD pipeline to ensure that every code release is automatically vetted for security compliance. This ensures that the application environment remains secure and compliant, not just in one cloud but across multiple cloud platforms.

- **Secure runtime environments**: Runtime security is a critical aspect that often gets overlooked. Containers, for instance, should be run with the least privilege to minimize the attack surface. Network policies can be configured to restrict unauthorized access to services and data. Moreover, runtime security monitoring tools can be enabled to provide real-time alerts on suspicious activities. These layers of protection are essential for detecting and preventing malicious activity during the application's operation.

By adopting these automation and configuration management practices, developers can significantly enhance the security posture of their cloud-native applications across multiple cloud environments. This not only minimizes the risk of security incidents but also simplifies the task of maintaining compliance with various regulatory standards.

Ensuring secure development practices

As we navigate the depths of the DevSecOps fortress, let's understand the essence of secure development practices—a treasury of knowledge to safeguard the core of cloud-native applications. Let's uncover some key aspects of it:

- **Secure coding practices**: In the realm of secure cloud-native development, secure coding practices are non-negotiable. These practices aim to identify and mitigate common vulnerabilities such as the following:

    - **SQL injection**: SQL injection is a type of cyberattack that occurs when an attacker injects malicious **Structured Query Language** (**SQL**) code into an input field or query in a web application. The goal of an SQL injection attack is to manipulate the application's database by injecting rogue SQL statements, often with malicious intent. SQL injection attacks are possible when an application doesn't properly validate or sanitize user inputs before using them in SQL queries.

    - **Cross-site scripting (XSS)**: XSS is a type of security vulnerability commonly found in web applications. It occurs when an attacker is able to inject malicious scripts (usually written in JavaScript) into web pages viewed by other users. These scripts can then run in the context of the victim's browser, potentially stealing sensitive information, such as cookies, session tokens, or other personal data. XSS attacks are particularly dangerous because they allow attackers to impersonate legitimate users and carry out malicious actions on their behalf.

    - **Buffer overflows**: A buffer overflow, also known as a **buffer overrun**, is a type of software vulnerability that occurs when a program writes more data into a buffer (a temporary storage area) than it can hold. This extra data can overflow into adjacent memory locations, potentially overwriting other data or even code. Buffer overflows are a common source of software security vulnerabilities and can lead to serious consequences, including crashes, data corruption, and security breaches.

    Utilizing **static application security testing** (**SAST**) tools such as Fortify or Checkmarx, developers can scan the code base for vulnerabilities during the development phase. These tools provide actionable insights and remediation advice, allowing developers to address issues before they escalate into more significant security risks.

- **Secure software supply chain**: The software supply chain is often an overlooked attack vector. Ensuring the security of the software supply chain involves multiple steps, from verifying the integrity of third-party components and libraries to continuously monitoring for vulnerabilities. Tools such as Snyk or WhiteSource can be integrated into the development pipeline to scan dependencies for known vulnerabilities. Additionally, digital signatures and checksums can be used to verify the integrity of these components, ensuring that they haven't been tampered with.

- **Secure containerization and image scanning**: Containerization has revolutionized the way applications are deployed and managed, but it also introduces its own set of security challenges. Container security is multi-faceted, involving everything from securing the container runtime to scanning container images for vulnerabilities. Tools such as Clair or Trivy can be used to scan container images as part of the CI/CD pipeline. For runtime security, solutions such as Aqua Trivy or Sysdig can be employed to monitor container behavior, enforce security policies, and provide real-time alerts on any security anomalies.

Now that we have a solid understanding of DevSecOps and how to integrate security seamlessly at each stage of the SDLC, let's shift our focus and delve into the importance of compliance across multiple cloud environments.

Managing compliance across multiple clouds environments

Remember—as cloud-native developers, we must uphold the highest standards of regulatory adherence and industry-specific compliance, ensuring that our applications flourish within the bounds of legal and ethical constraints. Developers should ensure that cloud-native applications adhere to and comply with consumer, industry, legal, and internal standards. Non-compliance might result in serious legal and financial consequences.

The following diagram proposes a continuous compliance cycle to ensure adherence to the corresponding standards and regulations:

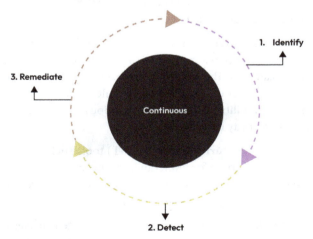

Figure 5.3 – Stages of the compliance cycle

This approach suggests four phases in the compliance cycle:

- **Identify**: Organizations should choose compliance frameworks that align with their industry and regulatory requirements. This framework should serve the organization to identify compliant security practices. Examples of frameworks include the **International Organization for Standardization (ISO)** *27001* and the **National Institute of Standards and Technology (NIST)** Cybersecurity Framework.

- **Detect**: Most cloud providers have built-in tools that ensure continuous compliance with security regulations. This becomes more important in cloud-native and DevOps cycles. Detecting security compliance should be a fast and preferably automated task to integrate compliance detection in the CI/CD cycle.

- **Remediate**: Detected compliance violations are also addressed with the help of compliance management platforms. These platforms usually sort violations by severity and propose recommended actions.

- **Continuous**: Compliance evaluation should not happen in an isolated and sporadic fashion but in a cyclic and continuous manner, integrated into other continuous practices.

Understanding the compliance landscape in multi-cloud environments

When it comes to compliance, it's not just about understanding the laws but also about knowing how to apply them in a variety of contexts. This section aims to provide a comprehensive guide to managing compliance across multiple clouds, focusing on industry-specific regulations, challenges, and cloud provider-specific offerings.

Overview of industry-specific regulations

It is also true that compliance is not a one-size-fits-all proposition. Different industries have their own sets of regulations that dictate how data should be handled, stored, and processed. For instance, healthcare organizations must comply with HIPAA, which has stringent requirements for the protection of patient data. Similarly, companies involved in payment processing must adhere to PCI DSS. For organizations operating within the European Union, GDPR sets rules for data protection and privacy. Understanding these regulations is not just a legal necessity but also a cornerstone for building compliant cloud-native applications.

Challenges and considerations

Compliance in a multi-cloud environment is a complex endeavor, fraught with challenges that range from data sovereignty to varying security standards among different cloud providers. Data sovereignty issues arise when data is stored or processed in a different jurisdiction than where it originated, potentially subjecting it to different laws and regulations. Additionally, each cloud provider may have its own set of security controls, which can complicate the task of maintaining a uniform compliance posture across multiple clouds. Therefore, a deep understanding of these challenges is crucial for devising effective compliance strategies that are both robust and flexible.

Cloud provider-specific compliance offerings

Each cloud provider offers a suite of tools and services specifically designed to assist with compliance. For example, **Amazon Web Services (AWS)** provides services such as AWS Config, which allows for real-time assessment of resource configurations, and AWS CloudTrail, which enables governance, compliance, and risk auditing. Azure, on the other hand, offers Azure Policy for enforcing organization-specific requirements and Azure Blueprints for orchestrating cloud resources with compliance and regulatory requirements in mind. Leveraging these tools effectively can significantly streamline compliance efforts, reducing the complexity and overhead associated with managing compliance in multi-cloud environments.

Implementing governance frameworks and controls

Establishing robust governance frameworks becomes imperative for maintaining a secure and compliant ecosystem.

Establishing governance frameworks

In multi-cloud compliance, governance frameworks serve as the compass and map, guiding organizations through an intricate maze of regulations and standards. Frameworks such as the NIST Cybersecurity Framework or ISO *27001* offer a structured approach, providing a set of guidelines that help organizations define policies, procedures, and controls that are in alignment with regulatory requirements. Adopting such frameworks is akin to following a well-marked trail on a hiking expedition; they provide the direction and markers that help you stay on the right path, ensuring that your cloud-native applications meet or exceed compliance standards.

Defining policies, procedures, and controls

If governance frameworks are the compass and map, then policies, procedures, and controls are the gear and supplies you carry on your compliance journey. Policies act as a rulebook, defining what needs to be done to achieve compliance. Procedures are the step-by-step guides, detailing how to implement these policies. Controls are the enforcement mechanisms, ensuring that policies and procedures are followed to the letter. In a multi-cloud environment, tools such as HashiCorp Sentinel or **Open Policy Agent (OPA)** can be invaluable. These tools allow you to define, enforce, and monitor policies, procedures, and controls, ensuring that your applications remain compliant across diverse cloud platforms.

Auditing and monitoring compliance posture

Continuous auditing and monitoring are the watchtowers and checkpoints on your compliance journey. They provide the visibility needed to assess the effectiveness of your compliance strategies in real time. Tools such as Splunk or Sumo Logic can aggregate logs from multiple cloud providers, offering a unified view of your compliance posture. These tools enable real-time monitoring and auditing, allowing you to set up automated alerts for any deviations from compliance norms. This proactive approach enables quick remediation, ensuring that your cloud-native applications remain compliant amid the ever-changing landscape of industry regulations and standards.

Figure 5.4 represents the high-level steps involved in auditing and monitoring compliance, start by identifying specific regulatory requirements applicable to your organization, which may include industry-specific standards such as HIPAA or GDPR.

The next step is to create comprehensive compliance policies and procedures based on these regulations, outlining rules and controls to enforce within your multi-cloud setup. You should also select appropriate compliance monitoring tools, whether built-in options from cloud providers or third-party solutions, to scan your cloud infrastructure for violations. It is important to configure monitoring rules within these tools to align with your compliance policies, covering aspects such as data encryption and access controls. Implement continuous monitoring through real-time or periodic scans to swiftly detect non-compliance issues.

Setting up automated alerts is essential for detecting violations to ensure prompt action by responsible teams. Following this, develop procedures for remediating compliance breaches, such as applying necessary configurations or security patches. You should also maintain detailed documentation of monitoring activities, including scans, alerts, remediation efforts, and compliance reports. Conduct regular compliance audits, both internal and external, to meet regulatory requirements.

It is essential that you generate compliance reports summarizing your posture for sharing with auditors and stakeholders, and periodically review and enhance your compliance monitoring processes and tools for improved efficiency. You should also ensure that teams are well trained in compliance procedures and stay informed about regulatory changes, updating policies and rules accordingly. Consider also third-party audits for an independent assessment of compliance, and collaborate with legal and risk management teams to align compliance efforts with legal obligations and risk mitigation strategies:

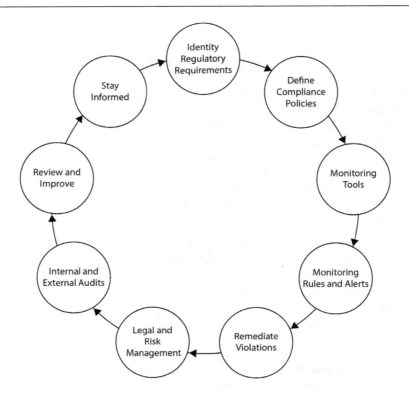

Figure 5.4 – High-level steps in auditing and monitoring compliance

In this section, we looked into the power of governance, policies, and audits—a triumvirate that stands resolute in safeguarding compliance across the expansive realms of multi-cloud environments. Through understanding the compliance landscape and implementing robust frameworks, you will emerge as a stalwart guardian of ethical practices and regulatory adherence, allowing your cloud-native applications to flourish under the virtuous light of compliance.

IAM across multiple clouds environments

IAM in the cloud is a security framework that can't be understated, especially in a multi-cloud environment. IAM is designed to authenticate and regulate user access, granting or denying access privileges. An effective cloud-based IAM solution allows organizations to implant such frameworks across different cloud environments.

IAM provides a powerful toolset ready to implement robust security practices in a multi-cloud environment. Let's make a quick introduction to some common capabilities of IAM frameworks:

- **Authentication**: IAM frameworks put different authentication strategies at our disposal. Authentication refers to the ability to verify that a user trying to log in to our system is legit and has not impersonated the actual user by guessing or accessing credentials that might have been compromised. IAM authentication aggregates additional authentication procedures, including **multi-factor authentication (MFA)**, an extension of **two-factor authentication (2FA)**. These strategies ensure additional layers of verification that can take multiple forms: fingerprint verification, an image scan, or a physical device that generates a one-time security token. Authentication solutions can authorize, deny, or challenge the user to provide additional authentication requirements:

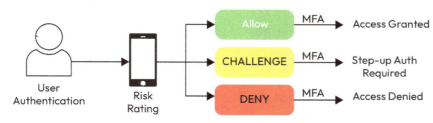

Figure 5.5 – MFA

- **Single sign-on (SSO)**: Usually works in collaboration with MFA capabilities and ensures that users have access to multiple services once authentication is verified.

- **Access management**: IAM frameworks offer the capability to restrict access to the fewest resources for a user. As we have discovered in previous sections, access can be restricted by the user's role or by defined attributes, such as time or location.

As we continue our journey through the multi-cloud landscape, we encounter the critical crossroads of IAM. Much like travelers who must secure their belongings and authenticate their identities at various checkpoints, cloud-native developers face the intricate task of managing user identities and access controls across a multitude of cloud platforms. This section serves as your guide through this complex terrain.

Centralized IAM

Typically, users traverse vast expanses of cloud platforms, each with its unique set of user identities and access controls. As we venture forth, we seek to unify this diversity and bring harmony to user **identity management (IM)**. Let's dive deeper and explore IAM capabilities in more detail:

- **Managing user identities across diverse cloud platforms**: In the world of multi-cloud computing, centralized IM is the passport that allows seamless travel across different cloud territories. Technologies such as SSO and identity federation protocols such as **Security Assertion Markup Language (SAML)** or **Open Authorization 2 (OAuth2)** act as a universal visa, enabling users to authenticate once and gain access to resources across various cloud platforms. This centralized approach is akin to a global entry system for travelers, streamlining the authentication process and enhancing the user experience.

- **Implementing centralized authentication and authorization**: Centralized authentication and authorization are the customs and immigration desks of our multi-cloud journey. Protocols such as OAuth2 or **OpenID Connect (OIDC)** serve as the master key, providing a **single source of truth (SSOT)** for user identities and permissions. These mechanisms streamline the process of verifying who you are (authentication) and what you are allowed to do (authorization) across different cloud environments. This unified approach simplifies management and enhances security, ensuring that users are who they say they are and have access only to the resources they are permitted to use.

- **RBAC and privilege management**: RBAC and privilege management are the travel advisories and restricted area signs in our multi-cloud expedition. They allow fine-grained control over who gets to do what within your cloud-native applications. RBAC enables you to define roles and permissions at a granular level, ensuring that users have only the access they need to perform their tasks. Tools such as AWS IAM, **Azure Active Directory (Azure AD)**, and Google Cloud Identity act as local guides, helping you implement these controls effectively across multiple cloud platforms.

MFA and secure access

As we delve deeper into the multi-cloud environment, we encounter the need for enhanced security measures, multiple locks and safeguards, one would use to secure valuable possessions during a journey. This section focuses on additional layers of security that can be implemented to fortify your cloud-native applications.

Introduction to MFA in multi-cloud environments

Consider MFA as an advanced lock system safeguarding the treasure chest of your multi-cloud environment. In a landscape where data breaches and unauthorized access are increasingly common, MFA serves as a critical line of defense. It enhances the basic authentication process by requiring two or more independent forms of verification, thereby significantly reducing the likelihood of unauthorized access.

The three pillars of MFA

MFA relies on a combination of the following three types of credentials:

- **Something you know**: This is usually a password or a PIN. It's essential to enforce strong password policies, such as a minimum length and the inclusion of special characters, to ensure this layer is as secure as possible.

- **Something you have**: This could be a physical device such as a security token, a smart card, or a smartphone that can generate or receive a **time-based one-time password (TOTP)**. Google Authenticator and Authy are popular apps that generate TOTPs.

- **Something you are**: This includes biometric data such as fingerprints, facial recognition, or retina scans. Biometric data offers a high level of security but requires specialized hardware and is generally used in more sensitive applications.

Figure 5.6 presents the three aforementioned types of credentials:

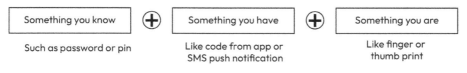

Figure 5.6 – MFA

Implementing MFA in cloud-native applications

Let us now explore some of the explore key aspects of implementing MFA, including identifying integration points, selecting the right technology, optimizing user experience, and ensuring compliance with industry regulations:

- **Integration points**: Identify critical points in your application where MFA should be implemented. This usually includes login pages, but you might also consider adding MFA for accessing sensitive features within the application.

- **Technology selection**: Choose an MFA solution that aligns with your needs. Google Authenticator and Authy are popular choices because they offer APIs and SDKs that are relatively easy to integrate into various types of applications and are supported across multiple cloud platforms.

- **User experience**: Implementing MFA should not come at the cost of user experience. Offer options such as **Remember this device** to minimize repeated MFA prompts and provide fallback mechanisms such as security questions or backup codes.

- **Compliance requirements**: Ensure that your MFA implementation complies with relevant regulations. For example, financial and healthcare industries often have specific guidelines around authentication.

Monitoring and auditing

We will now look into some of the essential practices for ongoing MFA security. This includes logging authentication activities, setting up alerts for suspicious events, and conducting regular security audits to ensure that your MFA configurations remain robust and resilient:

- **Logging**: Keep detailed logs of authentication attempts and regularly review them. This can help identify any suspicious activities early on.

- **Alerts**: Set up automated alerts for multiple failed authentication attempts from the same IP address or for any changes in authentication settings.

- **Regular audits**: Conduct regular security audits to ensure that the MFA settings are configured correctly and that there are no vulnerabilities.

In a nutshell, MFA is not just an optional add-on but a necessity in today's multi-cloud environments. By requiring multiple forms of verification, MFA significantly enhances the security posture of your cloud-native applications. Solutions such as Google Authenticator and Authy make it easier than ever to integrate robust MFA functionalities, providing an additional layer of security that is both effective and user-friendly.

Implementing secure access controls and session management

Secure access controls and session management are the surveillance cameras and alarm systems of our cloud-native security architecture. Techniques such as session timeout, session rotation, and IP whitelisting act as additional layers of security, ensuring that user interactions with applications are both secure and efficient. Cloud services such as Amazon Cognito or Azure AD B2C serve as security control centers, offering robust features for managing sessions and access controls across multiple clouds.

Managing access keys and credentials

Access keys and credentials are the master keys to your kingdom and managing them securely is paramount. Best practices include regularly rotating these keys, employing PoLP access, and using secrets management services such as AWS Secrets Manager or Azure Key Vault. These practices are akin to having a secure, tamper-proof safe for your most valuable items. By adhering to these best practices, you mitigate the risk of unauthorized access and ensure that your cloud-native applications remain secure across various cloud platforms.

Now that we have comprehensively explored MFA, delving into its significance, foundational pillars, and the practical steps to implement it within cloud-native applications, our journey continues into the next section, where we will shift our focus toward understanding data privacy and strategies for its safeguarding.

Data privacy and protection

As we continue our journey through the multi-cloud landscape, we arrive at a critical juncture of data privacy and protection, similar to the safeguarding of personal documents and valuables during international travel. This section aims to guide you through the labyrinthine regulations and technical complexities of ensuring data privacy and protection across multiple cloud platforms.

Understanding data privacy requirements

Navigating the multi-cloud environment without a deep understanding of data privacy regulations would be like traveling to foreign countries without knowing their laws. This section serves as your legal guidebook, helping you understand the intricacies of data privacy regulations and their implications for cloud-native applications.

Overview of data privacy regulations and their implications

Understanding data privacy regulations such as GDPR in the European Union or CCPA in the United States is not just a legal necessity but a cornerstone for building trust. These regulations set the legal framework for how data should be handled, stored, and protected. Non-compliance doesn't just risk financial penalties but can also erode customer trust, making it imperative for cloud-native developers to be well versed in these laws.

Identifying sensitive data and its protection requirements

Much like a traveler would separate their cash, passport, and other valuables for special attention, cloud-native applications must identify and specially handle sensitive data. This includes PII, financial records, and healthcare information. The protection requirements for these types of data are stringent and often involve multiple layers of encryption—both at rest and in transit—as well as strict access controls implemented through IAM solutions.

Data classification and handling of PII

Data classification is the process of sorting your valuables into different safes, each with its own set of locks and keys. In cloud-native applications, this involves categorizing data based on its sensitivity level. PII, for instance, requires the highest level of security measures. This not only includes robust encryption techniques but also strict access controls that are regularly audited and updated. Tools such as Amazon Macie or Varonis can automate the classification of PII and other sensitive data, ensuring that they are handled with the utmost care.

Implementing data privacy controls

Let's have a section that can serve as a guide to implementing data privacy controls that not only meet regulatory requirements but also go the extra mile in safeguarding sensitive data.

Data anonymization, masking, and pseudonymization techniques

Imagine you have a treasure map, but you don't want to reveal the exact location of the treasure to anyone who looks at it. *Data anonymization*, *masking*, and *pseudonymization* are akin to encoding that map. Let's take a closer look at these:

- **Data anonymization**: This process involves removing or altering PII or other sensitive data in a dataset to make it anonymous. Anonymized data cannot be traced back to individuals. Anonymization methods may include techniques such as randomization, aggregation, or generalization.

In the following example, the `anonymizeData` function takes an array of `data` objects and anonymizes sensitive information (such as names and emails). It's a basic representation of data privacy controls where personal identifiers are replaced to protect individual privacy:

```
function anonymizeData(data) {
    return data.map(item => {
      return {
        ...item,
        name: 'Anonymous',
        email: 'anonymized@example.com',
      };
    });
}


    // Example usage:
    const originalData = [
      { name: " packt user1", email: " packt_user1@example.com",
age: 30 },
      { name: " packt user2", email: " packt_user2@example.com",
phone: "1234567890" },
    ];


    const anonymizedData = anonymizeData(originalData);
    console.log("Original Data:", originalData);
    console.log("Anonymized Data:", anonymizedData);
```

- **Data masking**: Data masking, also known as data obfuscation or data redaction, involves concealing specific data elements in a dataset. This is often done by replacing sensitive data with fictional or scrambled values. The goal is to protect sensitive information while maintaining the structure and usability of the data for testing, development, or analytics.

The following example demonstrates data masking by taking an email address and replacing the characters before the domain with asterisks, preserving the first character and domain for recognizability:

```
function maskEmail(email) {
    const maskedEmail = email.replace(/^(.)(.*)(.@.*)$/,
      (_, firstChar, middleChars, lastPart) =>
        firstChar + middleChars.replace(/./g, '*') + lastPart
    );
    return maskedEmail;
}


    // Example usage:
    const email = 'packt_user1@example.com';
    const masked = maskEmail(email);
```

```
console.log("Original Email:", email);
console.log("Masked Email:", masked);
```

- **Pseudonymization**: Pseudonymization is a privacy-enhancing technique that involves replacing sensitive data with pseudonyms or tokens. Unlike anonymization, pseudonymized data can be reversed or re-identified using a separate mechanism, such as a lookup table. Pseudonymization allows for a level of data protection while still enabling specific use cases.

  In the following example, it takes a user ID and converts it into a hashed string using *SHA-256*, creating a pseudonym that can be used to reference the user without exposing the actual ID:

```
const crypto = require('crypto');

function pseudonymize(input) {
   const pseudonym = crypto.createHash('sha256').update(input).
digest('hex');
   return pseudonym;
}

// Example usage:
const userId = 'packt123';
const pseudonym = pseudonymize(userId);
console.log("Original ID:", userId);
console.log("Pseudonym:", pseudonym);
```

These techniques transform sensitive data into a format that is unintelligible to unauthorized users but can be reverted to its original state for authorized use. For example, data masking could replace a **Social Security number** (**SSN**) in a database with Xs, while pseudonymization could replace it with a random identifier. Tools such as Google's Cloud Data Loss Prevention or Microsoft's **Azure Information Protection** (**AIP**) can assist in implementing these techniques effectively.

Data loss prevention strategies and monitoring

Just as travelers use locks and tracking devices to prevent the loss of their valuables, **data loss prevention** (**DLP**) tools act as guardians of your data. These tools monitor and control data transfers within your cloud-native applications, identifying potential breaches or leaks. They can automatically block or quarantine suspicious activities, ensuring that sensitive data remains secure. Solutions such as Symantec DLP or McAfee Total Protection for DLP offer robust features for monitoring data in transit, at rest, or in use.

Consent management and privacy policy enforcement

In a world where data is the new currency, consent is the legal tender. **Consent management platforms** (**CMPs**) serve as gatekeepers for data collection and processing. They ensure that users are fully informed about how their data will be used and stored, providing them with the option to opt in or opt out. This is similar to customs declarations when entering a new country; you must declare what you are bringing in and for what purpose. Tools such as OneTrust or TrustArc can help manage user consent effectively, ensuring compliance with regulations such as GDPR and CCPA.

By implementing these data privacy controls, you are not just ticking off compliance checklists but are also building a fortress of trust around your cloud-native applications. This is crucial for navigating the complex terrain of data privacy and protection in a multi-cloud environment, ensuring that your journey is both secure and in compliance with global data protection regulations.

Summary

As we wrap up our journey through the multi-cloud landscape of data, security, and compliance, let's reflect on the wisdom and skills we've acquired. We've unlocked valuable insights to bolster cloud-native applications. In our pursuit of data security across diverse cloud platforms, we've fortified our defenses, mastering techniques such as encryption and access controls. Data integrity and confidentiality are our cornerstones. Navigating data privacy and compliance, we've embraced regulations such as GDPR and CCPA.

Now, we should be aware of the rules across various clouds and geographies, create robust plans, and keep a vigilant eye on things to ensure everything is in line. Data, security, and compliance are the bedrock of cloud-native applications. They safeguard users and trust in the multi-cloud world.

In our next chapter, we will explore strategies to manage cloud expenses effectively while maintaining performance and scalability. Stay tuned for insights into cost optimization in our dynamic cloud journey.

6

Maximizing Value and Minimizing Cost in Multi-Cloud

As a cloud-native developer, working with multiple cloud services can feel like navigating from one island to another, with each island representing a different cloud service that offers unique technological features to explore and weigh against each other. However, the costs associated with such services can be difficult to predict, making it crucial to keep a watchful eye on expenses throughout this journey. Therefore, it is crucial to navigate the unpredictable waters of multi-cloud environments with the support of platform and cloud engineers, who are responsible for the underlying platform and infrastructure. By finding innovative ways to keep costs low without compromising quality, you can take advantage of the exciting possibilities offered by multi-cloud environments while avoiding unnecessary expenses.

In this chapter, we'll explore the fundamental concepts and explore tips and strategies to make sure you use your resources wisely without spending more than you need to. We'll cover different aspects of cost optimization, from the impact of cost optimization on the very fabric of cloud-native app development to the art of right-sizing resources that align with functionality and performance requirements. We'll also cover how to detect and mitigate wasteful spending and how to choose the right cloud provider.

Throughout this journey, we hope to equip you with the necessary knowledge to sail through this journey of cost optimization, where each page brings you closer to the treasure of efficient, cost-effective, and strategic cloud-native application development. The following topics will be covered in this chapter:

- The shift-left cost for development in multi-cloud
- FinOps practices for cloud-native apps in multi-cloud
- Implementing shift-left cost management and FinOps practices
- Optimizing cloud resources and minimizing waste
- Selecting the right cloud provider based on cost and performance
- Data management cost strategies
- Governance and cost control

The shift-left cost for development in multi-cloud

When deploying workloads across a multi-cloud environment, cost optimization becomes a key factor. Just like designing a bridge, careful planning is required to ensure stability, functionality, and cost-efficiency without compromising safety. That's why shift-left cost optimization is crucial in the early stages of the development life cycle. It involves proactively considering cost-saving measures and strategies at the beginning of the development process rather than addressing cost concerns as an afterthought.

Shift-left cost optimization helps identify and mitigate potential cost overruns early in the development process. It ensures that cost considerations are integrated into the core of your cloud-native application's design and development from the outset. This approach reframes the development journey by acknowledging that every architectural choice made in the early stages can influence the project's financial landscape down the road. Here are some significances of opting for shift-left in development:

- **The significance of cost optimization in the development life cycle**: Cost control is paramount in today's dynamic technology landscape, where cloud services are consumed like utilities. By understanding the impact of cost during the design phase, developers can shape their cloud-native apps to be efficient not just in terms of performance but also financial resources. This approach ensures that solutions are both functional and fiscally responsible.

- **Cost analysis and predictions during development**: Developers can leverage cloud cost management tools to analyze and predict potential expenses. This analytical insight helps them make choices that align with their budget and performance goals.

- **Leveraging cost-focused development practices**: Efficient coding and resource utilization are key ingredients in the recipe for cost-conscious development. From optimizing code for performance to carefully provisioning cloud resources, every action can impact the bottom line. Developers, architects, and operations teams must collaborate to ensure that each line of code and every cloud instance serve a purpose without excess.

Regular cost-focused feedback helps developers adapt and optimize their coding practices, resulting in an application that is both finely tuned and financially prudent.

In the following section, we'll delve into **financial operations** (**FinOps**) practices, shedding light on how cloud-native developers can align their technical prowess with financial acumen to create efficient and cost-effective applications.

FinOps practices for cloud-native apps in multi-cloud

FinOps is a framework that's designed to manage operational expenditures related to cloud infrastructure and computing. The goal of FinOps is to promote collaboration among engineering, finance, business, and technology teams within the organization, ensuring they achieve business value and financial responsibility for cloud services.

FinOps revolves around cross-functional teamwork, cost visibility, performance monitoring, and benchmarking, with an emphasis on resource optimization. It's a discipline that aims to understand spending, optimize spending, and consistently evaluate cloud service performance that aligns with business objectives.

The FinOps cycle consists of three stages – inform, optimize, and operate:

- **Inform**: During the inform stage, organizations design cost allocation and management, establish visibility and monitoring of cloud resources, and lay the foundation for accurate benchmarking, forecasting, budgeting, and other business indicators.

- **Optimize**: The optimize stage addresses cost and resource utilization to reduce costs and minimize resource waste. Strategies to avoid overprovisioning or underutilized cloud resources can result in significant cost savings.

- **Operate**: The last phase of the cycle, operate, emphasizes collaboration among departments to make informed decisions about the performance, quality, and costs of cloud operations. This phase enables continuous validation and optimization of cloud usage and ensures adherence to the organization's business goals.

FinOps is a practice that aims to strike a balance between maximizing the value of cloud investments and controlling spending. It combines the expertise of finance, operations, and development teams to deliver cloud-native applications that excel in performance and thrive within budget constraints.

To learn more about FinOps, we suggest referring to the FinOps Foundation (`https://www.finops.org/`). Now, let's understand what the FinOps team operating model looks like, and the different roles involved in managing a company's cloud infrastructure:

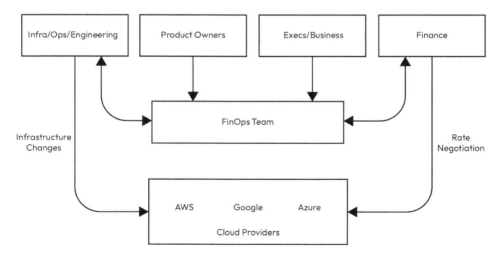

Figure 6.1 – FinOps team structure

Let's understand each role in detail:

- **Engineering/platform engineering**: These are the technical stakeholders responsible for designing, implementing, and managing cloud solutions. They work closely with the FinOps team to understand the cost implications of engineering decisions and optimize resource usage and efficiency.

- **Business/product owner**: These individuals focus on the product and business outcomes; this is where software developers could reside to design and develop the product. They collaborate with the FinOps team to ensure that the cloud spend is aligned with business objectives and delivers value.

- **Exec**: Executive stakeholders are responsible for the overall vision and direction of the organization's cloud strategy. They rely on the FinOps team for visibility into cloud spend and ensure that costs are managed in line with strategic goals.

- **Finance**: The finance department plays a critical role in budgeting, forecasting, and the financial governance of cloud spend. They work with the FinOps team to track cloud costs, allocate them accurately, and optimize financial operations related to the cloud.

- **FinOps team**: This is the central team that bridges the gap between all stakeholders. The FinOps team is responsible for managing cloud costs, ensuring that spending is transparent and that optimization strategies are in place. They work to balance and align the technical and financial aspects of cloud operations.

- **Infrastructure changes**: This indicates that the FinOps team is integral to managing and adapting to changes in cloud infrastructure, ensuring that cost efficiency and optimization are considered when changes are made.

- **Rate negotiations**: A specific function of the FinOps team where they negotiate with cloud providers to secure the best rates for services, which is essential for cost optimization.

- **Cloud provider**: The cloud provider is the entity that supplies cloud services to the organization. The FinOps team interacts with the cloud provider for various purposes, including cost management, service optimization, and negotiating rates.

> **Note**
> The placement of software developers within an organization depends on the specific structure and needs of that organization.

Now that we've covered the fundamentals of FinOps, let's see how we can practically apply these.

Implementing shift-left cost management and FinOps practices

As a developer, conquering technical challenges is only half the battle. Today's developers must wear multiple hats, embracing not just coding prowess but also financial responsibility. This topic explores two powerful philosophies – **shift-left cost management** and **FinOps** – empowering developers to become **budget heroes** who build applications that are both innovative and cost-effective.

Shifting costs left – prevention is key

Imagine catching a critical bug early in development, saving hours of frustration and costly fixes. Shift-left cost management applies this same principle to finances. Instead of waiting for hefty bills at the end of the project, it integrates *cost awareness and optimization seamlessly into the development life cycle*. It's not about policing developers; it's about *empowering them with knowledge and tools* to make informed decisions from the get-go.

So, how can you become a shift-left cost champion?

Let's find out:

- **Embed costs into code**: Tools such as Terraform and CloudFormation allow you to predict resource usage and costs directly within your code, giving you real-time feedback on infrastructure choices. Consider the impact of different instance types, storage options, and service configurations before they translate into hefty bills.

- **Code like a cost ninja**: Embrace serverless functions for event-driven tasks, leverage autoscaling to right-size resources based on demand and explore containerization options such as Docker and Kubernetes for efficient resource utilization. Remember, every line of code has a cost implication.

- **Become a monitoring maestro**: Don't be blindsided by unexpected expenses. Utilize cloud provider tools such as AWS Cost Explorer or Azure Cost Management to continuously monitor resource usage, identify cost anomalies, and set up alerts that notify you of potential overruns before they become major issues.

FinOps – collaboration is the secret sauce

FinOps goes beyond mere cost control; it's about *fostering a collaborative culture* where developers, finance, and operations teams work together toward a shared goal – *building cost-effective and sustainable* applications. It's about breaking down silos, sharing knowledge, and creating an environment where everyone feels responsible for optimizing cloud spend.

So, how can you be a FinOps champion?

Let's see:

- **Join the FinOps table**: Actively participate in regular FinOps meetings to discuss cost concerns, share best practices, and identify optimization opportunities with your colleagues from other teams. Remember, diverse perspectives often lead to the most innovative solutions.

- **Become a cost champion**: Don't just implement cost-saving practices; share your knowledge and success stories with your team! Motivate others to adopt FinOps principles and create a ripple effect of cost awareness.

- **Gamify the quest**: Foster a fun and engaging environment by launching friendly competitions with cost optimization challenges. Reward innovative solutions and celebrate collective achievements in reducing cloud costs.

The rewards of a cost-conscious mindset

By embracing shift-left cost management and FinOps, you're not just saving money – you're unlocking a treasure trove of benefits, such as the following:

- **Reduced cloud costs**: Proactive optimization throughout the development lifecycle leads to significant cost savings, freeing up resources for innovation and other critical initiatives

- **Improved financial transparency**: Gaining deeper insights into your application's resource usage fosters informed decision-making across all teams involved

- **Faster time to market**: Identifying and addressing cost issues early prevents delays and accelerates your time to market, giving you a competitive edge

- **Enhanced team collaboration**: Shared responsibility for cost optimization breaks down silos and fosters a more collaborative and engaged development environment

As an application developer, you might be wondering what your responsibility is when it comes to cost or FinOps. The **Responsibility Assignment Matrix (RACI)** is a crucial tool that defines the roles and responsibilities of departments involved in FinOps. It classifies an organization's departments and their involvement in FinOps according to four key roles: Responsible, Accountable, Consulted, and Informed. Let's have a look at the following example of RACI for an enterprise scenario:

Activities	FinOps Team	App Team	DevOps /SRE	Finance	Sourcing	Business
Implementing cloud cost management frameworks	A	I	C	C	-	-
Enforcing standards for cloud cost labeling and adherence	A	R	C	R	C	-
Defining keys for cloud expense distribution	A	R	C	R	-	-
Aligning actual and projected cloud expenditures with budgets	A	I	C	-	R	C
Assisting teams to set cost-effective goals for their workloads	A	R	I	-	-	C
Achieving cost efficiency at the workload level	C	A	I	-	-	C
Optimizing enterprise-level-cost through right-sizing	A	R	C	I	-	-
A Lead buying strategy to capture savings via reserved instance	A	C	C	-	R	C
IT planning, forecasting, and budgeting	C	R	A	R	-	C
Bottom-up planning and forecasting	C	R	A	R	-	C
Business unit economics	C	R	A	R	-	A

Figure 6.2 – FinOps RACI (R= Responsible, A=Accountable, C=Consulted, I=Informed)

In the next section, we will explore the art of right-sizing cloud resources. This is like choosing the right-sized canvas for a painting, where every resource contributes to the masterpiece while avoiding unnecessary excess.

Optimizing cloud resources and minimizing waste

Optimizing cloud resources is an ongoing process that demands constant monitoring, effective management, and relevant optimization to mitigate the risk of resource waste. Resource waste in the cloud environment refers to the overprovision of cloud resources that remain unused or idle. The following graph presents a simple relationship between reducing cloud resources waste and cost savings:

Figure 6.3 – Progressive cost savings through waste optimization

Let's understand the ways to optimize cloud resources and minimize waste:

- **Identify resource waste**: To identify resource wastage, do the following:

  - **Check your stuff**: Regularly look at your cloud resources. Are there any unused or outdated ones just hanging around, costing you money? Think of it like cleaning out your closet – getting rid of what you don't need!

  - **Track your spending**: Use tools such as AWS Cost Explorer or Azure Cost Management to see where your money's going. Are there any surprises? This helps you spot areas where you can tighten the belt.

  - **Look for code culprits**: Analyze your app's logs to see if any parts are using more resources than they should. Think of it like finding leaky faucets in your code – fix them and save that precious water (or in this case, money)!

- **Right-size cloud resources for efficiency**: Once you've identified waste, transform it into savings with rightsizing:

  - **Scale up and down automatically**: Use tools such as AWS Auto Scaling or Azure Autoscaling to adjust your resources based on how busy your app is. No more paying for resources you don't use, just like turning lights on and off in an empty room!

  - **Downsize when you can**: If you have resources that are barely used, shrink them down to a smaller size. Think of it as getting a smaller car if you only drive by yourself most of the time.

  - **Get deals on resources you use often**: If you know you'll need certain resources for a long time, consider buying them in advance at a discount. It's like buying groceries in bulk – cheaper in the long run!

- **Optimize your setup**: The third step is optimizing your application setup:

  - **Serverless functions**: Use these for small tasks that only run sometimes. You only pay when they run, so it's like paying for a taxi instead of owning a car.

  - **Containers**: Package your app in small, efficient containers with tools such as Docker or Kubernetes. It's like organizing your stuff in neat little boxes instead of dumping it all in a big pile.

  - **Storage**: Choose the right type of storage for your data and set up automatic cleanup for old stuff you don't need anymore.

> **Note**
> While most cloud providers have built-in tools for cloud cost optimization, third-party tools are also available. The following tables compile the most relevant in both groups.

Here are some cloud cost optimization tools that can help you apply these practices:

Service Providers	Cost Optimization Tools
AWS	AWS Pricing Calculator, AWS Cost Explorer, AWS QuickSight, AWS Budgets, and AWS Tag Editor
Azure	Azure Pricing Calculator, Azure Cost Management + Billing, Azure Power BI, Azure Policy, and Azure Budgets
Google Cloud Platform	Google Cloud Pricing Calculator, Google Cloud Billing Reports, Data Studio, Cost Forecasts, Cost Table Report, and Budget Alerts
Oracle Cloud Infrastructure (OCI)	OCI Cost Estimator, OCI Cost Analysis, OCI Cost Governance, Forecasting in cost analysis, OCI Tags, and OCI Budget Alerts
Third-party tools	Apptio Cloudability, CoreStack, CloudCheckr, VMware CloudHealth, Densify, Flexera, Kubecost, CloudVane, NetApp's Spot.io, Turbonomic, Nutanix Xi Beam, and CloudAdmin

Table 6.1 – Cost optimization tools

In the following section, we will discuss the crucial task of selecting the appropriate cloud provider while considering the balance between cost considerations and performance needs. Just as a traveler chooses the best route for their journey, cloud-native developers choose the cloud provider that best matches their application's requirements.

Selecting the right cloud provider based on cost and performance

In this section, we stand at the intersection of strategic decision-making (depicted in *Figure 6.5*), where cloud providers beckon with their offerings. Just as you would carefully choose a route that balances scenic beauty and efficiency, selecting the right cloud provider involves evaluating a blend of cost factors and performance metrics:

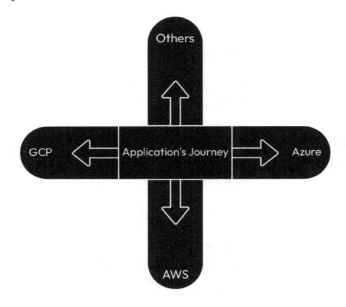

Figure 6.4 – Selecting the right cloud provider (a trade-off)

Evaluating cloud providers – cost factors and performance metrics

Choosing the right cloud provider for your workloads can have a significant impact on your cloud costs and performance. However, comparing cloud providers is not a straightforward task as each provider has its own pricing model, service offerings, and performance characteristics. In this section, we will review some of the key considerations when comparing cloud provider pricing models and how to assess performance and reliability metrics to inform your decision-making.

Cloud provider pricing models

One of the main challenges of comparing cloud providers is that they have different pricing models for their services. Some of the common factors that affect cloud provider pricing are as follows:

*   **Resource consumption**: This is the amount of resources (such as CPU, memory, disk, network, and so on) that you use for your workloads. Most cloud providers charge you based on the amount of resources you consume per hour or second. However, some providers may also charge you based on other factors, such as requests, transactions, operations, and others.

*   **Service type**: This is the type of service that you use for your workloads. Cloud providers offer different types of services, such as compute, storage, database, networking, analytics, and others. Each service type may have different pricing models and tiers, depending on the features and performance levels they offer.

*   **Region**: This is the geographic location where your workloads run. Cloud providers have different regions around the world where they operate their data centers and infrastructure. Each region may have different pricing rates and availability zones for their services.

*   **Commitment**: This is the duration of your contract with the cloud provider. Cloud providers may offer discounts or incentives for customers who commit to using their services for a certain period (such as 1 year or 3 years). Alternatively, some providers may also offer pay-as-you-go or spot pricing options for customers who want more flexibility and lower costs.

To compare cloud provider pricing models effectively, you need to understand how each factor affects your **total cost of ownership** (**TCO**) and **return on investment** (**ROI**). You also need to consider your workload requirements, such as scalability, availability, security, compliance, and so on, and how they align with each provider's service offerings.

Performance and reliability metrics

Another important aspect of comparing cloud providers is their performance and reliability metrics. Performance and reliability metrics measure how well a cloud provider delivers its services to its customers in terms of speed, quality, availability, and consistency. Some of the common performance and reliability metrics that you should consider are as follows:

*   **Latency**: This is the time it takes for a request to travel from your application to the cloud provider's service and back. Latency affects the responsiveness and user experience of your application. You should aim for low latency values for your workloads, especially if they are latency-sensitive or real-time.

*   **Throughput**: This is the amount of data that can be transferred between your application and the cloud provider's service in each period. Throughput affects the efficiency and performance of your application. You should aim for high throughput values for your workloads, especially if they are data-intensive or high-volume.

- **Availability**: This is the percentage of time that a cloud provider's service is operational and accessible to its customers. Availability affects the reliability and uptime of your application. You should aim for high availability values for your workloads, especially if they are mission-critical or SLA-bound.

- **Consistency**: This is the degree of variation in the performance and reliability metrics of a cloud provider's service over time. Consistency affects the predictability and stability of your application. You should aim for high consistency values for your workloads, especially if they are sensitive to performance fluctuations or anomalies.

To compare cloud provider performance and reliability metrics effectively, you need to collect and analyze data from various sources, such as benchmarks, tests, monitoring tools, reports, reviews, and more. You also need to consider your workload characteristics, such as workload type, workload pattern, workload distribution, and so on, and how they affect your performance and reliability requirements.

With this, let's get into data management cost strategies. Managing data efficiently is one of the most critical aspects for developers.

Data management cost strategies

When your application data volume grows, so does the potential for increased storage and transfer costs. For developers, implementing smart data management strategies is essential to control these costs without compromising on data accessibility or compliance. Here are some focused strategies that developers can use:

- **Choose the right data storage solution**:

  Assess the access patterns and criticality of your data. Based on the factors, choose between object storage, block storage, or file storage, and select the appropriate tier within these options:

  - **Example**: For data that is accessed infrequently but requires rapid access when needed, use Amazon S3's Infrequent Access tier or Azure's Cool Blob storage. This can significantly reduce storage costs compared to using standard storage options.

- **Implement data archiving and life cycle policies**:

  Define life cycle policies for your data. Automate the transition of data to cheaper storage classes or archival solutions as it ages and access patterns change:

  - **Example**: Set up a life cycle policy on your S3 buckets to automatically transition older files to Glacier for archival, reducing storage costs while keeping the data available for future needs

- **Optimize data transfer costs**:

  Be mindful of the costs associated with data transfer, especially in a multi-cloud environment. Optimize the data flow to minimize transfers between services and regions:

  - **Example**: If your application involves moving large amounts of data between AWS and on-premises regularly, consider setting up AWS Direct Connect to reduce data transfer costs and improve transfer stability

- **Leverage data compression and deduplication**:

  Implement data compression and deduplication to reduce the storage footprint. This not only saves on storage costs but can also reduce the bandwidth required for data transfer:

  - **Example**: Use data compression algorithms such as GZIP for your log files before storing them. For backups, use deduplication features available in backup services to store unique data, reducing storage needs.

- **Utilize caching mechanisms**:

  Use caching to reduce database load and minimize the need for larger, more expensive database instances. Cache read-heavy data or frequently accessed computations:

  - **Example**: Use Redis or Memcached to cache frequently queried database results or compute-intensive calculations, reducing the load on your databases and improving application performance

- **Monitor and optimize query performance**:

  Regularly monitor and optimize your database queries. Poorly optimized queries can lead to increased load and more expensive scaling needs:

  - **Example**: Use query performance insights and recommendations provided by cloud database services such as AWS RDS or Azure SQL Database to identify and optimize slow or inefficient queries

By adopting these data management cost strategies, developers can effectively control and reduce the costs associated with data storage and transfer in cloud-native applications. It requires a proactive approach, regular monitoring, and continuous optimization to ensure that your data management practices are both cost-effective and aligned with your application's needs.

Next, we'll look at the critical arena of governance and cost control.

Governance and cost control

As you build cloud-native applications in a multi-cloud environment, it's vital to manage governance and cost control effectively. This involves creating policies and frameworks that ensure compliance, security, and cost efficiency. To help you achieve this, we have outlined some practical steps:

1. **Establish clear governance policies**:

    Establish well-documented policies for cloud resource usage, security compliance, and cost management. Ensure that these policies are accessible and understood by all team members:

    *   **Example**: Create a policy that defines naming conventions, tagging requirements, and provisioning protocols for cloud resources. This ensures that resources are easily identifiable, correctly categorized, and consistently monitored for cost analysis.

2. **Implement role-based access control (RBAC)**:

    With the support of cloud and platform engineers, use RBAC to define and enforce access controls to cloud resources based on team members' roles. Ensure that individuals have the minimum necessary permissions to perform their tasks on your applications, reducing the risk of costly errors or security breaches.

3. **Leverage cost management tools**:

    Utilize built-in cost management tools provided by cloud providers. These tools help monitor, analyze, and optimize cloud spending for your application workload:

    *   **Example**: Use AWS Cost Explorer, Azure Cost Management + Billing, or Google Cloud's Cost Management tools to track spending patterns, set budgets, and receive alerts when your application spending exceeds predefined thresholds

4. **Automate policy enforcement**:

    With the support of cloud and platform engineers, automate the enforcement of governance and cost control policies wherever possible. This minimizes the reliance on manual processes and helps in maintaining consistent compliance and cost efficiency:

    *   **Example**: Use **Infrastructure as Code** (IaC) tools such as Terraform or AWS CloudFormation to automate the provisioning of cloud resources in compliance with your organization's governance policies. Implement scripts within the CI/CD pipeline or use cloud provider services to automatically shut down or scale down underutilized resources during off-peak hours.

By implementing these governance and cost control strategies, developers can ensure that their cloud-native applications in a multi-cloud environment are not only secure and compliant but also cost-efficient. It's about being proactive, leveraging the right tools, and fostering a culture of accountability and continuous improvement.

With this, let's look at some interesting use cases so that we can connect the dots.

Cloud provider comparison case studies

In this section, we will look at some real-world examples of cost and performance trade-offs in multi-cloud environments. We will see how different organizations have achieved cost savings through strategic cloud provider selection based on their workload requirements.

Case study 1 – eCommerce giant slashes costs by 50% with a multi-cloud microservices approach

A rapidly growing eCommerce platform faced soaring cloud bills due to a monolithic architecture and single cloud dependency. Scaling meant proportional cost increases, jeopardizing their growth ambitions:

- **Cost optimization tactics**:

  - **Microservices revolution**: They decoupled the monolith into modular, containerized microservices, enabling the following:

    - **Fine-grained scaling**: They scaled individual services based on real-time demand, maximizing resource utilization and minimizing idle costs.

    - **Multi-cloud cost targeting**: They matched cost-sensitive services with budget-friendly cloud providers. Static assets served efficiently on Google Cloud Storage, while mission-critical data resided in Azure's high-availability databases.

  - **Serverless-savvy**: They leveraged serverless functions for short-lived tasks, eliminating idle server costs and aligning expenses with usage patterns

  - **FinOps Foundation**: They implemented cost allocation, chargeback models, and financial governance to foster cost awareness and accountability across teams

- **Outcome**:

  - **50% cloud cost reduction**: By combining technical solutions with strong financial governance, they achieved significant cost savings

  - **Increased business agility**: Microservices facilitated faster deployments and improved scalability, supporting rapid growth without cost concerns

- **Key cost optimization takeaway**: Microservices, multi-cloud, and serverless functions, when coupled with FinOps principles, empower eCommerce businesses to achieve significant cost savings while maintaining agility

Case study 2 – social media app optimizes costs by 30% with containers and automation

A thriving social media app grappled with high infrastructure costs due to manual provisioning, inefficient resource utilization, and limited cost visibility:

- **Cost optimization tactics:**

  - **Containerization efficiency**: They packaged the app into standardized containers, enabling the following aspects:

    - **Cloud-agnostic deployments**: They moved containers between cloud providers based on cost, performance, and regional requirements, optimizing resource allocation

    - **Reduced resource footprint**: They shared the underlying operating system within containers, minimizing resource consumption and server costs

  - **IaC for cost control**: They utilized IaC to automate infrastructure provisioning, eliminating manual errors and ensuring consistent, cost-effective configurations

  - **Continuous cost monitoring**: They implemented cloud-native cost management tools for real-time cost insights, identifying and addressing cost inefficiencies proactively

  - **FinOps culture**: They invested in FinOps training and skills development, fostering collaboration and a shared understanding of cloud cost management across teams

- **Outcome:**

  - **30% infrastructure cost reduction**: Automation, containerization, and continuous cost monitoring delivered substantial cost savings

  - **Improved operational efficiency**: Automated processes minimized human error and freed up valuable developer time

  - **Enhanced resource utilization**: Standardized containers and IaC ensured optimal resource usage across cloud environments

- **Key cost optimization takeaway**: Containerization, automation, and continuous cost monitoring, combined with a FinOps culture, enable social media companies to achieve significant cost savings and operational efficiency while maintaining high availability and scalability

---

Remember

These case studies offer valuable insights, but your optimal approach depends on your specific cloud environment and workload patterns. Continuously explore new technologies, embrace a culture of cost awareness, and leverage a holistic FinOps approach to maximize your cloud cost optimization journey.

Summary

As we draw the curtains on our exploration of optimizing costs for cloud-native applications in a multi-cloud environment, it's imperative to reflect on the transformative journey we've undertaken. From understanding the intricacies of cost management to implementing sophisticated FinOps practices, and from right-sizing resources to selecting the perfect cloud provider, each step has been a stride toward achieving a harmonious blend of technical excellence and financial mindfulness.

The importance of cost optimization goes beyond mere budgetary considerations. It's about forging a symbiotic relationship between innovation and financial prudence. Much like an artist selects colors to bring a canvas to life, cloud-native developers orchestrate resources to bring their applications to fruition. But just as an artist plans brush strokes meticulously, developers must architect their solutions with an eye on cost efficiency from the very inception.

As a cloud-native developer, you're not just a coder; you're an architect of the digital kingdom. Your decisions shape the future of applications, infrastructure, and businesses. By implementing the principles of cost optimization, you're not only contributing to the fiscal health of your organization but also fostering an environment of responsible growth and continuous improvement.

With a heart brimming with newfound insights, turn the page to embark on the next leg of our journey. In the following chapter, we'll delve into the realm of troubleshooting cloud-native applications in multi-cloud environments. As you'll soon discover, the skills you've honed in optimizing costs will stand as pillars of resilience when navigating challenges in the cloud-native landscape.

7

Troubleshooting Multi-Cloud Applications

As we discussed in earlier chapters, **cloud-native applications** offer several advantages over traditional monolithic applications. Troubleshooting cloud-native applications is important because it can help to ensure that your applications are up and running and performing well. In this chapter, you will gain insights into the complexities that unfold when a cloud-native application in a multi-cloud environment doesn't function as anticipated. We'll explore the ripple effects of such issues and the challenges they pose, from degraded end user experiences to potential business disruptions. We'll delve into the use of dedicated cloud-native tools and techniques and how they can be leveraged to manage and rectify issues in this complex setup.

To bring these concepts to life, we'll be exploring some case studies that exemplify the common issues developers face in a multi-cloud environment. These scenarios will help illustrate how to streamline microservices communication, how to manage data consistency, and how to identify scaling challenges in multi-cloud environments. Throughout this chapter, we'll equip you with the knowledge and practical skills needed to effectively troubleshoot in a multi-cloud environment, fostering a robust, resilient, and efficient cloud-native application development journey.

The following topics will be covered in this chapter:

- Importance of troubleshooting in cloud-native development
- Challenges of troubleshooting cloud-native applications
- Tips for troubleshooting cloud-native applications
- Establishing an effective troubleshooting process for cloud-native applications
- Case studies
- SRE in multi-cloud environments
- Chaos engineering

Importance of troubleshooting in cloud-native development

As an organic outcome of the complexities within multi-cloud and cloud-native environments, troubleshooting is an essential skill. The ability to effectively diagnose and resolve issues is crucial, not only for maintaining the smooth operation of applications but also for safeguarding the broader interests of the business. Let's delve into why troubleshooting is vital and the impact of unresolved issues in cloud-native applications:

- **Reduced productivity and its implications**:

  - **Impact on developer efficiency**: Challenges in cloud-native applications can significantly hinder the productivity of developers. When applications malfunction, developers may face delays or spend excessive time resolving issues, leading to decreased efficiency and potential project setbacks.

  - **Business costs**: Reduced productivity due to application issues can translate into financial losses for businesses. Time spent troubleshooting could otherwise be used for development, innovation, or customer service, directly impacting the company's bottom line.

- **Lost revenue and customer trust**:

  - **Customer experience and sales**: Functional issues in cloud-native applications can directly affect customer interactions and sales. For instance, if an e-commerce platform experiences downtime or glitches, it may result in lost sales and dissatisfied customers.

  - **Long-term brand impact**: Consistent issues with cloud-native applications can erode customer trust and damage the company's reputation. In competitive markets, this can lead to a loss of clientele and long-term revenue decline as customers seek more reliable alternatives.

- **Damaged reputation and market position**:

  - **Perception of unreliability**: Frequent or unresolved issues in cloud-native applications can lead to a perception of unreliability and unprofessionalism, affecting the company's market position and ability to attract new customers.

  - **Case study**: Financial services reliability: For example, a financial services company with a frequently malfunctioning online banking app may lose customer trust, leading to a decrease in user base and revenue. This not only impacts immediate transactions but can also harm the company's long-term brand value and customer loyalty.

Next, we will explore the unique challenges of troubleshooting in cloud-native applications within multi-cloud environments. We'll examine common issues and provide practical strategies to effectively address these challenges, ensuring that cloud-native applications are reliable and efficient and contribute positively to the business's success.

Challenges of troubleshooting cloud-native applications

There are a number of challenges associated with troubleshooting cloud-native applications in a multi-cloud environment. These challenges include the following:

- **Complexity**: Cloud-native applications tend to have a higher level of complexity compared to traditional monolithic applications. These applications are often composed of multiple microservices and components, which can be distributed across different cloud providers and platforms. As a result, managing and monitoring the performance, reliability, and security of these applications can be quite challenging.

  The intricate nature of cloud-native applications often makes it difficult to pinpoint the source of a problem, as issues can stem from various components, such as the infrastructure, networking, or the application code itself. Furthermore, the diverse range of cloud services, APIs, and tools used in these applications can complicate troubleshooting, as engineers may need to go through multiple logs, metrics, and alerts to identify and resolve issues.

- **Heterogeneity**: The diverse landscape of cloud providers presents its own set of challenges when managing and monitoring cloud-native applications. Each cloud provider offers a unique set of features, services, and tools that cater to specific use cases and requirements. This heterogeneity can lead to difficulties when troubleshooting problems that are specific to a particular cloud provider, as the root cause of an issue may be tied to a provider's unique infrastructure or service offering.

  The varying features and services across cloud providers can also complicate the process of creating a unified monitoring and management strategy. Engineers may need to familiarize themselves with multiple monitoring tools, APIs, and management consoles to effectively diagnose and resolve issues. Additionally, the lack of standardization in logging and metrics formats can further hinder the process of correlating and analyzing data across different cloud providers.

- **Data silos**: In cloud-native applications, data is often distributed across various storage systems, databases, and services, creating isolated pockets of information known as data silos. These data silos can impede the ability to efficiently gather, analyze, and correlate the necessary data for troubleshooting problems and making informed decisions.

  The disparate nature of data silos can lead to several challenges, including the following:

  - **Inefficient data access**: Developers may need to access multiple data sources and systems to retrieve the required information, which can be time-consuming and labor-intensive

  - **Incomplete insights**: Data silos can result in a fragmented view of the application's performance, making it difficult to identify trends and correlations across different components and services

  - **Data inconsistencies**: As data is stored in different formats and structures across various systems, reconciling and normalizing this information for analysis can be a complex and error-prone task

- **Collaboration barriers**: Data silos can hinder collaboration between different teams within an organization, as each team might have access to only a subset of the overall data, leading to disjointed problem-solving efforts

After learning about the challenges of troubleshooting cloud-native applications in multi-cloud environments, let's review some tips for overcoming them.

Tips for troubleshooting cloud-native applications

Despite the challenges, there are a number of things that you as a developer can do to troubleshoot cloud-native applications in a multi-cloud environment. Here are some tips:

- Use a centralized monitoring tool
- Use a cloud-native logging tool
- Use a cloud-native debugging tool
- Use a cloud-native observability platform

Let us understand each one of them one by one.

Use a centralized monitoring tool

To handle the complexities, it is more important than ever to have a comprehensive monitoring solution in place. A centralized monitoring tool, such as the open source **Zabbix** or the paid offering from **Datadog**, can help you collect and view data from all of your cloud-native applications in one place, making it easier to identify and troubleshoot problems. In addition to its overarching benefits, employing a centralized monitoring tool offers a host of specific advantages:

- **Streamlined data collection**: A centralized monitoring tool collects data from multiple sources, including microservices, cloud providers, and third-party services. By aggregating data in one place, developers can save time and resources that would otherwise be spent on managing multiple monitoring systems.

- **Consistent monitoring metrics**: Centralized monitoring ensures that all data collected follow a consistent format and structure, making it easier for developers to analyze and compare performance metrics across different services and cloud providers. This consistency allows developers to identify trends, anomalies, and bottlenecks more effectively.

- **Comprehensive visibility**: With a centralized monitoring tool, developers gain a comprehensive view of their application's performance and health across multiple cloud providers. This increased visibility enables them to quickly identify and diagnose issues, reducing the time it takes to pinpoint and resolve problems.

- **Customizable dashboards and alerts**: Centralized monitoring tools often provide customizable dashboards and alerting systems, allowing developers to tailor the monitoring experience to their specific needs. This customization enables developers to focus on the most critical aspects of their application, ensuring that potential issues are identified and addressed promptly.

- **Simplified troubleshooting**: By consolidating monitoring data in one place, developers can more easily correlate events and identify the root cause of problems. This streamlined approach to troubleshooting reduces the time and effort required to resolve issues and minimizes the impact on application performance.

- **Scalability and flexibility**: Centralized monitoring tools are designed to handle large volumes of data and adapt to the growing needs of cloud-native applications. As the application scales, the monitoring tool can easily accommodate new services and cloud providers without compromising performance or reliability.

There are a number of different centralized monitoring tools available, so it is important to choose and consider a trade-off that meets your specific needs.

Choosing a centralized monitoring tool for your needs

When choosing a centralized monitoring tool, consider the following factors:

- **Data types**: Determine the types of data the tool can collect, such as logs, metrics, and traces. Ensure that it can gather the necessary information to provide comprehensive insights into your application's performance and health.

- **Features and functionality**: Assess the features offered by the tool, such as data visualization, alerting, anomaly detection, and integrations, in accordance with other systems. The tool should provide a robust set of capabilities to streamline monitoring and troubleshooting tasks.

- **Pricing and scalability**: Consider the cost of the tool, taking into account not only the initial investment but also any additional expenses associated with scaling or adding new features. Choose a tool that fits within your budget and can grow with your organization's needs.

- **Compatibility**: Verify that the tool supports the various cloud providers, platforms, and technologies you're using in your multi-cloud environment. This ensures seamless integration and consistent monitoring across different cloud services.

- **Configure alerts**: One of the most crucial aspects of using a centralized monitoring tool is setting up alerts to notify you when problems arise. This enables you to quickly identify and resolve issues before they impact your users.

- **Regularly review data**: It's essential to routinely analyze the data collected by your centralized monitoring tool. This proactive approach helps you detect potential problems before they escalate into outages.

- **Leverage data for application improvement**: The data gathered by your centralized monitoring tool can be instrumental in enhancing your applications. For instance, you can identify bottlenecks and performance issues by analyzing the data, which allows you to make informed decisions for optimizing your application's performance.

- **Collaborate with team members:** Share monitoring insights with your team members to encourage collaborative problem-solving and foster a culture of continuous improvement. This collective approach helps teams identify and resolve issues more efficiently, ultimately enhancing the overall performance and reliability of cloud-native applications.

- **Collaborative problem-solving**: A centralized monitoring tool enables developers to share data and insights with other team members, fostering collaboration and knowledge sharing. This collaborative approach helps teams identify and resolve issues more quickly and efficiently, leading to continuous improvement and the optimization of the application.

By considering these factors, you can make an informed decision when choosing a centralized monitoring tool that meets your organization's needs and enhances the monitoring and troubleshooting process in a multi-cloud environment. The following illustration (*Figure 7.1*) highlights some of the common key features of a central monitoring tool designed to streamline data collection, provide consistent metrics, offer comprehensive visibility, and simplify troubleshooting across cloud-native applications:

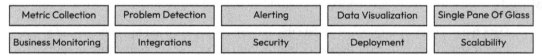

Figure 7.1 – Common features of a centralized monitoring tool

Use a cloud-native logging tool

Apart from monitoring, leveraging a cloud-native logging tool is crucial for efficiently managing, troubleshooting, and maintaining applications in a cloud environment. These tools have been specifically engineered to address the intricacies and unique requirements of cloud-native applications, offering advanced features for log collection, aggregation, analysis, and storage.

Logging is an essential technique for troubleshooting cloud-native applications. In a multi-cloud environment, logging encourages the collection and centralization of computer logs across the application's services. Computer logs usually contain designed attributes that reflect the state of the application at a given timestamp. Additional abstraction layers can be added to facilitate data analysis and extract decisive clues about the application's incidents. Some of the best practices for logging cloud-native applications are listed here:

- **Centralized logging**: In a multi-cloud environment, it becomes essential to define strategies for centralized logging with the purpose of simplifying log management. Different cloud providers and services distributed across the realm of the multi-cloud can provide logs that are different in format and content. The figure that follows depicts how logs from different services are received by a centralized unit. Log aggregation techniques ensure that the logs of different providers are standardized before being visualized and analyzed in troubleshooting tools.

- **Design logging attributes**: It is important to carefully design the attributes that will be collected during a logging routine. Logging customer data can put compliance at risk. Remember that the purpose of logging is to troubleshoot application instabilities, so make sure to log only essential attributes for technical analysis. Overcharged log files may impact application performance and hardware consumption, which, in the multi-cloud environment, can result in additional computing costs.

- **Real-time logging**: Logging in real time can provide invaluable insights for service failure or shutdowns. Real-time logging ensures that your application records computer events as they happen, reducing the risk of losing logs when services shut down.

With a cloud-native logging tool, such as the open source **Elasticsearch, Logstash, and Kibana (ELK)** stack, as well as the paid offering from **Splunk**, you can centralize logs from a wide range of components and services, allowing for the quick identification of issues, patterns, and areas of concern. Many of these tools support real-time log analysis and visualization, which empowers teams to detect anomalies and proactively tackle potential problems before they escalate.

Additionally, cloud-native logging tools often facilitate seamless integration with other cloud-native services and tools, enhancing overall workflow efficiency and collaboration among team members. These tools also provide customizable dashboards and reporting features, enabling the easy sharing of insights and trends with various stakeholders across the organization.

By incorporating a cloud-native logging solution into the technology stack, organizations can strengthen application reliability, reduce downtime, and streamline debugging processes, ultimately ensuring a high level of service quality in a complex cloud environment.

Let's take a visual tour (*Figure 7.2*) of the ELK stack—a prominent cloud-native logging solution for managing, analyzing, and visualizing logs in cloud environments—architecture overview:

Figure 7.2 – High-level architecture of the ELK stack

Use a cloud-native debugging tool

As we continue digging deeper, the cloud-native debugging tools are essential for effectively managing and resolving issues in cloud environments. These tools are specifically developed to address the unique challenges of cloud-native applications, offering advanced features tailored for distributed systems and microservices, such as **Kubernetes** or **serverless architectures**.

A cloud-native debugging tool, such as the open-source project **Telepresence** or the paid offering from **Rookout**, enables you to inspect application behavior in real time, trace requests across services, and swiftly identify the root causes of issues. These tools often provide interactive debugging capabilities, breakpoints, and code-stepping functionality, empowering teams to proactively address potential problems and gain a deeper understanding of their application's inner workings.

Additionally, cloud-native debugging tools typically integrate seamlessly with other cloud services and platforms, such as container orchestration systems, monitoring tools, and logging solutions, ensuring smooth workflows and collaboration among team members.

By incorporating a cloud-native debugging solution, such as Telepresence or Rookout, into their technology stack, organizations can enhance application reliability, minimize downtime, and optimize development and troubleshooting processes, ultimately maintaining highly available and reliable services in a complex cloud environment.

Figure 7.3 provides a visual glimpse of a Rookout environment, a powerful cloud-native debugging tool, in action. In the following screen capture, the routing system directed a user request to `homePage.js`, reaching a breakpoint in line 5. When the code execution reaches this line, it will take a live snapshot of a collection of runtime attributes, including variables, processes, execution chains, and tracing of services. In the bottom-right section, we can observe the value of multiple variables. For example, at the time of the breakpoint, the value of the data variable was an object with some filtering options and the value of some text fields.

Observing runtime attributes in real time provides valuable information about the state of our application in a time-stamp:

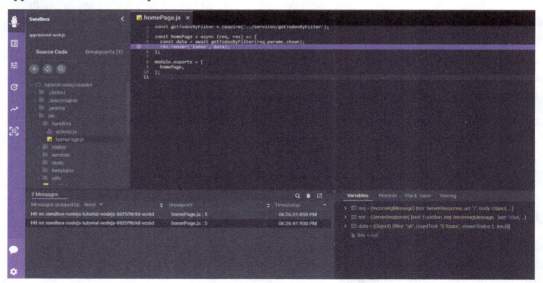

Figure 7.3 – Sample Rookout environment

Use a cloud-native observability platform

For cloud platform engineers, utilizing a cloud-native observability platform, such as **Prometheus** (open source) or **Dynatrace** (paid), is essential for effectively managing, monitoring, and troubleshooting applications in a cloud environment. These platforms are designed to address the unique challenges of cloud-native applications, providing comprehensive insights into system health and performance across distributed systems and microservices.

With a cloud-native observability platform, developers can collect, analyze, and visualize metrics, logs, and traces from various components and services, enabling rapid identification of issues and trends. These platforms often support real-time data analysis, alerting, and anomaly detection, helping development teams proactively address potential problems.

Additionally, cloud-native observability platforms, such as **Grafana** (open source) or **New Relic** (paid), offer seamless integration with other cloud-native services and tools, facilitating streamlined workflows and collaboration for developers. They provide customizable dashboards and advanced visualization capabilities, allowing developers to create tailored views of their applications' performance.

By adopting a cloud-native observability solution, organizations can maintain application reliability, minimize downtime, and optimize resource usage in a cloud environment. Furthermore, developers are empowered to create and maintain high-quality applications, ensuring seamless user experiences and efficient development processes.

Leveraging these observability platforms not only accelerates troubleshooting but also fosters a culture of continuous improvement, enabling developers to learn from past incidents and proactively optimize their applications for better performance and resilience.

Figure 7.4 illustrates the Prometheus architecture, an open source cloud-native observability platform, showcasing its core components and their interactions. Let's have a closer look at each of the components of Prometheus:

- **Prometheus server**: This is the core element of Prometheus and is responsible for scraping and collecting metrics from configured endpoints at specified intervals. The Prometheus server is designed to be highly available and reliable, and it is usually deployed as a standalone server, ensuring its correct functioning when other parts of the architecture are broken.

- **Service discovery**: Prometheus can be integrated with Kubernetes thanks to a service discovery unit. File-based service discovery is implemented to provide Prometheus with a list of targets—usually exposed through defined endpoints—from which to scrape metrics.

- **Pushgateway**: This unit is used to handle short-lived jobs. If a job might disappear before Prometheus scrapes its metrics, then it can push the metrics to the pushgateway, and Prometheus will pull the metric from there.

- **Alerting**: This component manages the alerts sent by Prometheus. It collects the alerts from the server and duplicates them before sending them to configured channels (email, PagerDuty, etc.).

The following figure illustrates the Prometheus architecture:

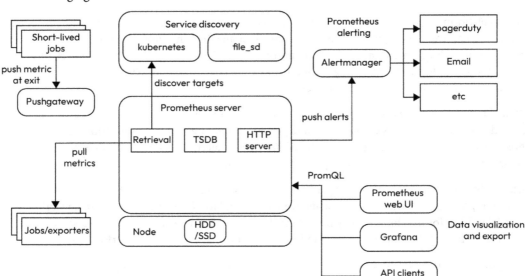

Figure 7.4 – Prometheus architecture

Use a service mesh

Service mesh could be one option when developing applications in a cross-cloud environment. Since we have covered the fundamentals in earlier chapters, let's take a look from a troubleshooting point of view. A **service mesh** is a network of software components that can help you manage and secure your cloud-native applications. A service mesh, such as **Istio** (open source) and **Linkerd** (open source), can be a valuable tool for a cloud-native developer in a multi-cloud environment when it comes to troubleshooting. By providing a consistent and unified layer of communication, monitoring, and security for microservices, a service mesh can simplify and streamline the troubleshooting process. A service mesh can help a cloud-native developer in a multi-cloud environment with troubleshooting in the following ways:

- **Observability**: A service mesh collects telemetry data, such as request traces, logs, and metrics from all microservices, making it easier to monitor the performance and health of services across multiple cloud providers. This increased visibility allows developers to quickly identify and diagnose issues, pinpointing the root cause of a problem.

- **Tracing and debugging**: A service mesh enables distributed tracing, which helps developers follow the flow of requests across microservices and gain insights into latency, errors, and bottlenecks. This can help identify issues related to interservice communication or performance, even in complex and distributed multi-cloud environments.

- **Traffic management**: With a service mesh, developers can control and shape the traffic between microservices using features such as load balancing, circuit breaking, and retries. This helps to manage and isolate issues during troubleshooting, ensuring minimal impact on the rest of the application.

- **Consistent security**: A Service mesh provides a consistent security layer across all microservices, regardless of the cloud provider. By managing authentication, authorization, and encryption, developers can troubleshoot security-related issues more effectively and maintain secure communication between services.

- **Fault injection and chaos testing**: A service mesh allows developers to inject faults and perform chaos testing to proactively identify and address potential issues before they occur in production. This helps to improve the resilience and reliability of applications deployed in multi-cloud environments.

- **Centralized control plane**: A service mesh comes with a centralized control plane that allows developers to configure and manage microservices across different cloud providers. This simplifies troubleshooting by providing a single point of control and visibility for the entire application.

- **Multi-cloud compatibility**: Service mesh solutions are designed to work across different cloud providers, ensuring that developers can consistently apply troubleshooting techniques and best practices, regardless of the underlying infrastructure.

By leveraging a service mesh, a cloud-native developer can simplify and streamline the troubleshooting process in a multi-cloud environment, reducing the complexity and time required to diagnose and resolve issues.

Choosing the right service mesh for your needs

There are many service meshes available in the market, so it's essential to select one that caters to your specific requirements. When choosing a service mesh, consider the following factors:

- **Features and functionality**: Evaluate the features offered by the service mesh, such as traffic management, security, observability, and resilience. The service mesh should provide a comprehensive set of capabilities that help you effectively manage and monitor your microservices architecture.

- **Pricing and scalability**: Consider the cost of implementing a service mesh technology, taking into account not only the initial investment but also the recurrent and additional costs related to new features or scaling your application. The costs should adjust to your budget and organizational goals.

- **Compatibility and interoperability**: Ensure that the service mesh supports the various platforms, technologies, and programming languages used within your organization. This guarantees seamless integration and consistent management across your microservices environment.

- **Community and support**: Investigate the service mesh's community, documentation, and support options. A strong community and accessible resources can help you quickly address any issues or questions that arise during implementation and ongoing management.

By considering these factors, you can make an informed decision when choosing a service mesh that meets your organization's needs and enhances the management and observability of your microservices in a multi-cloud environment.

Figure 7.5 depicts Istio, employed as an ingress gateway within a service mesh. The accompanying flowchart was generated using **Kiali**, an open source observability and visualization tool. Kiali can help us visualize the complex flow of traffic between microservices and the complex architectures established through Istio that rule microservices intercommunication in our application. The following diagram provides the microservice architecture for the products page, which then either leads to expanded details or to the reviews of the product. Each of the microservices is independent and can communicate with each other through APIs or other protocols. The ingress Gateway is a component from Istio that helps manage incoming and outgoing traffic to the service mesh. It is the entry point to the service mesh and provides an additional layer for policy reinforcement and better traffic management:

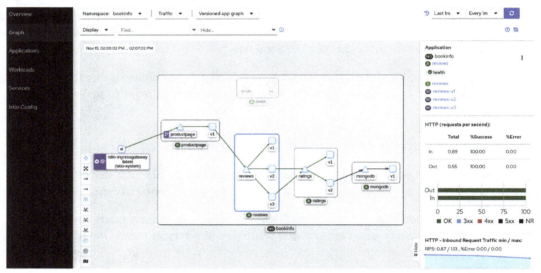

Figure 7.5 – Kiali graph tab with Istio Ingress gateway

Use a cloud-native configuration management tool

For platform engineers, employing a **cloud-native configuration management** tool, such as **Ansible** (open source) or **Terraform** (open source), is crucial for managing and automating the configuration of cloud-native applications across multi-cloud environments. These tools help ensure that applications are always configured correctly, which can help to prevent problems like manual errors and reduce the time spent on manual configuration tasks. Here's how such tools can be helpful:

- **Centralized configuration**: These tools help manage the configuration settings for all services, making it easy to track, modify, and maintain configurations across different environments. This can help in identifying and resolving issues caused by misconfigurations.

- **Version control**: By integrating with version control systems, these tools allow developers to track changes to configuration files, making it easier to identify when a change may have introduced an issue. This enables faster rollback to a previous, stable state.

- **Consistency and automation**: The tool ensures consistency for configuration settings across all instances of a service or application, reducing the risk of environment-specific issues. The automated deployment of configuration changes also reduces the likelihood of human errors during manual updates.

- **Monitoring and auditing**: Configuration management tools can monitor and audit configuration changes, enabling developers to detect unauthorized or unexpected changes that may lead to issues. This feature also helps in maintaining compliance with security and industry regulations.

- **Faster problem resolution**: By providing visibility to the configuration state of the services, developers can quickly identify misconfigurations or inconsistencies that may be causing issues. This accelerates the troubleshooting process and reduces downtime.

By adopting these tools, it helps developers collectively maintain application reliability, minimize downtime, and optimize resource usage in a cloud environment. Moreover, developers can focus on delivering value through their applications, ensuring seamless user experiences and efficient development processes. These tools also contribute to troubleshooting by enabling the rapid detection and resolution of configuration-related issues, thereby accelerating incident response and recovery times. *Figure 7.6* illustrates the high-level components of Terraform, The Terraform configuration files describe the resource allocation and infrastructure to be created by the cloud provider. After that, the core element of Terraform takes and interprets the configuration files and prepares the corresponding request for each cloud provider. Finally, Terraform stores the state of the managed architecture and infrastructure, and this contains a mapping between resources in your configuration files and the real-world entities they represent. This can be viewed in *Figure 7.6*:

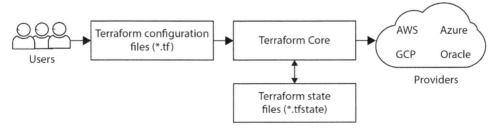

Figure 7.6 – Terraform components

In addition to these tools in place, it is also important to have a well-defined process for troubleshooting cloud-native applications. This will be discussed in the next section.

Establishing an effective troubleshooting process for cloud-native applications

To effectively tackle problems in a multi-cloud environment, it is essential to have a clearly defined approach for debugging cloud-native apps. The following are the steps to set up such a procedure:

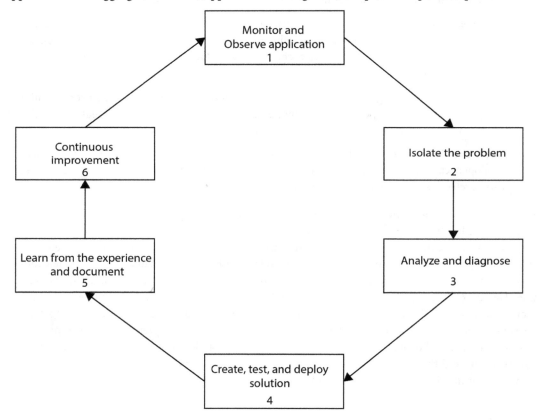

Figure 7.7 – Flowchart for troubleshooting cloud-native applications for developers

Step 1 – Detecting the issue

Detecting an issue is the first and most crucial step in the troubleshooting process. By identifying and acknowledging problems quickly, you can minimize the impact on end-users and application performance. In this context, detecting an issue consists of two primary methods:

- **Receive an alert** from monitoring and observability tools: Cloud-native developers should rely on well-configured monitoring and observability platforms to detect issues proactively. These tools collect, analyze, and visualize metrics, logs, and traces from various application components and services. By setting up alerting rules based on **key performance indicators (KPIs)**, error rates, latency thresholds, or resource utilization, developers can be notified as soon as an issue arises. Alert notifications can be delivered through various channels such as email, SMS, or chat platforms, ensuring that the responsible team members are informed and can take immediate action.

- **Observe abnormal behavior** in logs or metrics: In addition to automated alerts, cloud-native developers can receive support from platform engineers to review the logs, metrics, and visualizations provided by their observability tools. Regularly examining these data allows developers to spot abnormal behavior or anomalies that may not have triggered an alert but could still indicate a potential issue. For example, a sudden spike in resource usage or an increase in error rates may warrant further investigation. By proactively monitoring the health and performance of their applications, developers can identify and address issues before they escalate into more significant problems or impact end-users.

Detecting issues in a timely manner is a critical aspect of maintaining and enhancing cloud-native applications. Cloud-native developers should leverage monitoring and observability tools, configure effective alerting mechanisms, and actively review application data to ensure quick identification and response to any issues that arise in their multi-cloud environments.

Step 2 – Isolate the problem

Isolating the problem is the next crucial step in the troubleshooting process. Pinpointing the root cause of an issue helps to minimize the time spent on debugging and ensures that the appropriate corrective measures are taken.

In the context of isolating the problem, developers should focus on identifying the affected component(s) or service(s) within your application or external dependencies. As was covered in earlier chapters, cloud-native applications often consist of multiple microservices and components that interact with one another, as well as external dependencies (e.g., cloud provider services or third-party APIs). As a cloud-native developer, you should first determine which component or service within your application is affected by the issue. This can be achieved by analyzing the logs, metrics, and traces collected by your observability tools. Look for error messages, increased latencies, or any other anomalies that may help pinpoint the problematic component(s) or service(s).

In addition to examining your application components, it's essential to consider the role of external dependencies in the issue. Cloud-native applications often rely on various cloud provider services and third-party APIs, and problems in these dependencies can also impact your application. Review the status pages, documentation, and support channels of these external dependencies to identify any known issues or outages that may be contributing to the problem.

Isolating the problem area in a cloud-native application is a critical aspect of effective troubleshooting. Cloud-native developers should leverage their observability tools and insights from logs, metrics, and traces to identify the affected component(s) or service(s) within their application or external dependencies. By doing so, developers can focus their efforts on the most relevant areas and work towards resolving the issue more efficiently, ultimately minimizing the impact on end-users and application performance.

Step 3 – Analyze and diagnose

The **analysis and diagnosis** step is critical in the troubleshooting process for cloud-native developers. It involves a systematic approach to understanding the nature and cause of issues encountered in cloud-native applications, particularly in multi-cloud environments. As a developer, you should perform the following actions:

- Examine application logs, metrics, and traces to understand the issue: it's crucial to thoroughly **examine logs, metrics, and traces** collected from your application and its components. These data sources provide valuable insights into the application's behavior, helping you understand the nature and scope of the issue at hand. By analyzing this information, you can identify patterns, anomalies, and possible correlations that can guide your troubleshooting efforts.

- **Review recent changes** in the code, configuration, or deployment: Investigate any recent changes made to the codebase, configuration files, or deployment process that could be contributing to the issue. Comparing the current state of the application with a previous, stable version can reveal discrepancies that may be causing the problem. Identifying and reverting or fixing these changes can help resolve the issue.

- Consult relevant documentation, forums, or known issues related to your tech stack: **Research and consult** documentation, online forums, and known issue repositories related to your technology stack to gain insights into the issue you're facing. Others in the cloud-native community might have encountered similar problems and shared their solutions, workarounds, or insights. Gathering information from these sources can help you diagnose the problem more effectively and efficiently.

- **Utilize debugging tools** to pinpoint the root cause: Employ cloud-native debugging tools to dive deeper into your application's behavior and identify the root cause of the issue. Debugging tools can provide real-time insights into application execution, allowing you to trace requests across services, set breakpoints, and step through the code. By using these tools, you can gain a comprehensive understanding of the issue, which can help you develop a targeted solution.

In summary, analyzing and diagnosing issues in a cloud-native application involves a combination of examining logs, metrics, and traces, reviewing recent changes, consulting external resources, and using debugging tools. As a cloud-native developer, mastering these techniques is essential for efficiently diagnosing and resolving issues in a multi-cloud environment.

Step 4 – Create, test, and deploy the solution

Implementing the solution is an essential step in the troubleshooting process. After developing and testing the fix or workaround, it is crucial to deploy it in the production environment and monitor its impact on the application. In the context of implementing the solution and verifying its effectiveness, developers should consider the following:

- **Deploy** the fix or workaround in the production environment: Using your application's CI/CD pipeline, deploy the tested solution to the production environment. This process should involve automated deployments, configuration updates, or any necessary adjustments to external dependencies. Ensure that you follow best practices for deployment, such as using blue-green or canary deployments, to minimize the potential impact on users and facilitate rollback if needed.

- **Monitor** the impact of the changes on application **performance and stability**: After deploying the solution, actively monitor the application's performance, stability, and relevant metrics to ensure that the fix or workaround has had the desired effect. Use your monitoring and observability tools to track any changes in performance, error rates, or other relevant indicators. This helps you verify that the issue has been resolved without negatively impacting other aspects of the application.

- **Confirm** that the issue has been resolved: Based on your monitoring and observability data, confirm that the deployed solution has effectively addressed the identified issue. Check that the original symptoms have disappeared and that the application is functioning as expected.

- **Ensure** no new issues have been introduced: While verifying that the issue has been resolved, also ensure that no new problems have been introduced because of the fix or workaround. Continuously monitor the application's performance, stability, and metrics to identify any potential side effects or unexpected consequences of the solution. If new issues are detected, the troubleshooting process may need to be repeated to address these additional problems.

By carefully implementing and verifying the effectiveness of the solution, cloud-native developers can ensure that the identified issue is resolved and that the application remains stable, performant, and reliable, providing a seamless user experience and reducing the likelihood of future issues.

Step 5 – Learn from the experience and document

Learning from the experience and **documenting it** is a vital step. This practice allows developers to continuously improve their applications and troubleshooting skills, ensuring long-term application resilience and stability. By learning from past experiences and documenting key insights, teams can prevent similar issues from recurring and share valuable knowledge with the broader development community. The details to achieve this goal are as follows:

1. **Update the internal documentation and knowledge base** with the issue details and resolution: After resolving the issue, it's crucial to update your internal documentation and knowledge base

to include the details of the problem and its resolution. This helps create a valuable reference for your team and future developers, enabling them to quickly identify and resolve similar issues.

2. **Share the experience and lessons learned** with your team and the cloud-native community: Communicate the issue and its resolution to your team members to help them learn from your experience. You may also consider sharing your findings with the wider cloud-native community through blog posts, forums, or conference presentations. This contributes to the collective knowledge and helps others avoid or address similar issues more effectively.

3. **Identify opportunities** for **improving application design, monitoring, and alerting** to prevent similar issues in the future: Reflect on the issue and its resolution to identify potential improvements in your application design, monitoring, and alerting practices. Implementing these improvements can help prevent similar issues from occurring in the future and further enhance your application's overall resilience and performance.

By focusing on documentation, knowledge sharing, and continuous improvement, cloud-native developers can enhance their troubleshooting capabilities and contribute to the success of their team and the broader cloud-native community. This approach ultimately results in more robust and maintainable cloud-native applications, benefiting both developers and end-users.

Step 6 – Continuous improvement

By adopting a continuous improvement mindset, developers can proactively address potential issues, reduce downtime, and optimize the overall development process. The following points are some key aspects to consider when focusing on continuous improvement:

1. **Analyze trends and patterns** in incidents to identify areas for improvement in your cloud-native applications: Regularly review incident data, trends, and patterns to identify recurring issues or areas of weakness in your applications. Use this information to prioritize areas for improvement and focus your development efforts on enhancing application resilience, performance, and maintainability.

2. **Implement proactive measures** to enhance application resilience, performance, and maintainability: Based on your analysis of incident data, implement proactive measures to address identified areas of improvement. This may include refining application architecture, improving error handling, optimizing resource usage, or updating dependencies.

3. **Refine monitoring, alerting, and troubleshooting processes** based on experience and feedback: Continuously review and refine your monitoring, alerting, and troubleshooting processes based on your team's experiences and feedback from the cloud-native community. This iterative approach ensures that your processes remain effective, efficient, and up-to-date with the best practices in the rapidly evolving cloud-native ecosystem.

By following these steps, we foster a culture of continuous improvement and learning, enabling the applications to become more resilient, performant, and maintainable over time. This approach ultimately results in better user experiences and more robust cloud-native applications.

In this section, we've explored how to create an effective troubleshooting process, starting with identifying the problem and journeying toward continuous improvement.

But our adventure doesn't stop here. In the next part, we'll dive into real-world case studies. These stories will show how cloud-native developers put their troubleshooting skills to work while managing applications in a multi-cloud environment.

Case studies

Let's now get into some practical examples. Real-world scenarios, or case studies, serve as a valuable resource to understand the application of concepts we have discussed thus far. They allow us to examine specific instances where troubleshooting methodologies are employed to resolve issues that arise in a multi-cloud setup.

In this section, we will walk through a series of case studies. These studies are designed to mirror typical situations that cloud-native developers might encounter while managing applications across different cloud platforms. By studying these cases, we will gain insights into how the effective use of monitoring and observability tools, along with sound troubleshooting strategies, can address complex problems that surface in a multi-cloud environment.

Each case study will present a problem scenario, discuss the approach taken to diagnose and resolve the issue, and highlight the key takeaways and best practices. While these case studies are hypothetical, they are built on common challenges that developers and operations teams frequently face. By the end of this section, you will have a better understanding of how to apply the principles and techniques of troubleshooting to real-world situations, thereby enhancing your skills in managing and maintaining cloud-native applications in a multi-cloud environment.

Let's get started and see these troubleshooting strategies in action!

Case study 1 – Streamlining microservices communication in multi-clouds

Consider a leading e-commerce company that uses a microservices-based architecture for its application, deployed across multiple cloud providers. They started experiencing intermittent downtime in their application, leading to a significant impact on their business. Each microservice was developed and managed by different teams, and the application was deployed across **AWS** and **Google Cloud**. The errors were sporadic and seemed to be originating from various services, making it challenging to isolate the exact source of the problem:

- **Approach**: The DevOps team decided to employ a service mesh to better manage and monitor the microservices communication. They chose Istio for its robust capabilities in traffic management, security, and observability. With Istio, they could gain detailed insights into the application's network traffic, identify the problematic services, and manage the communication between different services effectively.

They also integrated their service mesh with their centralized logging and monitoring system to correlate the telemetry data from Istio with their application logs and metrics. This helped them trace the errors back to a handful of services that were experiencing high latencies due to inefficient database queries.

- **Resolution**: Once the problematic services were identified, the respective development teams optimized the database queries, significantly reducing the latencies. They also introduced circuit breakers and retries in their service mesh configuration to manage network-related failures better.

The team then monitored the application closely to ensure that the fixes were effective. Over the following weeks, the application's stability improved significantly, and the intermittent downtimes were eliminated.

- **Takeaways**:

  - A service mesh can provide valuable insights into microservices communication and help diagnose complex issues in a multi-cloud, microservices-based application

  - Centralized logging and monitoring are crucial for correlating different data types (logs, metrics, and traces) and identifying the root cause of the problem

  - The effective management of microservices communication using techniques such as circuit breakers and retries can significantly improve application stability

Case study 2 – Managing data consistency in a multi-cloud environment

This case involves a global healthcare provider that leverages a multi-cloud strategy to serve its patients across different geographical locations. They use a cloud-native approach for developing and deploying their patient management application, which is used by doctors and patients worldwide.

However, they started facing challenges with data consistency across different cloud platforms. The issue became prominent when patients moved between countries and their health records were not synced timely across the clouds. The resulting data inconsistency led to delayed or incorrect medical care, causing a significant impact on the patient experience and potentially on their health:

- **Approach**: To resolve this, a cloud-native developer decided to incorporate a global transaction protocol into the application, ensuring data consistency across all cloud platforms. The developer also decided to use a distributed database system that could effectively operate and synchronize across different clouds.

- **Resolution**: The developer implemented the global transaction protocol, which ensured that all transactions across different clouds were atomic, meaning they were either fully completed or fully rolled back, ensuring data consistency. A distributed database system was also introduced, which helped to maintain the real-time synchronization of patient records across the clouds.

- **Takeaways**:

  - The case study highlights the crucial role of data consistency in multi-cloud environments, especially when dealing with sensitive data such as healthcare records

  - It emphasizes the need for cloud-native developers to account for data-related challenges when designing applications for multi-cloud deployments

  - The case study shows that utilizing appropriate protocols and distributed database systems can significantly aid in managing data consistency across various cloud platforms

Case study 3 – Scaling challenges in a multi-cloud environment

This case involves a prominent online education provider that offers a suite of online courses to a global audience. The platform uses a cloud-native approach for its application development and employs a multi-cloud strategy to cater to its worldwide user base.

However, with a sudden increase in user traffic due to a global event, EdTech Global started facing application scaling issues. The platform wasn't scaling efficiently across all cloud providers, leading to poor application performance and a subpar user experience:

- **Approach**: A cloud-native developer at EdTech Global suggested implementing an automatic scaling solution that could function efficiently across multiple cloud platforms. The developer proposed to leverage Kubernetes, a container orchestration platform, to manage and scale the application seamlessly across different clouds.

- **Resolution**: The developer deployed Kubernetes across the multi-cloud environment and configured the auto-scaling feature. This change enabled the platform to handle the varying load efficiently, as resources were automatically scaled up or down based on the demand across different clouds. As a result, the application performance improved, and users had a consistent experience, irrespective of the surge in traffic.

- **Takeaways**:

  - The EdTech Global case study accentuates the importance of robust scalability strategies in multi-cloud environments.

  - It draws attention to the fact that user traffic can greatly fluctuate and be unpredictable; thus, cloud-native applications must be designed to scale effortlessly across diverse cloud platforms.

  - The case study reveals that tools such as Kubernetes can be instrumental in achieving this scalability, thereby guaranteeing a consistent user experience, irrespective of the platform load.

In wrapping up our case study exploration, we've seen firsthand how different organizations have navigated the complexities of troubleshooting in a multi-cloud environment. These real-world situations underscore the importance of robust monitoring, observability, and the appropriate use of cloud-native tools.

These case studies illustrate not only the challenges but also the successful strategies employed in addressing them. They highlight the significance of proactive monitoring, the need for efficient observability tools, and the benefit of implementing service meshes in a multi-cloud setup. Importantly, each case study reinforces the necessity for teams to continuously learn, adapt, and improve their applications and processes.

As we move forward in our cloud-native journey, let these case studies serve as a roadmap, offering practical insights and effective strategies. Remember, every challenge encountered is an opportunity to learn and enhance our understanding, leading to more resilient and efficient cloud-native applications. Let us now learn about SRE, a discipline that incorporates aspects of software engineering and applies them to infrastructure and operations problems.

SRE in multi-cloud environments

Site reliability engineering (**SRE**) is a key discipline in managing cloud-native applications, especially in a multi-cloud environment. SRE originated at Google when a team of software engineers was tasked to make Google's already highly reliable services even more reliable. The goal was not just to maintain uptime but to create scalable and highly reliable systems that could support Google's rapid growth and the increasing complexity of its services. This team approached operations from a software engineering perspective, applying principles of computer science and engineering to operational problems. This methodology was a departure from traditional IT operations, focusing on automating and improving the reliability of systems through engineering solutions rather than manual intervention.

The principles of SRE

SRE emanates from the challenges of managing large-scale, complex, and dynamic production systems. At its core, SRE operates on a few foundational principles that set it apart from traditional IT operations. These principles are as follows:

- **Service-level indicators** (**SLIs**): These are the quantitative measures of a service's reliability and performance, such as latency or uptime. Based on these SLIs, SREs define **service-level objectives** (**SLOs**) for targeted levels of reliability and performance. For instance, an SLO might state that a service should successfully handle 99.9% of its requests. Importantly, SLOs are not meant to drive a service to a perfect reliability score but rather to align it with business needs and user expectations, balancing reliability with other goals, such as feature velocity.

- **Error budgets**: In the realm of SRE, the concept of error budgets stands as a sentinel guarding the equilibrium between reliability and innovation. Think of it as a buffer zone, a carefully defined margin of allowable mishaps within the grand scheme of your SLOs. Imagine a system with an SLO of 99.95%. Within this, there's an error budget of 0.05%, which signifies the permissible risk threshold. This is a game-changer, as it furnishes engineering teams with a dynamic framework. It allows them to push the boundaries of innovation while always keeping a vigilant eye on the acceptable margins of failure. Consider it akin to a trapeze artist performing daring maneuvers high above the circus floor. The safety net is the error budget, which is essential for pushing the boundaries and trying out new, bold acts. It encourages calculated risks and fosters a culture of experimentation, all while maintaining a safety net to prevent catastrophic falls. In the world of SRE, error budgets are the essence of controlled innovation.

- **Reducing toil**: In the intricate world of SRE, the term **toil** carries substantial weight. It doesn't merely describe the mundane or repetitive tasks but signifies a relentless pursuit of liberation. Toil, in this context, encompasses all those manual, repetitive, and often frustrating chores that consume valuable engineering hours. These are hours that could otherwise be invested in endeavors that bring lasting value to your systems and organization.

  Imagine engineers mired in the monotony of routine server patching or responding to countless alarms triggered by avoidable incidents. These are hours spent merely keeping the system afloat, not making it better. SRE aims to systematically root out such toil, replacing it with automated processes, smart tooling, and efficient workflows. It's about liberating your skilled engineers from the shackles of repetitive tasks, enabling them to focus on what truly matters—innovation and the creation of features that enhance your system's reliability.

- **Shared responsibility**: In the SRE model, both developers and SRE engineers are accountable for the software they produce. This shared ownership ensures that reliability considerations are integrated throughout the software lifecycle. Developers might take part in on-call rotations, understanding firsthand the implications of their code in production. Conversely, SRE can be embedded in development teams, contributing to features and improvements with a reliability-focused perspective.

- **Blameless culture**: In the traditional landscape of operations, the aftermath of an incident is often echoed with finger-pointing and blame. The SRE paradigm, in stark contrast, advocates for a blameless culture. In the world of SRE, when something goes awry, the spotlight shines not on identifying the culprit but on understanding what transpired and why.

  Imagine a courtroom where the goal isn't to accuse but to uncover the truth. When an incident occurs, the primary question becomes, "What went wrong?" rather than "Who did it?" This subtle shift in perspective fosters a profound change in organizational culture. It promotes transparency, encourages individuals to come forward with their findings, and empowers the entire team to learn from the experience.

  In a blameless culture, the focus is on continuous improvement. It's about using incidents as valuable learning opportunities, not occasions for assigning guilt. This approach not only accelerates the resolution of issues but also cultivates an environment where everyone strives for betterment, collaboration, and, ultimately, greater reliability.

Before we move on to the benefits of SRE, let's view a comparison with DevOps, which was explored in detail in previous chapters. As the two disciplines may intersect at some point, it becomes important to draw a line between the two concepts.

The benefits of SRE

There are many benefits to implementing SRE in a multi-cloud environment; let's dive into some of them:

- **Improved service reliability**: By focusing on SLOs and error budgets, SRE ensures that services maintain a consistent level of reliability across multiple cloud providers. This consistent approach to reliability helps teams anticipate and mitigate potential issues specific to each cloud environment.

- **Optimized cost management**: Multi-cloud deployments can quickly become cost-intensive due to differences in pricing models among cloud providers. SRE practices such as reducing toil and automating operations can optimize resource usage and reduce wastage. Efficient resource allocation means organizations only pay for what they truly need.

- **Enhanced flexibility and avoidance of vendor lock-in**: SRE emphasizes automation and standardization. When combined with IaC, this ensures that configurations and deployments are consistent across different cloud providers, reducing dependency on a single vendor and allowing flexibility in choosing the best services from each provider.

- **Improved incident management**: With the principle of blameless postmortems, SRE promotes a culture of learning from incidents. When working across multiple clouds, this means a cohesive and unified approach to incident management, regardless of where the issue originates.

- **Efficient scalability**: Automated scaling is a core component of SRE. In a multi-cloud environment, this means that services can automatically scale up or down based on demand across all cloud platforms, ensuring optimal performance and cost-effectiveness.

- **Reduced operational toil**: By focusing on eliminating repetitive and manual tasks, SRE can significantly reduce the operational overhead that often comes with managing services across different cloud providers. This leads to more time for innovation and improving the system's overall health.

- **Enhanced security and compliance**: Standardized tools, processes, and automated checks ensure that security measures are consistently applied across all cloud environments. Automated audits, logging, and monitoring help maintain compliance standards regardless of the cloud provider.

- **Faster time-to-market**: The use of automation and CI/CD integration, as well as a focus on delivering features without compromising reliability, means that products or features can be rolled out quickly across all cloud platforms.

- **Continuous improvement**: The iterative nature of SRE, especially with blameless postmortems and error budgets, fosters a culture of continuous improvement. In multi-cloud environments, this means constantly optimizing deployments, configurations, and operations across all cloud providers.

Implementing SRE in multi-cloud settings ensures that organizations can harness the unique benefits of multiple cloud providers while maintaining consistent, reliable, and efficient operations. Now, it's time to understand chaos engineering, increasingly recognized as one of the best practices for cloud-native applications, especially in multi-cloud environments.

Chaos engineering

Chaos engineering is a discipline in systems engineering where engineers intentionally introduce failures into systems to ensure they can withstand unexpected disruptions. The process was born out of the need to improve system resilience in increasingly complex distributed architectures, and its roots can be traced back to companies, such as Netflix, that created related tools, such as **Chaos Monkey** (a tool designed to induce one specific type of failure – it randomly shuts down instances in order to simulate random server failure), to randomly terminate instances in their production environment to ensure that engineers continuously reinforce their systems against failures. Here are some key points about chaos engineering:

- **Proactive approach**: Instead of waiting for an unplanned disruption, chaos engineering takes a proactive approach to identify weaknesses before they cause bigger issues.

- **Understanding provider-specific failures**: Every cloud provider has its unique architecture, services, and potential points of failure. By conducting chaos engineering experiments on each platform, teams can gain insights into specific failure modes that might only occur on that particular platform. For instance, **AWS** might have different latency issues or service disruptions compared to **Azure** or **Google Cloud**.

- **Experiments, not accidents**: Despite the term "chaos," this engineering practice is methodical. Before introducing any failures, a hypothesis is formed about the system's behavior. Then, the failure is introduced, and the system's actual behavior is observed and compared to the hypothesis. If the system behaves differently than expected, there's a resilience gap that needs to be addressed.

- **Safety first**: Experiments are designed to be as safe as possible. The blast radius (or the potential impact area of the experiment) and magnitude (or the severity of the experiment) are carefully controlled. Automated rollbacks and safeguards are put in place to ensure that things can quickly return to normal if the experiment goes awry.

- **Network complexity**: In a multi-cloud setup, there might be inter-cloud communication. Chaos experiments can simulate network failures, latency, or packet loss between cloud providers. This allows teams to design and validate failover mechanisms, redundancy, and resiliency in these cross-cloud communications.

- **Continuous learning**: The goal isn't to break things for the sake of breaking them; it's to learn from these breaks. By continuously testing systems in this way, teams can uncover and fix unknown issues, leading to more robust and resilient systems.

- **Standardization amidst diversification**: While each cloud provider has its quirks, there's also a need for standardization to ensure smooth operations. Chaos engineering can help validate whether **standard operating procedures (SOPs)** are working across different cloud environments. For example, if you have a standard rollback mechanism, does it work as efficiently in AWS as it does in Google Cloud?

  By deliberately introducing failure into these systems, you can observe whether the rollback triggers correctly, operates within the expected time frame, or restores services to the desired state with minimal disruption in both settings.

- **Security and compliance**: Different cloud providers might have different security postures and compliance assurances. Chaos engineering can also encompass security experiments (sometimes called **chaos security**) to validate whether the security measures, such as encryption and access controls, remain consistent and effective across providers.

- **Tools and platforms**: Over time, a plethora of tools and platforms have emerged to assist with chaos engineering. Examples include Netflix's **Simian Army** (which includes Chaos Monkey), **Gremlin**, **Litmus**, and many more.

Chaos engineering is a four-step process that strengthens systems by deliberately injecting controlled chaos and observing how they handle it. Let's have a look at the following diagram and explore the lifecycle of chaos engineering:

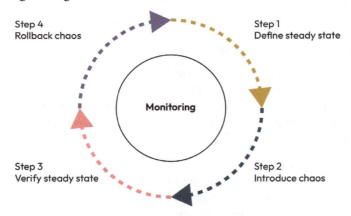

Figure 7.8 – The lifecycle of chaos engineering

The steps are as follows:

1. **Define the steady state**: Establish normal operating conditions for the system.

2. **Introduce chaos**: Simulate real-world failures such as network delays or disk outages.

3. **Verify steady state**: Monitor how the system handles the disruptions.

4. **Rollback**: Restore the system to its original state.

By iterating through these steps, engineers can identify and fix weak points, making systems more resilient to real-world chaos.

In essence, chaos engineering in a multi-cloud environment doesn't just validate the application's resilience; it validates the entire operational strategy, from networking to data replication, security, monitoring, and even cost management. By introducing failures intentionally in a controlled environment, teams can proactively address the complex challenges that come with managing multiple cloud providers.

Summary

In conclusion, troubleshooting cloud-native applications in a multi-cloud environment can be a complex task, but with the right strategies and tools, it is certainly manageable. As a cloud-native developer, it's crucial to understand that issues in such a dynamic environment are inevitable. However, the key to effective troubleshooting lies in robust monitoring, comprehensive observability, and efficient debugging tools, all working in tandem with a well-planned troubleshooting workflow.

This chapter has delved into the intricacies of the multi-cloud environment and has shown how to navigate its complexities when things go awry. We've covered the ripple effects of application malfunctioning, the unique challenges posed by multi-cloud setups, and a range of strategies for effective troubleshooting. Real-world scenarios were discussed to exemplify these principles in action, and various tools and practices were highlighted.

The goal is not merely to solve the problem at hand but to learn from each issue and iteratively improve the resilience and reliability of your applications. As the final takeaway, remember the importance of continuous improvement. Every troubleshooting incident is an opportunity to refine your applications and your approach, enhancing the overall quality and reliability.

As we progress further into the cloud-native and multi-cloud era, the demand for effective troubleshooting skills will only grow. Therefore, developing these skills and staying abreast of best practices is not just beneficial; they're essential for any developer aiming to excel in this evolving landscape.

In the upcoming chapter, we'll explore real-world examples of multi-cloud and cloud-native success stories and best practices. Join us in the next chapter!

Part 4:
Best Practices, Case Studies, and Future Trends for Multi-Cloud and Cloud-Native

This final part of the book brings together real-world success stories, best practices, and a forward-looking perspective on multi-cloud and cloud-native applications. It showcases case studies of companies that have effectively implemented these technologies and distills the lessons learned and recommendations for future projects. The chapters provide hands-on guidance for planning, designing, and optimizing cloud-native applications in a multi-cloud environment. Lastly, it offers a glimpse into the future, discussing emerging technologies and trends and the evolving role of the community and community in shaping the next wave of cloud computing.

This part has the following chapters:

- *Chapter 8, Learning from Pioneers and Case Studies*
- *Chapter 9, Bringing Your Cloud-Native Application to Life*
- *Chapter 10, Future-Proofing Your Cloud Computing Skills*

8

Learning from Pioneers and Case Studies

Our journey so far has been a mixture of multiple interesting topics around cloud-native development and multi-cloud. Now, it is time to embark on a journey to conquer the highest peaks in the world. You've done your research, gathered your gear, and trained relentlessly.

But this journey doesn't have to be a solitary expedition. Instead, we can draw from the experiences of pioneers who've navigated these paths before us.

Welcome to *Chapter 8, Learning from Pioneers and Case Studies*, where we're about to explore real-world success stories in the realm of multi-cloud and cloud-native applications. Just as those mountaineers shared their tales of ascent and descent, we're here to unveil stories of organizations that have successfully harnessed the power of multi-cloud and cloud-native technologies.

Why are these stories important? They offer more than just inspiration; they provide actionable insights. They represent a blueprint for success in a realm where the landscape constantly shifts, much like the mountainscape. These stories reveal the best practices, the strategies that work, and the pitfalls to avoid. They equip you, the cloud-native developer, with a unique perspective that can distinguish between a successful ascent and a strenuous struggle.

In this chapter, we'll delve deep into the annals of real-world case studies, dissecting the journeys of companies that have seamlessly scaled their applications, optimized costs with precision, and built unwavering resilience into their systems. We'll extract the essence of their success, distilling it into actionable advice you can implement in your projects.

But we won't stop at just these stories; we'll also explore the best practices that underpin the successes. From architectural considerations and deployment strategies to effective management and monitoring, we'll provide you with a comprehensive toolkit for your cloud-native toolkit. The following topics will be covered in this chapter:

- Real-world case studies

- Deployment strategies and best practices

- Lessons learned and recommendations

Real-world case studies

The case studies in this section will offer a glimpse into how companies from diverse industries harnessed the power of multi-cloud and cloud-native technologies to overcome unique challenges, achieve remarkable feats, and set new standards for innovation.

Each case study is a testament to the transformative potential of these approaches. We delve into the challenges these organizations faced, the ingenious strategies they employed, the tools and practices that powered their solutions, and the profound cultural shifts that paved the way for success. Let's dive into the case studies one by one.

Capital One – accelerating decision-making applications with Kubernetes

Capital One Financial Corporation is an American bank holding company that specializes in credit cards, auto loans, banking, and savings accounts, primarily operating within the United States. This case study demonstrates how Capital One effectively leveraged cloud-native technologies to address and surmount its challenges:

- **Challenges**:

  - **Complex application portfolio**: Capital One needed to develop a provisioning platform for applications with varying degrees of complexity, from real-time streaming to big data decision-making and machine learning. One critical application processed millions of daily transactions, including vital functions such as fraud detection and credit decisions.

  - **Resilience and speed**: Ensuring the resilience of these applications, particularly those involved in mission-critical tasks while maintaining high-speed performance, was a paramount challenge.

  - **Cluster rehydration**: The team faced the challenge of achieving the full rehydration of the cluster from base **Amazon Machine Images** (**AMIs**), a process that is essential for maintaining the health and reliability of the applications.

- **Strategies**:

  - **Strategic adoption of Kubernetes**: Capital One strategically adopted Kubernetes as a foundational technology for their application provisioning platform

  - **Kubernetes as an operating system**: Kubernetes was utilized as a substrate or operating system for their applications, providing a unified foundation for various workloads

  - **Degree of affinity**: The team integrated Kubernetes into their product development process, emphasizing its role in their technology stack

- **Tools and practices**:

  - **Kubernetes**: The adoption of Kubernetes as a container orchestration platform was pivotal in addressing the challenges

  - **Automation**: Kubernetes automation and declarative configuration played a crucial role in streamlining processes

  - **Provisioning platform**: The company developed a provisioning platform for managing applications and clusters

- **Cultural shift**:

  - **Productivity multiplier**: Kubernetes became a significant productivity multiplier for Capital One, leading to a shift in how they approached application development and deployment

  - **Cost-efficiency**: The adoption of Kubernetes resulted in cost-efficiency, significantly reducing operational expenses

  - **Agility**: The time-to-market for new applications and features improved drastically

- **Lessons learned**:

  - **Productivity impact**: Kubernetes had a profound impact on productivity and cost optimization, emphasizing its strategic importance

  - **Cost reduction**: Running the platform without Kubernetes would have substantially increased costs, highlighting the cost-saving potential of container orchestration

  - **Time-to-market**: Kubernetes significantly reduced the time required to deploy new applications and updates, enhancing agility

  - **Automation benefits**: Automation, as facilitated by Kubernetes, streamlined critical processes, making tasks more efficient

  - **Operational enhancements**: The automation of the rehydration/cluster-rebuild process resulted in faster and more reliable operations

> **Note:**
> For more information, please check https://www.cncf.io/case-studies/capitalone/.

Ygrene – using cloud-native tech to bring security and scalability to the finance industry

Ygrene Energy Fund, Inc. is a financing corporation that provides property-assessed clean energy financing to residential and commercial properties for energy efficiency projects. This case study demonstrates how Ygrene effectively leveraged cloud-native technologies to address and surmount their challenges:

- **Challenges**:

  - **Data aggregation and processing**: Ygrene, a **property-assessed clean energy** (PACE) financing company, faced challenges related to aggregating data from various sources and processing it efficiently

  - **Scalability limits**: They were using large servers but reached the vertical scaling limit, leading to system instability and performance issues, especially during real-time background data processing

  - **Security in finance**: As a finance company, Ygrene had to ensure the security of its applications and data

- **Strategies**:

  - **Adoption of Kubernetes**: Ygrene transitioned from their existing **Engine Yard** platform and **Amazon Elastic Beanstalk** to Kubernetes to achieve vertical scalability and distribute workloads effectively

  - **Build-time controls**: The company implemented **Notary** for build-time controls to establish trust in **Docker** images, particularly those using third-party dependencies

  - **Comprehensive observability: Fluentd** was employed for observing all parts of their technology stack, enhancing monitoring capabilities

  - **Amazon EC2 Spot**: Ygrene's setup ran on Amazon EC2 Spot Instances for cost optimization

- **Tools and practices**:

  - **Kubernetes**: Kubernetes played a pivotal role in enabling vertical scaling and workload distribution

  - **Notary**: Notary was used for ensuring trust and control in Docker image usage

  - **Fluentd**: Fluentd provided comprehensive observability across the technology stack

  - **Amazon EC2 Spot**: Leveraging EC2 Spot Instances contributed to significant cost savings

- **Cultural shift**:

  - **Deployment speed**: Kubernetes drastically improved deployment times from hours to minutes, enabling more frequent and agile deployments

  - **Zero downtime**: Ygrene could now deploy, ship code, and migrate databases without downtime, enhancing overall system availability

- **Lessons learned**:

  - **Deployment efficiency**: Kubernetes significantly reduced deployment times and allowed for more frequent code releases

  - **Operational resilience**: The shift to Kubernetes enhanced the system's stability and ability to handle real-time data processing

  - **Cost optimization**: Running Kubernetes clusters on Amazon EC2 Spot Instances resulted in substantial cost reductions

  - **Security and trust**: Implementing Notary and other controls improved the security and trustworthiness of their Docker images

  - **Agility**: Ygrene gained the flexibility to deploy code and make database migrations without system downtime, increasing overall agility

> **Note:**
>
> For more information, please check https://www.cncf.io/case-studies/ygrene/.

T-Mobile – scaling up for peak with Kubernetes

In the ever-evolving landscape of telecommunication, agility and scalability are essential. *T-Mobile*, one of the largest mobile companies in the United States, faced challenges originating from traditional monolithic applications. The company's slow development cycles and rigid architectures were insufficient to meet surging market needs. The T-Mobile case study is an excellent showcase of adopting Kubernetes to improve application development and infrastructure management:

- **Challenges**:

  - **Slow delivery**: T-Mobile was suffering from slow delivery rates. In 2015, it took T-Mobile seven months to deploy new code updates, which is a very slow rate for responding promptly to increasing market demand.

  - **PaaS limitations**: T-Mobile successfully improved deployment times thanks to Pivotal Cloud Foundation, a multi-cloud PaaS running on top of Kubernetes. However, the Docker containers didn't run smoothly, and new solutions were required.

- **Availability and reliability**: As a major telecommunication provider, T-Mobile has to ensure uninterrupted service, especially during peak times.

- **Strategies**:

  - **Adopting Kubernetes**: T-Mobile initially developed their own open source Kubernetes platform. However, it was after adopting Pivotal Cloud Foundation's **Pivotal Kubernetes Services (PKSs)** that efficiency and scalability became more tangible.

  - **Phased launch**: T-Mobile adopted a phased migration to the cloud, starting with a small portion of the production traffic in 2018 being balanced to Kubernetes and gradually scaling to intake more traffic.

- **Tools and practices**:

  - **Kubernetes**: The cornerstone of T-Mobile's cloud-native solution was based on Kubernetes, which was used to improve container orchestration and enable increased scaling and deployment.

  - **Pivotal Cloud Foundation (PCF)**: Adopted for improved and agile development cycles and shorter deployment times.

  - **Pivotal Kubernetes Service (PKS)**: Kubernetes cluster technologies, such as PKS, were necessary for T-Mobile to automate multi-cluster operations. It plays an important role in centralizing in-cluster services for monitoring, logging, networking, and other services needed for cloud-native applications.

- **Cultural shift**: Beyond the technical advantages brought by Kubernetes, T-Mobile had to adapt its organizational paradigm to host agile and innovative developers, fostering rapid development cycles and deployments.

- **Lessons learned**:

  - **High availability**: Thanks to the adoption of Kubernetes and PKS, T-Mobile was able to automatically manage the scaling of services, especially during peak times, ensuring high availability and reliability of services

  - **Agile deployment**: The role of modern development cycles that came hand-in-hand with the new technologies acquired by T-Mobile incentivized agile development practices that were able to cope with rapidly changing market needs

> **Note:**
> For more information, please check https://www.cncf.io/case-studies/t-mobile/.

Uber – cloud-native transformation for agility

Uber Technologies, Inc. provides ride-hailing services, food delivery, and freight transport. It is headquartered in San Francisco. The company operates across approximately 72 countries and 10,500 cities worldwide. This case study demonstrates how Uber effectively leveraged cloud-native technologies to address and surmount their challenges:

- **Challenges**:

  - **Scale and complexity**: Uber was dealing with the monitoring of around 4,000 proprietary microservices and a growing number of open source systems. The existing monitoring tools, **Graphite** and **Nagios**, were proving inadequate for handling this scale and complexity.

  - **Maintenance challenges**: Teams had to use pre-packaged Graphite monitoring software and create Nagios scripts to monitor metrics from these packages. This approach was challenging to maintain as the number of services and metrics increased.

- **Strategies**:

  - **Adoption of Prometheus**: Uber chose Prometheus as its monitoring solution because it aligned well with the preferences and requirements of Uber engineers

  - **Open sourcing M3 platform**: Uber's technical team developed and open sourced the M3 platform. This platform served as a scalable and configurable store for Prometheus metrics

  - **Scalability and global persistence**: M3 was implemented to accommodate the massive scale at Uber, handling billions of time series and millions of metrics per second, helping them to persist globally

- **Tools and practices**:

  - **Prometheus**: Uber adopted Prometheus as its primary monitoring tool

  - **M3 platform**: The open source M3 platform was utilized as a scalable metric store

  - **Client libraries**: Engineers used Prometheus client libraries to facilitate metric collection and monitoring

- **Cultural shift**:

  - **Operational efficiency**: The adoption of Prometheus and M3 significantly improved operational efficiency. Setting up monitoring systems became faster and less burdensome for operational maintenance.

- **Lessons learned**:

  - **Cost efficiency**: The use of Prometheus and M3 resulted in substantial cost savings, making metric ingestion significantly more cost-effective

- **Rapid deployment**: Monitoring systems for Uber's Advanced Technologies Group were deployed much faster than before, enhancing agility

- **Reduced maintenance:** The team experienced a drastic reduction in operational maintenance tasks, leading to improved overall efficiency and reduced alert fatigue

> **Note:**
> For more information, please check https://www.cncf.io/case-studies/uber/

Now that we have witnessed some real-world success stories, it's time to understand what deployment strategies is and why is it important.

Deployment strategies and best practices

In the dynamic world of cloud-native application development, where agility, scalability, and resilience are paramount, embracing strategies and best practices is not just a choice but a necessity. This section delves deep into the time-tested strategies, approaches, and principles that will empower you to craft robust, efficient, and adaptable applications tailored for the multi-cloud era. Let's learn about the deployment strategies in the multi-cloud environment.

Deployment strategies

Deployment patterns in cloud-native application development play a pivotal role in ensuring the reliability, scalability, and maintainability of your software. These patterns dictate how your application is rolled out, updated, and managed in a dynamic, often multi-cloud, environment. In this section, we'll delve into the intricacies of some deployment patterns, providing you with a comprehensive understanding of when and how to use them effectively.

Canary deployments

Canary deployments involve releasing a new version of your application to a subset of your user base while the majority of users still interact with the old version. This subset of users is referred to as the "canary group." The idea is to monitor and gather real-world data on how the new version performs in a controlled environment. *Figure 8.1* illustrates a canary deployment, a strategic method employed to reduce the risk associated with deploying new software versions:

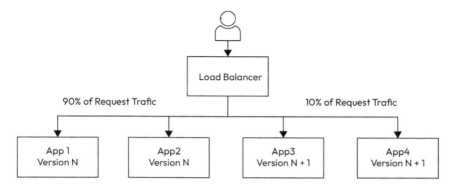

Figure 8.1 – Canary deployment

In this approach, instead of updating the entire system at once, a small percentage of the traffic—in this case, 10%—is directed to the new version of the application. The remaining 90% of traffic continues to be served by the old version. As we explored in the case studies, this is the same spirit that motivated T-Mobile, where they began by balancing some of the network with the new architecture before implementing full deployment. This technique allows real-world exposure to the new release with minimal impact on the overall user base. Monitoring tools are used to carefully analyze the performance and stability of the new version based on the feedback from this subset of traffic. If no issues are detected, the new version can gradually take on more traffic until it eventually serves all users. This incremental process provides a safety net, enabling quick rollback if any problems arise and ensuring a smoother, more controlled deployment:

- **Use cases**: Canary deployments are particularly valuable in the following instances:

  - Introducing major updates or changes to your application

  - Ensuring the new version performs well under real-world usage

  - Minimizing the risk of widespread issues by catching problems early

  - Gradually rolling out new features or changes to a subset of users for feedback

- **Implementation**: Implementing canary deployments often involves the following:

  - Diverting a small portion of incoming traffic or users to the new version

  - Monitoring key performance metrics, error rates, and user feedback for both versions

  - Gradually increasing the canary group's size if the new version proves stable

  - A potential rollback if issues arise or further deployment to the entire user base if successful

Blue-green deployments

Blue-green deployments maintain two identical environments: one as the "blue" production environment (the current live version) and the other as the "green" staging environment (the new version). Traffic is initially directed to the blue environment, but when a new release is ready, traffic switches to the green environment. *Figure 8.2* showcases a blue-green deployment strategy, an approach designed to reduce downtime and risk by running two identical production environments, only one of which is live at any given time:

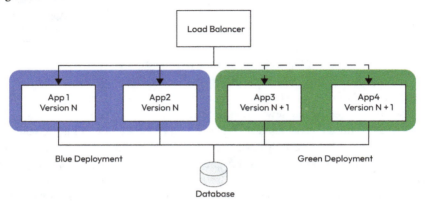

Figure 8.2 – Blue-green deployment

In this model, "blue" represents the current, active version of the application, receiving all user traffic via a load balancer. When a new version of the application, "green," is ready to be deployed, it's carried out in a parallel environment to Blue. After thorough testing and once Green is verified to be stable, the load balancer seamlessly shifts all traffic from Blue to Green. This switch can be instantaneous and allows for an immediate fallback to the Blue environment if any issues arise with Green, ensuring uninterrupted service and providing a robust mechanism for updates and rollbacks:

- **Use cases**: Blue-green deployments are suitable in the following instances:
  - Minimizing downtime is critical during updates
  - Ensuring the ability to rollback quickly in case of issues
  - Gradually transitioning users to a new version for a seamless experience

- **Implementation**: Implementing blue-green deployments often occurs in the following instances:
  - Setting up identical blue and green environments
  - Directing traffic to the blue environment initially
  - Deploying the new version to the green environment

- Switching traffic from blue to green when ready

- Monitoring issues and rolling back to blue if necessary

Rolling deployments

Rolling deployments update a running application incrementally by replacing instances one at a time. This process maintains continuous availability while introducing new features or fixes gradually. *Figure 8.3* depicts the process of a rolling deployment, a technique that facilitates the gradual replacement of an older version of an application with a new release:

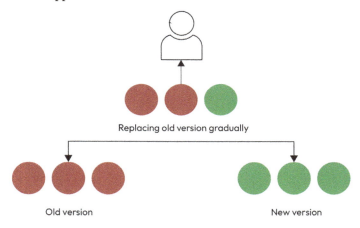

Figure 8.3 – Rolling deployment

During this procedure, the update occurs incrementally, with each instance of the application being updated one after the other. This systematic approach ensures that there is no downtime, as only a subset of instances is taken offline for the update at any given time. As each instance is updated, it rejoins the pool of active servers, serving the new version of the application. This method allows for a smooth transition and provides the ability to monitor the deployment for any issues, thereby minimizing risk and ensuring service continuity for end users:

- **Use cases**: Rolling deployments are useful in the following instances:

  - Ensuring high availability and minimal disruption is critical

  - Incrementally releasing updates to a running application

  - Gradually scaling up or down based on demand

- **Implementation**: Implementing rolling deployments often occurs in the following instances:

  - Dividing your application instances into smaller groups

  - Replacing instances in one group at a time with new versions

- Monitoring performance and health after each replacement
- Gradually moving through all groups until the update is complete
- Rolling back to previous versions if issues arise

Shadow deployments

Shadow deployments duplicate incoming requests to a new version of the application without serving them to users. The primary goal is to monitor and test the new version's behavior under real-world conditions without impacting users. *Figure 8.4* illustrates the concept of a shadow deployment, a strategy employed to test a new version of an application in the live production environment without impacting end users:

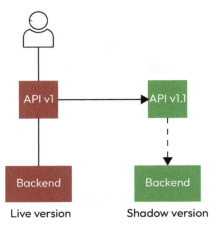

Figure 8.4 – Shadow deployment

In this deployment, when users access the existing API (version *v1*), their requests are handled by the current backend as usual, ensuring that the user experience remains unchanged. Simultaneously, these requests are duplicated and routed to the newer API version (*v1.1*), which operates in parallel. This shadow version processes the traffic in real time but does not affect the actual response returned to the user. This approach allows developers to observe the behavior of the new version under actual load conditions, verifying its performance and stability before fully transitioning to it:

- **Use cases**: Shadow deployments are beneficial in the following instances:

  - Introducing significant changes or updates to an application
  - Validating the new version's performance, stability, and compatibility
  - Ensuring a smooth transition to a new version without affecting user experience

- **Implementation**: Implementing shadow deployments often occurs in the following instances:

  - Creating a mirrored environment for the new version

  - Diverting a portion of incoming traffic to the shadow environment

  - Monitoring and analyzing how the new version behaves under real usage

  - Comparing the metrics and outcomes between the shadow and production environments

  - Gradually transitioning users to the new version based on performance analysis

These deployment strategies empower cloud-native developers to update applications efficiently, manage risks, and maintain high availability. When combined with robust rollback strategies, they ensure that updates can be safely and promptly reversed in case of deployment failures or unexpected issues, minimizing disruptions to users and businesses.

In the next section, we will see some of the lessons learned from real-world experiences in cloud-native development and recommendations.

Lessons learned and recommendations

This section distills valuable insights from real-world experiences in cloud-native development and management. It delves into the challenges faced, the strategies employed, and the outcomes achieved by organizations and individuals working in the cloud-native space. By examining these lessons, readers gain a deeper understanding of best practices and the pitfalls to avoid when embarking on cloud-native projects. Moreover, this section provides actionable recommendations for future initiatives, covering critical aspects such as security, compliance, automation, scalability, budgeting, and innovation. It serves as a comprehensive guide for anyone looking to make the most of cloud-native technologies and ensure the success of their projects.

Lessons learned

This section aims to summarize the key takeaways, highlight the common challenges and pitfalls encountered, and offer practical advice based on these lessons. Drawing from case studies and industry expertise, it provides a rich resource for individuals and organizations embarking on similar cloud-native journeys:

- **Embrace cloud-native principles**: Embracing cloud-native principles, such as microservices and containerization, has been shown to significantly enhance scalability and resilience in case studies. However, it's essential to approach these transitions methodically, as they can be challenging to implement effectively.

- **Plan for failure**: By recognizing that the cloud is not infallible, organizations have learned the importance of planning for failure. This includes implementing redundancy and disaster recovery strategies, as well as conducting thorough testing to minimize downtime and data loss in the event of failures or outages.

- **Security is paramount**: The case studies underscore the critical importance of integrating security from the outset of cloud-native projects. Cloud-native applications require robust security measures and continuous monitoring to defend against evolving threats in the dynamic cloud environment.

- **Cost optimization is continuous**: Achieving cost optimization in cloud-native projects is an ongoing process. It entails the continuous monitoring of resource usage, adjusting resource allocations as needed, and adopting **financial operations** (**FinOps**) practices to prevent overspending and ensure efficient resource utilization.

- **Collaboration is key**: Successful cloud-native projects have highlighted the significance of cross-team collaboration. Breaking down organizational silos and fostering collaborative DevOps practices are essential for driving innovation and efficiency, ultimately leading to project success. Such collaboration leads to streamlined workflows, improved problem-solving, and faster delivery of products to market. This unity not only boosts product quality and reliability but also cultivates a resilient and adaptive organizational culture, providing a significant competitive advantage in a rapidly evolving digital landscape.

Recommendations for future projects

By drawing on the insights and lessons learned in the previous section, this section offers a roadmap for success in a holistic cloud-native development and management. It covers essential areas such as security, compliance, automation, scalability, budgeting, innovation, and more. By embracing these recommendations, individuals and organizations can navigate the complex landscape of cloud-native technologies with confidence, ensuring their projects are not only efficient but also positioned for long-term growth and adaptability:

- **Start with a cloud strategy**: Developing a comprehensive cloud strategy is the cornerstone of a successful cloud adoption journey. It begins with a thorough assessment of an organization's business goals, ensuring that the cloud strategy aligns perfectly with these objectives. This alignment is critical as it lays the foundation for demonstrating how cloud technology can empower and support broader business goals, whether they involve cost reduction, scalability, global expansion, or customer experience enhancement. The next pivotal step is crafting a cloud migration roadmap, a detailed plan that outlines the migration process's phases, timelines, and expected outcomes. Prioritizing workloads based on their business value and complexity is essential.

- **Prioritize security and compliance**: Prioritizing security and compliance is paramount. It's essential to weave these critical elements into the very fabric of your project, permeating every stage of its development and operation. Firstly, robust **identity and access management (IAM)** practices should be adopted to ensure that only authorized personnel can access resources and data. This not only safeguards sensitive information but also prevents potential breaches. Encryption, both at rest and in transit, is another foundational layer of security. By encrypting data, you protect them from unauthorized access, even if a breach were to occur. Additionally, compliance with industry standards and regulations should be diligently observed. Adherence to these standards not only ensures that your cloud-native project operates within legal boundaries but also aligns with best practices in safeguarding data and maintaining trust with stakeholders. Overall, the fusion of these security and compliance measures throughout the project lifecycle establishes a resilient and trustworthy cloud-native environment.

- **Embracing automation, orchestration, and compliance as code**: Adopting robust automation and orchestration practices is imperative. By investing in automation and orchestration tools, organizations can streamline the deployment, scaling, and day-to-day management of cloud-native applications. This not only accelerates processes but also minimizes manual labor, reducing the risk of errors and enhancing overall operational efficiency.

  Furthermore, to ensure security and regulatory compliance in cloud-native environments, it's crucial to embrace "compliance-as-code" practices. This involves integrating compliance checks and policy enforcement seamlessly within your **continuous integration/continuous deployment (CI/CD)** pipelines. By automating compliance checks, organizations can proactively identify and rectify compliance issues, thus strengthening their overall security position and ensuring adherence to industry-specific regulations and standards. This holistic approach to cloud-native development combines the benefits of automation, orchestration, and compliance, fostering a secure, efficient, and agile environment for application development and deployment.

- **Enhancing application performance and adaptability**: To optimize your cloud-native applications, it's imperative to focus on two key aspects: monitoring and scalability. First, establish robust monitoring and observability practices by selecting appropriate tools that offer deep insights into application performance and user experience. This proactive approach enables your team to identify and resolve issues swiftly, ensuring the seamless operation of your systems.

  Simultaneously, design your applications with scalability and elasticity at the forefront. By doing so, you prepare your infrastructure to adapt to fluctuating workloads and dynamic conditions. Scalability ensures that your applications can efficiently handle increased demand, while elasticity guarantees performance consistency regardless of varying circumstances. Together, these strategies enhance your application's performance and adaptability, contributing to a resilient and high-performing cloud-native environment.

- **Data strategy**: A robust data strategy is essential for cloud-native applications. It encompasses various critical elements, such as data governance, storage, and analytics. The strategy should be meticulously designed to make data accessible to those who need them while upholding stringent security measures and compliance with relevant regulations. By doing so, organizations can harness the power of their data to drive insights, innovation, and informed decision-making in a secure and compliant manner, ultimately contributing to the success of their cloud-native projects.

*   **Financial efficiency and innovation**: Achieving the delicate balance between financial efficiency and innovation is a hallmark of successful cloud-native projects. By implementing FinOps practices, organizations can gain better control over their cloud expenditure through regular cost analysis and optimization efforts while setting transparent budgets. Simultaneously, fostering a culture of experimentation and innovation encourages teams to explore novel technologies and methodologies, driving continuous improvement in their cloud-native applications while maintaining cost-effectiveness.

*   **Culture of continuous learning and knowledge sharing**: In the rapidly evolving landscape of cloud-native technologies, it is paramount to **instill a culture of continuous learning** within your organization. Encourage your team members to stay abreast of the latest industry trends and best practices by regularly updating their skill sets. Consider investing in certifications and training programs to build and certify their expertise, ensuring they remain well versed in cutting-edge cloud-native advancements. To facilitate seamless knowledge transfer and ensure continuity, prioritize documentation and knowledge sharing. Documenting processes, architectures, and best practices serves as a valuable resource for your team, enabling them to reference and replicate successful approaches. Promote a culture of knowledge sharing, where team members freely exchange insights, challenges, and solutions. By doing so, you not only harness the collective intelligence of your organization but also foster collaborative learning, which is fundamental in navigating the ever-changing cloud-native landscape effectively.

So far, we've explored several recommendations to guide you on your cloud-native journey. As we come to the conclusion of this chapter, let's take a moment to summarize the key takeaways and reinforce the knowledge we've acquired.

Summary

In this chapter, we took a deep dive into real-world case studies, meticulously dissecting the journeys of successful companies. These stories reveal how these organizations seamlessly scaled their applications, optimized costs with surgical precision, and fortified their systems with unwavering resilience. We also unveiled the best practices that underpin these remarkable achievements. From architectural insights and deployment strategies to effective management and vigilant monitoring, we provide you with a comprehensive toolkit for your cloud-native endeavors. This chapter covers critical topics, including real-world case studies, best practices for multi-cloud and cloud-native approaches, and the invaluable lessons learned.

As we move forward into the next chapter, we will transition from theory to practical implementation. You will learn how to design, deploy, and operate cloud-native applications across different cloud environments, putting the knowledge and best practices from the previous chapters into action.

Bringing Your Cloud-Native Application to Life

From the previous chapters, you've gained a strong foundation in the principles and concepts of building modern, scalable applications. Now, it's time to take your skills to the next level by delving into the complexities and opportunities presented by multi-cloud architecture.

In this chapter, we'll explore holistically how to plan, design, and deploy cloud-native applications that seamlessly operate across multiple cloud service providers. You'll discover strategies for ensuring resilience, optimizing performance, and managing costs effectively in this dynamic and demanding environment.

This chapter can be your hands-on guide, providing practical insights and actionable steps to empower you as a cloud-native developer in the era of multi-cloud computing. Whether you're a beginner looking to grasp the fundamentals or an intermediate practitioner aiming to refine your skills, this chapter is designed to provide valuable insights and practical guidance. Our goal is to equip you with the knowledge and expertise needed to succeed.

The following topics will be covered in this chapter:

- Project planning
- Designing cloud-native applications for multi-cloud
- Security best practices for deployment
- Troubleshooting and optimization
- Hands-on exercise

Project planning

For any project, project planning is a fundamental phase in the life cycle of any successful endeavor, in any development. This phase involves a series of crucial steps that lay the foundation for smooth and efficient project execution. Each step is vital for ensuring that your multi-cloud project is well-prepared, well-managed, and well-executed.

Throughout this book, we have explored areas of vital interest to get you ready for the multi-cloud ecosystem. The perspectives provided in each of the sections provide a unique consideration to remember when designing a cloud-native application. When you are planning for a cloud-native project, you should have a global view on multiple fields of the multi-cloud realm, compiled in the following figure (*Figure 9.1*), and evaluate their impact on your cloud-native application. Depending on the business project, some areas may require more attention than others, but you should always consider all areas of multi-cloud, even if they initially seem secondary to your specific project.

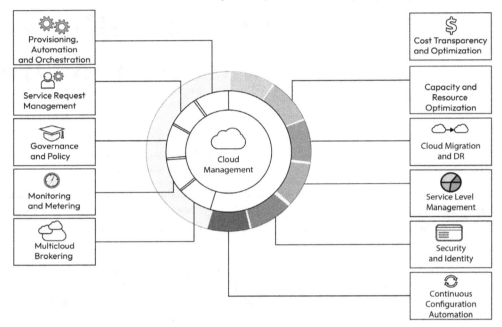

Figure 9.1 – Typical multi-cloud ecosystem

It is important to remember that understanding the intricacies of project planning is essential for achieving your goals effectively and efficiently. Let's look into the key aspects of project planning:

1. **Define clear project objectives and requirements**: At the outset of any project, it's essential to have a crystal-clear understanding of what you want to achieve. Begin by defining your project's objectives, which should be **specific, measurable, achievable, relevant, and time-bound (SMART)**. These objectives serve as your guiding star throughout the project and help you stay focused on what matters most. Additionally, outline the project's requirements, including functional and non-functional aspects. This step ensures that everyone involved understands the project's goals and scope.

- **Example**: Imagine a healthcare organization aiming to implement a multi-cloud solution to improve patient data accessibility and reduce administrative overhead. The specific project objective is to create a secure patient portal that allows users to access their medical records and schedule appointments online. A key requirement is that the patient portal must comply with healthcare regulations such as HIPAA to ensure patient data privacy.

2. **Identify key stakeholders and establish communication channels**: Typically, any live project requires multiple stakeholders, each with their interests and expectations. Identify who these key stakeholders are, whether they are team members, management, clients, or external partners. Establish effective communication channels to facilitate collaboration and ensure everyone is on the same page. Regular meetings, reports, and clear lines of communication are essential to address concerns, provide updates, and make informed decisions.

   - **Example**: Key stakeholders in the healthcare multi-cloud project include the IT department, medical staff, patients, and cloud service providers (e.g., AWS, Azure, Google Cloud). Effective communication channels are established through regular meetings, emails, and a secure online portal for patients to communicate with their healthcare providers.

3. **Create a multi-cloud strategy**: In a multi-cloud environment, choosing the right cloud service providers (CSPs) is crucial and challenging as well. Start by assessing your project's specific needs, such as performance requirements, compliance considerations, and geographical reach. Based on these factors, select the CSPs that align best with your goals. Your multi-cloud strategy should outline how you plan to leverage the strengths of each CSP while managing any potential complexities. Consider factors such as data integration, security, and cost management in your strategy.

   - **Example**: The multi-cloud strategy involves using AWS for scalable data storage and analytics, Azure for hosting the patient portal application, and Google Cloud for machine learning-based predictive analytics on patient health data. The strategy emphasizes data encryption, access controls, and regular security audits to ensure compliance with HIPAA regulations.

4. **Set a budget and allocate resources**: Managing costs is a fundamental aspect. Define a clear budget that includes not only the expected cloud costs but also other resources such as personnel and tools. Allocate resources wisely to ensure that you have the necessary skills and technology at your disposal. Keep in mind that effective resource allocation can prevent overspending and project delays.

   - **Example**: A budget of $2 million is allocated for the healthcare multi-cloud project. Resources include cloud infrastructure costs ($1 million), salaries for a team of cloud architects, developers, DevOps engineers, project managers, and security experts ($800,000), and cybersecurity tools and training ($200,000). The allocation ensures that the project has the necessary financial and human resources to meet its objectives.

5.   **Risk assessment and mitigation**: Identifying potential risks and developing strategies to mitigate them is crucial for any cloud transformation project's success. Conduct a comprehensive risk assessment specific to your multi-cloud project. Anticipate challenges related to security, compliance, technology integration, and external dependencies. Once identified, outline mitigation plans to address these risks effectively. Regularly revisit and update the risk assessment throughout the project life cycle to adapt to changing circumstances.

   - **Example**: For the example of healthcare services adopting a multi-cloud solution, potential risks could include, for example, data breaches or non-compliance with healthcare regulations. Mitigation strategies may involve implementing robust encryption protocols, regular compliance audits, and establishing contingency plans for switching cloud providers if necessary. Continuous monitoring and adaptation of mitigation plans will help maintain project resilience.

6.   **Establish project timelines and milestones**: It is key to develop a detailed project timeline that outlines when specific tasks and milestones should be completed, where these milestones serve as checkpoints to track progress and ensure that the project stays on course. Break down larger objectives into smaller, manageable tasks and assign responsibilities to team members. This approach enhances accountability and helps you identify and address issues early.

   - **Example**: Key project milestones include completing a security risk assessment within the first month, deploying the patient portal on Azure within six months, conducting penetration testing and obtaining HIPAA compliance certification within nine months, and rolling out the portal to patients within a year. These milestones ensure that the project progresses on schedule while maintaining data security and regulatory compliance.

By following these steps, you'll lay a strong foundation for your cloud-native project in a multi-cloud environment. Effective planning sets the stage for successful design, deployment, and operation of cloud-native applications across multiple cloud platforms.

Designing cloud-native applications for multi-cloud

Designing cloud-native applications for a multi-cloud environment is a complex task that requires careful planning and consideration of various factors. Here are detailed explanations of some of the key considerations when designing cloud-native applications for multi-cloud:

- **Portability**: Portability is a foundational principle when designing cloud-native applications. It entails creating applications that can seamlessly run on various cloud platforms without requiring significant modifications. To achieve this, developers should adopt cloud-agnostic technologies and standards. Technologies such as containers and container orchestration platforms such as Kubernetes, which is mentioned in detail in *Chapter 2, Building the Backbone of Cloud-Native Applications*, have gained popularity for their ability to abstract away cloud-specific intricacies. By avoiding vendor lock-in through the use of proprietary services, developers ensure that their applications remain adaptable and flexible, capable of migrating between cloud providers as needed.

- **Resilience**: Resilience is a critical aspect of cloud-native application design, especially in multi-cloud environments. It involves building applications that can withstand failures on any one cloud platform or in any region. To accomplish this, a distributed architecture is key. Applications should be architected to operate across multiple cloud regions or providers, minimizing single points of failure. Additionally, implementing failover mechanisms is crucial. These mechanisms enable automatic redirection of traffic to an operational cloud platform if one experiences issues, ensuring continuous service availability.

- **Performance**: Performance optimization is imperative to deliver a consistent user experience across all cloud platforms. Cloud-native applications must be designed to be scalable and capable of dynamically allocating resources based on varying workloads. Cloud-native technologies such as auto-scaling and load balancing play a vital role in efficiently distributing traffic and resources. By adopting these practices, applications can maintain high performance levels, regardless of the cloud platform they are hosted on.

- **Cost**: Managing costs is a fundamental consideration when operating in a multi-cloud environment. We've explored in detail, in *Chapter 6, Maximizing Value and Minimizing Cost of Multi-Cloud*, that cost optimization involves regular analysis and optimization of resource utilization to minimize wastage. Cloud cost management tools and cost monitoring services provide insights into resource spending, allowing organizations to make informed decisions. Cost control strategies, such as rightsizing resources and leveraging reserved instances, can further help in optimizing cloud expenses. Ultimately, being mindful of cost implications ensures that cloud-native applications are not only technically sound but also financially sustainable in a multi-cloud setup.

> **Note**
>
> Dynamic management of resources of cloud-native applications can be an inflection point for cost management in multi-cloud. The flexibility of scaling cloud resources according to fluctuating needs eliminates the risk of both overprovisioning and underutilizing resources.

These were the few considerations that are required for designing cloud-native applications. Now, we will see the steps required to design a cloud-native application on multi-cloud.

Designing a cloud-native application on multi-cloud

Cloud-native applications are emerging as the gold standard and these applications are designed to leverage cloud computing to their advantage, offering unparalleled flexibility and performance. The journey of designing cloud-native applications on multi-cloud encompasses various facets, from defining requirements to optimizing for performance and cost. Let's delve into them:

1. **Define your requirements**: Before embarking on the design process, it's crucial to define your application's requirements clearly. This includes both functional requirements (what the application should do) and non-functional requirements (how well it should perform). Understanding your performance and cost targets is vital. Are you building a high-availability system that requires low-latency responses, or is cost-efficiency your primary concern? Defining these requirements upfront helps guide your design decisions.

    *   **Example**: Suppose you're developing an e-commerce platform. Your functional requirements may include features such as user registration, product search, and payment processing. Non-functional requirements could involve handling 10,000 concurrent users, ensuring transactions complete within 2 seconds, and keeping operational costs below $10,000 per month.

2. **Choose the right cloud platforms**: Selecting the appropriate cloud platforms is a critical decision. Evaluate different cloud providers based on their features, pricing models, and support services. Ensure that the chosen platforms align with your application's requirements. For example, if you need advanced machine learning capabilities, a cloud provider with robust AI services might be essential. Conversely, if cost optimization is paramount, consider providers with flexible pricing structures.

    *   **Example**: Imagine you're building a data analytics application. **Amazon Web Services (AWS)** offers a range of analytics tools such as Amazon Redshift and Athena, while **Google Cloud Platform (GCP)** provides BigQuery. Depending on your application's compatibility and pricing structure, you might choose AWS for data warehousing and GCP for machine learning services.

3. **Design a cloud-agnostic architecture**: To ensure multi-cloud compatibility, design your application with a cloud-agnostic mindset. Use technologies and frameworks that are not tied to a specific cloud provider. Containers and container orchestration tools such as Kubernetes are popular choices for achieving this portability. Moreover, tools such as Terraform, explored in *Chapter 4, Crafting and Deploying in the Multi-Cloud as a Developer,* can automate cloud configuration across multiple providers, and your deployment will be ruled by a centralized file, increasing the portability of your cloud-native application across the multi-cloud. Later in this chapter, we will also visit a practical example of deploying a cloud-native application across different cloud providers. By avoiding vendor-specific services and APIs, you can seamlessly deploy your application across multiple clouds.

- **Example**: Instead of relying on proprietary databases, you can choose open source databases such as PostgreSQL or use cloud-neutral storage solutions such as Amazon S3 or Google Cloud Storage. By avoiding vendor-specific services, your application can easily migrate between clouds.

4. **Design for resilience**: Resilience is a core aspect of multi-cloud design. Develop your application with a distributed architecture that can gracefully handle failures on any cloud platform. Implement mechanisms for automatic failover to alternate cloud providers in case of downtime or issues. This approach guarantees uninterrupted service delivery, even in the face of unexpected disruptions.

   - **Example**: Consider an online collaboration tool. If the cloud provider hosting your chat service experiences an outage, your application should seamlessly switch to an alternate provider, ensuring uninterrupted communication for users.

5. **Design for performance**: Performance optimization is essential to meet user expectations across various cloud platforms. Design your application to be inherently scalable, capable of efficiently utilizing cloud resources. Implement auto-scaling capabilities that dynamically adjust resource allocation based on workload fluctuations. Ensure your application can accommodate different types of workloads, from steady-state operations to sudden traffic spikes.

   - **Example**: If you're developing a content delivery application, optimize your application for global distribution. Use a **content delivery network** (**CDN**) to cache and serve content from edge locations, ensuring low latency for users worldwide.

6. **Design for cost**: Cost management is crucial in a multi-cloud environment. Evaluate the cost implications of deploying and operating your application on multiple cloud platforms. Choose a pricing model that aligns with your budget and usage patterns. Implement cost-control strategies such as resource rightsizing and utilization monitoring. Regularly analyze cost data to optimize spending and ensure cost-effectiveness in a multi-cloud setup.

   - **Example**: Let's say you run a media streaming service. Depending on usage patterns, you might choose a mix of on-demand and reserved instances on AWS, Azure, and GCP to balance cost and performance.

> **Note**
>
> Remember that in *Chapter 3*, *Designing for Diversity with Multi-Cloud Application Strategies*, we provided a compilation of design patterns for cloud-native applications. Depending on the priorities of your business logic, you can opt for one pattern or another.

This section taught us the key considerations and steps of designing a native cloud app on multi-cloud platforms. Now, we will focus on how to build a cloud-native application.

Building your cloud-native application

Building your cloud-native application involves crafting an application architecture and structure that leverages cloud technologies and principles to maximize scalability, flexibility, and resilience. This process encompasses decisions about programming languages, frameworks, microservices design, and integrations with cloud-native tools and services. Building a cloud-native application is not only about writing code but also about embracing a cloud-first mindset, enabling your application to thrive in dynamic multi-cloud environments. Here are the few points to consider while building a cloud-native application:

- **Choosing the right programming languages and frameworks**

  Choosing the right programming languages and frameworks for building a cloud-native application is a critical decision that significantly impacts your project's success. Here's a detailed explanation of this aspect:

  - **Team's expertise**: Consider the skills and expertise of your development team. Choosing a language and framework that your team is familiar with can boost productivity and reduce the learning curve. It enables developers to work efficiently, write high-quality code, and troubleshoot issues effectively.

  - **Application requirements**: Understand the specific requirements of your cloud-native application. Different applications have different needs. Consider factors such as the following:

    - **Performance**: If your application requires high performance, you might choose languages that are known for speed and efficiency, such as Go or Rust

    - **Scalability**: For applications that need to scale horizontally, consider languages and frameworks that support microservices architecture, such as Java with Spring Boot or Node.js with Express.js

    - **Data processing**: If your application involves heavy data processing or analytics, languages such as Python are ideal due to their rich ecosystem of data processing libraries (e.g., pandas and NumPy)

    - **Real-time processing**: For real-time applications with low-latency requirements, consider languages such as Node.js, which is event-driven and suitable for handling many simultaneous connections

  - **Community support**: Evaluate the community support and ecosystem around the programming language and framework. A vibrant and active community can provide resources, libraries, and solutions to common problems. It's also an indicator of the framework's longevity and relevance.

- **Microservices architecture and containerization**: This approach involves breaking down your application into small, independently deployable services. Containerization, facilitated by technologies such as Docker, plays a crucial role in this context as it encapsulates these services, making them portable and efficient. For more details, please refer to *Chapter 2, Building the Backbone of Cloud-Native Applications*

- **Integrating cloud-native tools and services**: When building a cloud-native application, it's crucial to leverage the tools and services provided by cloud providers. These cloud-native services are specifically designed to simplify and optimize various core functionalities within your application. They cover a wide range of needs, from data storage and computation to security and scalability.

    In *Chapter 4, Crafting and Deploying in the Multi-Cloud as a Developer*, we introduced the concept of the service mesh and highlighted its importance in managing an increasing number of services, and their respective communications, a typical scenario in a cloud-native application deployed in the multi-cloud.

    For instance, if you're using a cloud provider such as AWS, you have access to services such as Amazon S3 for scalable object storage or AWS Lambda for serverless computing. By integrating these cloud-native services into your application, you can offload complex tasks and processes to the cloud platform, benefiting from its robust infrastructure and scalability. This, in turn, allows your development team to focus more on the application's business logic and less on managing infrastructure.

- **Ensuring cross-cloud compatibility**: As you are aware, multi-cloud deployments involve using more than one cloud provider to ensure redundancy, avoid vendor lock-in, and optimize costs. However, different cloud providers have their unique services, APIs, and infrastructure.

    To make your application compatible with multiple cloud providers, you should design it to be cloud-agnostic. This means building the application in a way that it can seamlessly run on different cloud platforms without requiring significant modifications.

    To achieve this, you can use cloud-agnostic databases, storage solutions, and APIs. For example, you might opt for databases such as PostgreSQL, which is compatible with various cloud providers. Similarly, you can design your application's storage layers to be independent of a specific cloud provider's storage service, making it easier to switch between providers or use multiple providers simultaneously.

By ensuring cross-cloud compatibility, you reduce the risk of vendor lock-in, allowing you to choose the best services and pricing models from different providers based on your application's needs and cost-efficiency. This flexibility is essential in multi-cloud environments where adaptability and optimization are key considerations.

Practical examples: building effective cloud-native applications

Now that we know what points to consider while building a cloud-native application, let's consider a few examples to understand them:

- **Internet of Things (IoT) sensor data analytics platform**: Imagine you're developing an IoT platform that collects data from thousands of sensors deployed in various locations. This platform needs to efficiently gather, process, and analyze sensor data in real time to provide insights and trigger actions. In this scenario, a combination of programming languages and frameworks can be utilized:

  - **Java for scalability**: Java is known for its robustness and scalability. It could be used for building the backend services of the IoT platform, especially when dealing with a large number of sensor data inputs. The use of Java's multithreading capabilities can help handle concurrent data streams effectively.

  - **Apache Kafka for data streaming**: Apache Kafka, often used with Java, can be employed as a data streaming platform. It can handle the ingestion of data from sensors and distribute it to various processing modules in real time. Kafka provides fault tolerance and high throughput, making it suitable for handling sensor data streams.

  - **Apache Spark for data processing**: Apache Spark, typically used with Scala or Python, can be employed for real-time data processing and analytics. It can process incoming sensor data streams, perform analytics, and generate insights in real time. Scala, being compatible with Java and designed for distributed data processing, is a suitable choice for developing Spark applications.

  - **React.js for dashboards**: On the frontend, React.js can be used to create a user-friendly dashboard that allows users to visualize and interact with the sensor data. React's component-based architecture and virtual DOM make it a popular choice for building dynamic and responsive web interfaces.

- **Ride-sharing and navigation service**: Imagine you are developing a ride-sharing and navigation service similar to Uber or Lyft, where users can request rides, drivers can accept those requests, and passengers are provided with real-time navigation. To efficiently build such a service with microservices architecture, you can consider the following choices of programming languages and frameworks:

  - **Java for microservices**: Java is a robust and widely adopted language for building microservices due to its strong typing, excellent performance, and rich ecosystem of libraries. Each microservice in your application can be developed using Java.

  - **Spring Boot for microservices**: Spring Boot is a popular framework for building microservices in Java. It simplifies the development of standalone, production-grade Spring-based applications.

You can create microservices for user registration, ride requests, driver management, and more using Spring Boot.

- **Node.js for real-time features**: For real-time communication between drivers, passengers, and the central server, Node.js can be an excellent choice. Node.js, with libraries such as Socket.io, can handle real-time notifications, such as ride requests, driver updates, and route calculations, efficiently.

- **React Native for cross-platform mobile apps**: To provide a seamless mobile experience to both passengers and drivers, React Native can be used. React Native allows you to build cross-platform mobile applications for iOS and Android using JavaScript and React. This ensures that users on different platforms can access your service.

- **Docker for containerization**: Containerization is essential for deploying microservices independently and ensuring consistency across various cloud platforms. Docker can be used to containerize each microservice, making it easy to manage and scale.

- **Kubernetes for orchestration**: Kubernetes can be employed to orchestrate and manage the deployment of microservices. It provides features for auto-scaling, load balancing, and monitoring microservices across multi-cloud environments.

In the preceding examples, the choice of programming languages and frameworks aligns with the specific requirements of the applications, showcasing the importance of considering factors such as data processing, scalability, and real-time capabilities when making these decisions in the context of cloud-native development for multi-cloud environments.

Deployment best practices

In this section, we will learn about deployment best practices for cloud-native applications in a multi-cloud environment. Deployment is a critical phase in the application life cycle, ensuring that your application is delivered reliably and efficiently to your target cloud platforms. Let's delve into some key aspects of it:

- **Continuous Integration/Continuous Deployment (CI/CD) pipelines**: CI/CD pipelines are the backbone of modern software development. They automate the steps from integrating new code into your application to deploying it into production environments. In multi-cloud scenarios, CI/CD ensures that your application is consistently and efficiently delivered across different cloud platforms. CI/CD promotes consistency in code integration, testing, and deployment, which is crucial when targeting multiple cloud providers. It helps eliminate variations in deployment processes across different platforms. Here are some best practices that can be implemented to achieve optimal results in CI/CD space:

  - **Automate testing**: Implement automated testing suites, including unit tests, integration tests, and end-to-end tests. Tools such as Selenium, JUnit, or Jest can be integrated into your pipeline.

- **Automate deployment**: Utilize deployment scripts and tools to automate the deployment process. Docker and Kubernetes can help manage containerized applications consistently across clouds.

- **Git repository**: Maintain a Git repository for your code base. Git is widely used and integrates seamlessly with CI/CD tools. Use branching and tagging strategies for version management.

- **Code reviews**: Enforce code reviews as part of your pipeline. This ensures code quality and reduces the likelihood of introducing issues.

- **Artifact repository**: Utilize artifact repositories such as JFrog Artifactory or Nexus Repository to store and manage build artifacts. This ensures that you're using the correct versions of dependencies.

- **Pipeline as code**: Treat your CI/CD pipeline as code using tools such as Jenkins Pipeline DSL or GitLab CI/CD YAML. This allows you to version and reproduce your pipeline configurations.

Let's consider an example to understand CI/CD usage. You're deploying a microservices-based e-commerce application to multiple clouds. Your CI/CD pipeline consists of stages for code integration, automated testing (unit tests, API tests), building container images, and deploying to cloud environments. If a new feature is added, the pipeline automatically builds, tests, and deploys it to each cloud platform, ensuring consistency and reliability.

- **Infrastructure as Code (IaC) for reproducible deployments**: Introduced in *Chapter 4, Crafting and Deploying in the Multi-Cloud as a Developer*, was a methodology for managing and provisioning infrastructure components using code and automation. In multi-cloud scenarios, IaC allows you to define, configure, and provision cloud resources consistently across different providers. The following are some best practices that can be implemented to achieve optimal results in the IaC space:

  - **Declarative IaC**: Use tools such as Terraform or AWS CloudFormation to declare your infrastructure's desired state. These tools work based on the principle of declarative IaC, where you specify what you want (e.g., a database server with specific configurations), and the tool handles provisioning and management.

  - **Version control**: Store IaC scripts alongside your application code in a version control repository, such as Git. This practice ensures that changes to your infrastructure are versioned and can be tracked alongside code changes.

  - **Modularization**: Organize your IaC scripts into reusable modules. These modules can represent common infrastructure components (e.g., databases, virtual networks) and can be shared across projects, enhancing efficiency.

  - **Parameterization**: Parameterize your IaC scripts to make them adaptable to different environments or cloud providers. This allows you to reuse scripts with slight variations for each cloud platform.

Let's consider a simple example to understand IaC usage. Suppose you're deploying a web application to both AWS and GCP. With IaC, you can define the required cloud resources, such as virtual machines, databases, and networking components, in code. Here's a simplified example using Terraform (Git repo: `https://github.com/PacktPublishing/Multi-Cloud-Handbook-for-Developers/tree/main/Chapter-9`):

```
# Define an AWS EC2 instance
resource "aws_instance" "web_server_aws" {
  ami           = «ami-0c55b159cbfafe1f0
  instance_type = «t2.micro»
  tags = {
    Name = "MyWebServer-AWS"
  }
}


# Define a GCP Compute Engine instance
resource "google_compute_instance" "web_server_gcp" {
  name         = "my-web-server-gcp"
  machine_type = "f1-micro"
  zone         = "us-central1-a"

  boot_disk {
    initialize_params {
      image = "debian-cloud/debian-9"
    }
  }

  network_interface {
    network = "default"
  }
}
```

In this example, the same infrastructure components (web servers) are defined using Terraform for AWS and GCP. When you apply this IaC script to each cloud provider, it provisions the corresponding resources, ensuring consistency in your multi-cloud deployments.

Security best practices for deployment

As we presented in *Chapter 5, Managing Security, Data, and Compliance on Multi-Cloud*, security is paramount when deploying cloud-native applications in multi-cloud environments. In this section, we'll explore key security measures such as encryption and IAM and security audits, to safeguard your applications:

- **Encryption**: This is fundamental for securing data both in transit and at rest. It ensures that even if unauthorized access occurs, the data remains unreadable. Let's consider some examples:

  - **Transport Layer Security (TLS)/Secure Sockets Layer (SSL)**: Implement TLS/SSL for data in transit. For instance, you can configure NGINX as a reverse proxy with Let's Encrypt to automatically manage SSL certificates, securing communication between users and your application.

  - **Encryption-at-rest**: Employ encryption mechanisms provided by cloud providers. In AWS, use Amazon S3 server-side encryption to protect data stored in S3 buckets. This ensures that data files, backups, and logs are encrypted.

- **Identity and Access Management (IAM)**: IAM helps control access to cloud resources and services. It ensures that only authorized entities can interact with your application. Let's consider some examples:

  - **AWS IAM roles**: In AWS, define IAM roles with specific permissions for services or applications. For instance, create a role that allows EC2 instances to access necessary S3 buckets. Attach this role to the instances.

  - **Azure Active Directory (Azure AD)**: Utilize Azure AD to manage user identities and access control in Azure. Configure **role-based access control (RBAC)** to define who can perform actions on specific Azure resources.

- **Regular security audits**: Continuous monitoring and security audits are essential for identifying vulnerabilities and ensuring compliance:

  - **Vulnerability scanning**: Employ tools such as Nessus or Qualys to scan your application and infrastructure for vulnerabilities. Schedule regular scans and address identified issues promptly.

  - **Penetration testing**: Conduct penetration tests to simulate attacks on your application. Identify weaknesses in your security measures and patch them. Services such as AWS Security Hub offer automated vulnerability and threat detection.

By implementing these security measures and examples, you can significantly enhance the security of your cloud-native applications across multiple cloud platforms. However, remember that security is an ongoing process, and staying updated on best practices and emerging threats is crucial.

Load testing and performance optimization

In the context of multi-cloud cloud-native application development, load testing and performance optimization play a vital role in ensuring your application delivers a seamless experience to users. Let's delve into what load testing is, its significance, and provide detailed examples of its implementation:

- **Load testing**: It is the process of evaluating how a system or application performs under specific conditions of load or stress. It involves simulating a large number of concurrent users or requests to assess the application's responsiveness, scalability, and stability. In multi-cloud environments, where applications are distributed across various cloud providers, load testing becomes even more critical due to potential variability in cloud performance. Now, let's understand the significance of load testing:

  - **Identify performance bottlenecks**: Load testing helps pinpoint performance bottlenecks, allowing you to optimize critical components before deploying to multiple cloud platforms.

  - **Ensure scalability**: Multi-cloud environments require the ability to scale resources dynamically. Load testing ensures your application can scale efficiently to meet traffic demands.

  - **Optimize resource allocation**: Optimizing resource allocation across different cloud providers ensures cost-effectiveness.

- **Performance optimization**: Performance optimization is a crucial aspect of developing multi-cloud cloud-native applications. It involves a set of practices and techniques aimed at enhancing the speed, responsiveness, and efficiency of your application. In the context of multi-cloud, where applications span multiple cloud providers, optimizing performance becomes even more critical to deliver a seamless user experience across diverse cloud environments. Now, let's understand its significance:

  - **User experience**: Performance directly impacts user satisfaction. Faster response times and smoother interactions lead to happier users.

  - **Cost efficiency**: Efficient applications consume fewer cloud resources, translating to cost savings, especially in multi-cloud scenarios where resource costs may vary across providers.

  - **Scalability**: Performance optimization ensures your application can scale effectively to handle increased traffic or workloads in multi-cloud environments.

Now that we have an understanding of load testing and performance optimization, let's consider an example to understand them.

Performing load testing and performance optimization

In this section, we will look at some examples to understand load testing and performance optimization:

- **Load testing with Apache JMeter**: Apache JMeter is a widely used open source tool for load testing. You can simulate heavy loads by configuring test plans with various scenarios. Run tests against your application deployed on different cloud providers to assess its performance under different conditions.

- **Database query optimization**: Analyze and optimize database queries to reduce response times. Use database indexing and caching to enhance query efficiency.

- **Content Delivery Networks (CDNs)**: Utilize CDNs to distribute static assets (e.g., images, stylesheets) to edge locations, reducing latency for users across different regions and cloud providers.

- **Caching mechanisms**: Implement caching layers for frequently accessed data. Tools such as Redis and Memcached can be used to store and retrieve data quickly, reducing the load on your application's backend.

Troubleshooting and optimization

As we delve into the critical aspects of troubleshooting and optimization for multi-cloud cloud-native applications. This section is essential for maintaining the reliability and efficiency of your applications across diverse cloud environments. For more information about troubleshooting strategies for cloud-native application, you can refer back to *Chapter 7, Troubleshooting Multi-Cloud Applications*, of this book.

Let's see some common deployment issues as these issues can occur frequently in multi-cloud scenarios due to variations in cloud providers and infrastructure. Identifying and addressing these issues promptly is crucial. Common deployment issues include the following:

- **Resource mismatch**: Resource mismatch occurs when cloud providers offer similar services with varying specifications. For example, AWS and Azure may both offer **virtual machines (VMs)**, but their available VM sizes, performance characteristics, and pricing structures can differ significantly. This can lead to compatibility problems when migrating or scaling applications across clouds.

  To address the challenges faced with resource mismatch, the following measures can be taken:

  - **Cloud-agnostic configurations**: Develop configurations that abstract cloud-specific details. Instead of defining VM sizes explicitly, use variables or parameters that can be mapped to specific sizes in different clouds.

  - **Automated translation**: Implement scripts or tools that can automatically translate resource definitions from one cloud provider to another. For example, if your application uses AWS's `t2.micro`, the script can map it to an equivalent Azure VM size.

- **Networking challenges**: Inconsistent network configurations or firewall rules can disrupt communication between application components when deploying across multiple clouds. Each cloud provider has its networking and security services, which may require different settings and rules.

To address the challenges faced with networking, the following measures can be taken:

- **Use cloud-agnostic networking**: Deploy networking components that are cloud-agnostic and can adapt to different cloud environments. For example, use Kubernetes for container orchestration, which abstracts network complexities.

- **Automate network setup**: Implement automation scripts or templates that configure networking resources based on your application's requirements. Tools such as Terraform or Ansible can be helpful.

- **Data consistency**: Maintaining data consistency across multi-cloud data storage solutions can be challenging. Data synchronization issues can arise when data is replicated or moved between different cloud storage systems.

To address the challenge faced with data consistency, the following measures can be performed:

- **Multi-cloud database solutions**: Consider using databases designed for multi-cloud use cases, such as Google Cloud Spanner or CockroachDB. These databases are built to ensure data consistency across clouds.

- **Data replication strategies**: Implement data replication strategies that synchronize data between cloud databases in near real time, ensuring consistency.

- **Scaling problems**: Scaling an application across clouds may encounter challenges such as load balancing or auto-scaling configuration discrepancies. Each cloud provider offers its load balancing and scaling services with unique configurations.

To address the challenges faced with scaling, the following measures can be performed:

- **Load balancer abstraction**: Use load balancer abstraction layers that can adapt to different cloud providers. Kubernetes built-in load balancing or services such as AWS **Elastic Load Balancer** (**ELB**) provide this abstraction.

- **Auto-scaling templates**: Create templates or scripts that define auto-scaling rules in a cloud-agnostic way. These templates can be translated to cloud-specific auto-scaling configurations during deployment.

Optimization and scaling

In cloud-native application development across multi-cloud environments, optimization and scaling are paramount. These practices ensure that your applications run efficiently and cost-effectively, and can handle varying workloads. Let's delve into details of how to achieve optimization, scaling, and tuning a multi-cloud environment:

Cost-optimization strategies

Cost optimization is a foundational principle in multi-cloud development. *Chapter 6, Maximizing Value and Minimizing Cost of Multi-Cloud,* provided a comprehensive view about optimizing costs when developing cloud-native applications, thanks to advanced techniques such as FinOps. We came to understand that cost optimization involves balancing the allocation of cloud resources with budget constraints to maximize value:

- **Implementing FinOps practices**: **FinOps** (short for **Financial Operations**) practices are a set of principles and techniques used to manage cloud costs effectively. They promote a culture of financial responsibility within organizations using cloud services.

  - **Example**: When implementing FinOps, you can create cost-aware teams responsible for managing their cloud resources. Each team can be assigned a specific set of cost allocation tags, such as "environment," "owner," or "project." For example, tagging a resource as "production" helps in tracking its cost within the multi-cloud environment, making cost allocation transparent and accountable.

- **Cloud cost management tools and techniques**: Cloud cost management involves leveraging various tools and methodologies to control, analyze, and optimize cloud expenses. These tools help organizations gain insights into their cloud spending and make informed decisions to reduce costs.

  - **Example**: AWS Cost Explorer is a powerful tool that provides detailed cost and usage reports. By setting up budgets and alerts, you can proactively monitor your cloud spending. For instance, if your budget for a specific project is exceeded, you will receive an alert, allowing you to take immediate action to prevent unexpected overruns.

- **Right-sizing resources for cost efficiency**: Right-sizing is the practice of aligning your cloud resources with the actual needs of your applications. It involves selecting the appropriate instance types, storage capacities, and other cloud services to meet your performance requirements while optimizing costs.

  - **Example**: Suppose your application experiences variable workloads with periods of high and low demand. In such cases, you can leverage AWS EC2 instances with burstable performance (e.g., T2 or T3 instances). These instances provide burstable CPU capacity, allowing you to pay only for the CPU power you use during peak periods while reducing costs during low-demand times.

- **Monitoring and optimizing cloud spend**: Continuous monitoring of cloud spend is a fundamental practice. It involves regularly reviewing cost reports, tracking changes in resource usage, and making necessary adjustments to optimize cloud spending.

  - **Example**: Let's say you observe a sudden spike in storage costs within your multi-cloud environment. To optimize spending, you can investigate the cause, which might be redundant data storage or outdated backups. By identifying and addressing these issues promptly, you can reduce costs by deleting unnecessary files, ensuring efficient resource usage.

Scalability and elasticity

Scalability and elasticity ensure that your applications can adapt to varying workloads while maintaining high availability and performance:

- **Auto-scaling policies for dynamic workloads**: Auto-scaling policies are dynamic resource management mechanisms that automatically adjust computing resources based on real-time workload changes. This allows applications to efficiently handle fluctuations in traffic.

  - **Example**: Consider an e-commerce website that experiences increased traffic during holiday sales. By configuring AWS Auto Scaling, you can set policies that monitor application metrics (e.g., CPU utilization, request latency). When traffic surges, additional server instances are automatically added to distribute the load effectively. During quieter periods, excess instances are removed, optimizing resource utilization and cost-efficiency.

- **Load balancing across multi-cloud environments**: Load balancing is essential for evenly distributing incoming network traffic across multiple cloud instances or regions. It ensures high availability, minimizes response times, and prevents overloading of individual resources.

  - **Example**: AWS (ELB) can distribute incoming traffic to resources in both AWS and Azure. By defining routing rules, you can efficiently allocate traffic across clouds, ensuring optimal resource utilization. This not only enhances performance but also adds a layer of fault tolerance to your multi-cloud setup.

- **Designing for elasticity and high availability**: Designing for elasticity involves implementing redundancy and failover mechanisms. High availability strategies ensure that your application remains accessible even in the face of failures.

  - **Example**: To achieve high availability in a multi-cloud scenario, deploy your application in multiple regions on both AWS and Azure. Implement data replication mechanisms to ensure data consistency between regions. If one region encounters issues, the other can seamlessly take over, providing uninterrupted service to users.

- **Handling traffic spikes and surges**: To handle unexpected traffic spikes and surges in demand, it's crucial to employ strategies such as burstable resources, caching, and **content delivery networks (CDNs)**.

  - **Example**: Consider a news website that utilizes a CDN to cache and serve static content such as images. When a breaking news event leads to a sudden surge in traffic, the CDN efficiently delivers cached content to users, reducing the load on origin servers. This ensures that the website remains responsive and accessible, even during traffic spikes.

Performance monitoring and tuning

Performance monitoring and tuning are paramount for maintaining optimal application performance in multi-cloud environments. These practices enable you to ensure that your applications run efficiently, deliver excellent user experiences, and meet service-level objectives.

- **Setting up comprehensive monitoring systems**: Establishing comprehensive monitoring systems involves the implementation of tools and processes to capture data on various aspects of your application, including resource utilization, response times, and overall application health.

  - **Example**: Use cloud-native monitoring services such as AWS CloudWatch and Azure Monitor to collect metrics and monitor the health of critical application components, such as databases, web servers, and microservices. Configure custom alarms to proactively detect and respond to performance anomalies, ensuring the reliability of your multi-cloud applications.

- **Real-time performance dashboards**: Real-time performance dashboards provide a visual representation of **key performance indicators (KPIs)** and resource utilization in your multi-cloud environment. They offer immediate insights into the health and performance of your applications.

  - **Example**: Create custom dashboards using visualization tools such as Grafana, which can integrate with various cloud providers and data sources. Alternatively, leverage cloud-native solutions such as AWS CloudWatch dashboards to build real-time dashboards that display critical metrics, enabling your teams to respond promptly to performance deviations and optimize resource allocation.

- **Identifying bottlenecks and latency issues**: Identifying bottlenecks and latency issues involves analyzing performance metrics, logs, and application behavior to pinpoint areas where performance is suboptimal. Latency issues can result from inefficient code, resource limitations, or other bottlenecks.

  - **Example**: Analyze application logs and performance metrics to identify slow database queries that contribute to latency. Optimize these queries by restructuring them or scaling the database tier horizontally or vertically. This optimization can significantly improve response times and overall application performance in a multi-cloud setup.

- **Tuning applications for optimal multi-cloud performance**: Continuous tuning of your applications is essential for achieving the best possible performance in a multi-cloud environment. This includes refining code, configurations, and resource allocation to balance performance and cost-effectiveness.

  - **Example**: If your multi-cloud application relies on serverless functions, regularly review and adjust settings such as memory allocation and execution time. Fine-tuning these parameters can optimize performance and resource utilization, ultimately enhancing the user experience while controlling costs.

Hands-on exercise: e-commerce in multi-cloud architecture

In today's digital era, e-commerce is rapidly transforming, propelled by consumers' increasing preference for online shopping experiences. This shift is further supported by advanced logistics infrastructure and seamless delivery options. However, e-commerce platforms encounter challenges reminiscent of those faced by physical retail stores, particularly in managing peak demand periods. Unlike traditional stores, which scale up through additional personnel and stock, e-commerce platforms rely on the strategic provisioning of computing resources, a domain where cloud-native applications excel.

Multi-cloud architectures enable e-commerce platforms to seamlessly scale and optimize resources to meet surging demand, ensuring highly available applications and ultimate customer satisfaction. Additionally, cloud-native applications prioritize security and create safe, secure environments for online transactions. To illustrate this, let's explore a practical example on GitHub (`https://github.com/GoogleCloudPlatform/microservices-demo`) for an e-commerce store. This comprehensive example delves into various aspects, from project planning and architecture to monitoring and **Site Reliability Engineering** (**SRE**), providing a valuable blueprint for building high-performing, resilient e-commerce platforms. Let's take a look in detail.

Project planning:

- **Project objective**: Modernize the online boutique e-commerce platform by improving performance and scalability to handle increased user traffic and product offerings. Enhance the user experience with faster browsing, checkout, and order processing. Reduce operational costs by adopting a cloud-native architecture.

- **Key requirements**:

  - The platform must be able to handle increased user traffic and product offerings without performance degradation

  - The platform must be highly available and resilient to ensure minimal downtime and an uninterrupted user experience

  - The platform must comply with all relevant data privacy and e-commerce regulations

- The platform should leverage cloud-native technologies to optimize resource utilization and reduce costs

- **Example**: Increase the page load speed by 20% (measured with tools such as WebPageTest), reduce the checkout time by 15% (tracked through checkout process analytics), and achieve 99.5% uptime during peak hours (monitored with the cloud provider's uptime statistics)

- **Project plan**:

  - **Phase 1: planning and design (1 month)**

    - Define detailed project objectives and KPIs. Tools such as Jira and Trello can be used for project management.

    - Identify key stakeholders and their roles.

    - Develop a detailed system architecture using microservices and cloud-native technologies.

    - Estimate project costs and resource requirements.

  - **Phase 2: development and implementation (3 months)**

    - Develop and test individual microservices

    - Implement CI/CD pipeline for automated builds and deployments

    - Integrate the platform with payment gateways and other third-party services

    - Conduct security audits and penetration testing

  - **Phase 3: testing and deployment (1 month)**

    - Perform thorough functional and non-functional testing of the platform

    - Deploy the platform to a production environment and monitor performance

    - Train users on the new platform and its features

  - **Phase 4: monitoring and optimization (ongoing)**

    - Continuously monitor platform performance and identify areas for improvement

    - Optimize cloud resources to reduce costs and improve efficiency

    - Implement new features and updates based on user feedback and market trends

Budgeting and FinOps:

- **Budget allocation**: The company allocates a budget of $5 million for this project, with cost monitoring throughout the project life cycle

- **Cost control strategies**:

  - Implement resource tagging for cost allocation and tracking

  - Use cloud cost management tools to monitor spending

  - Implement policies for resource rightsizing and decommissioning underutilized resources

  - Regularly review and optimize cloud infrastructure

Architecture:

- **Cloud providers**:

  - Evaluate multiple cloud providers based on:

    - Cost-optimization opportunities

    - Regional availability requirements

    - Unique service offerings (e.g., specialized AI services)

    - Disaster recovery and business continuity strategies

- Consider a multi-cloud approach with GCP as the primary provider and a secondary provider such as AWS or Azure

- **Cloud-native design**:

  - Employ cloud-agnostic technologies to facilitate portability:

    - Kubernetes for multi-cloud deployments (e.g., using Anthos or EKS Anywhere)

    - Istio for service meshes across multiple providers

    - Vendor-neutral observability tools (Prometheus, Grafana)

- Plan for data replication and synchronization between clouds if needed

- **Example**: The architecture of the boutique e-commerce platform contains 11 microservices written in various languages that communicate with each other via gRPC protocol

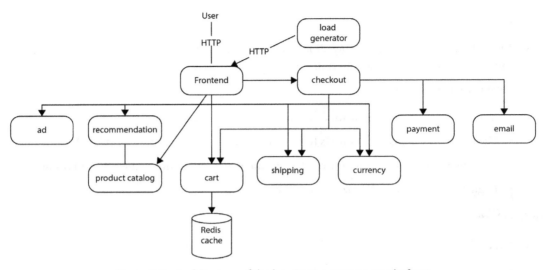

Figure 9.2 – Architecture of the boutique e-commerce platform

Compliance requirements:

- **Identify applicable regulations:**

  - Determine any e-commerce or data privacy regulations applicable to the boutique

- **Implement compliance measures:**

  - Adapt compliance measures to the boutique's context, potentially involving data encryption and access controls
  - Keeps audit logs for monitoring and compliance reporting

DevSecOps and CI/CD:

- **DevSecOps practices:**

  - Integrate security into every stage of the development pipeline
  - Conduct regular vulnerability scanning and threat modeling
  - Implement automated security testing (e.g., static and dynamic code analysis)
  - Enforce RBAC and least privilege principles

- **CI/CD pipeline:**

  - Explore cloud-agnostic CI/CD tools (e.g., Jenkins and GitLab CI) for multi-cloud deployments
  - Configure pipelines to deploy to different cloud environments seamlessly

- Automate testing, code review, and deployment

- Enforce deployment policies and rollback procedures

- Monitor and log every deployment

- **Example**: In the code snippet is a continuous deployment workflow (GitHub actions), and it runs on every commit to the main branch:

```
name: "Push and Deploy"
on:
  push:
    # run on pushes to main
    branches:
      - main
jobs:
  push-deploy:
    runs-on: [self-hosted, is-enabled]
    steps:
    - uses: actions/checkout@v4
    - name: Push latest images to GCR
      timeout-minutes: 20
      run: |
        skaffold config set --global local-cluster false
        # tag with git hash
        skaffold build --default-repo=gcr.io/$PROJECT_ID \
                    --tag=$GITHUB_SHA
      env:
        PROJECT_ID: ${{ secrets.PROJECT_ID }}
```

Monitoring and observability:

- **Monitoring stack**:

- Prioritize tools that integrate with multiple clouds (e.g., Datadog and New Relic)

- Correlate metrics and logs across cloud environments for unified visibility

- **Observability practices**:

- Set up centralized logging and monitoring dashboards

- Implement distributed tracing with OpenTelemetry

- Utilize synthetic monitoring tools for user experience monitoring

- Implement automated alerting for incidents and performance anomalies

Site Reliability Engineering (SRE):

- **Error budgets and SLIs/SLOs:**

  - Define **service-level indicators** (SLIs) and **service-level objectives** (SLOs) for critical services

  - Establish an error budget for permissible service disruptions

- **Incident management:**

  - Implement an incident management process with defined roles and responsibilities

  - Utilize incident tracking tools and post-mortems for continuous improvement

  - Set up automated responses to common incidents

- **Capacity planning:**

  - Monitor resource utilization across clouds and adjust capacity as needed

  - Consider cloud bursting for handling peak loads

- **Example:** The `locustfile.py` file (`https://github.com/GoogleCloudPlatform/microservices-demo/blob/main/src/loadgenerator/locustfile.py`) demonstrates synthetic load generation for testing and monitoring user experience:

```
class UserBehavior(TaskSet):

    def on_start(self):
        index(self)

    tasks = {index: 1,
        setCurrency: 2,
        browseProduct: 10,
        addToCart: 2,
        viewCart: 3,
        checkout: 1}

class WebsiteUser(HttpUser):
    tasks = [UserBehavior]
    wait_time = between(1, 10)
```

This hands-on example demonstrates how an e-commerce platform can achieve scalability, resilience, and cost-efficiency through a cloud-native, multi-cloud architecture, while prioritizing security, observability, and continuous delivery practices.

Summary

In this chapter, we've examined the critical facets of project planning, covering everything from setting precise project objectives and requirements to identifying key stakeholders, establishing effective communication channels, devising a robust multi-cloud strategy, defining budgetary parameters.

Next, we ventured into the realm of designing cloud-native applications for multi-cloud. Here, we explored pivotal elements such as requirement definition, the selection of the most fitting cloud provider, crafting a cloud-agnostic architecture, resilience-centric design, performance optimization, and ensuring cost-efficiency in the development of cloud-native applications tailored for multi-cloud environments.

Following this, we delved into the intricacies of deployment best practices. We unraveled the concepts underpinning **Continuous Integration/Continuous Deployment** (**CI/CD**) pipelines and demystified **Infrastructure as Code** (**IaC**) while addressing associated security considerations. Furthermore, we delved into practical examples of load testing and performance optimization, providing insights into troubleshooting strategies to maintain a resilient application.

The next and final chapter will provide a glimpse into the future of multi-cloud and cloud-native development. We will explore emerging trends and innovative technologies, community involvement in platform engineering, and the role of the **Cloud Native Computing Foundation** (**CNCF**) in shaping the landscape of multi-cloud applications.

10

Future-Proofing Your Cloud Computing Skills

Welcome to the final chapter in our exploration of multi-cloud and cloud-native technologies. Here, we synthesize our journey's insights and look ahead to the transformative potential of these evolving technologies. Before we move further into the chapter, let us have a quick recap of what we have gone through so far.

Our exploration began with cloud-native technologies, revealing a paradigm shift in application development and management, emphasizing elasticity, distribution, and agility. We delved into containerization, microservices, and dynamic orchestration, foundational elements that enhance scalability, resilience, and manageability.

In parallel, we examined multi-cloud environments, focusing on strategic combinations of cloud services for robust, versatile infrastructures. This approach enhances **disaster recovery** (**DR**) and performance optimization and reduces vendor lock-in, also from a broader picture of where multi-cloud meets cloud-native and how they both collectively add value.

As we pivot toward the future, let's look into emerging trends and cutting-edge technologies that are reshaping cloud computing. We'll explore how these advancements enhance technical capabilities and influence the broader ecosystem of the digital and IT landscape in the realm of cloud-native and multi-cloud paradigms.

As we look ahead to the future of cloud computing, these groundbreaking topics will define the next wave. Let's explore the following areas one by one:

- Next-generation cloud-native infrastructure and platforms

- Introduction to **artificial intelligence** (**AI**) and **machine learning** (**ML**) in cloud-native evolution

- The emergence of serverless architecture and **event-driven architecture** (**EDA**)

- Advanced security paradigms for cloud-native applications

- **Quantum computing (QC)** and its impact on cloud technologies
- Sustainable cloud computing – a new era
- The convergence of telco and edge computing with cloud-native
- Blockchain integration with cloud-native development
- The rise of **low-code (LC)/no-code (NC)** platforms
- Cloud-native governance and compliance in the future
- Conclusion – preparing for a cloud-native future

Before we proceed, let's embrace this journey with an open mind, a spirit of innovation, and a readiness to adapt. The future of cloud computing is not just an unfolding reality but a landscape we are actively shaping with our ideas, creativity, and visionary aspirations. Let's step forward with anticipation and enthusiasm, ready to explore and harness the transformative potential that lies ahead in the world of multi-cloud and cloud-native technologies.

Next-generation cloud-native infrastructure and platforms

Platform engineering is transforming in exciting ways, reshaping how we think about cloud-native development. It's no longer just about using cloud services. Now, it's about building ecosystems that boost efficiency and spark innovation. This shift marks a move away from traditional IT methods toward a more integrated, holistic approach. The focus is on making everything automated and user-friendly, with a strong emphasis on DevOps practices.

Throughout this book, we have covered topics related to platform engineers and how they partner with developers. Looking ahead, it is important to understand that the aim of platform engineering is to create systems that are not only strong and scalable but also quick to adapt to the ever-changing needs of businesses. We're steering toward platforms that can foresee future trends and adjust seamlessly. These platforms are designed to be more than technical structures; they are enablers of business growth and innovation. In the coming years, platform engineering will likely play a crucial role in the digital transformation of companies, making it an exciting field to watch.

Evolution of platform engineering

The traditional paradigm for deploying applications requires slow and hierarchical routines to approve and deploy new features. This scenario was often deemed slow and not responsive enough to surging market needs. After that, DevOps proposed more agile development paradigms proven to be more resilient and easily scalable to cope with current market demands.

With a strong collaboration with DevOps practices, platform engineering has intensified its focus on studying architectural and platform needs for modern application developments. The main focus of platform engineering is to design tailored workflows and toolchains that will define a native cloud ecosystem for the application in question. Platform engineering creates abstract environments ready for developers to start developing top-notch applications right away without worrying about the underlying platform and architecture.

Let us now delve into a practical illustration of these principles: a detailed exploration of Netflix's strategic transformation, which epitomizes the remarkable potential of platform engineering when executed with vision and precision.

Case study – Netflix's strategic shift in platform engineering

Netflix's transformation to a cloud-native powerhouse is a prime example of platform engineering's evolution. Initially constrained by scalability and reliability limitations, its shift to a cloud-native model, predominantly utilizing **Amazon Web Services** (**AWS**), marked a pivotal change in service delivery mechanisms. This move was characterized by the following:

- **Microservices architecture**: Transitioning from a monolithic framework to microservices, Netflix achieved modular scalability and expedited development, enabling distinct services to evolve independently

- **Embracing AWS**: The choice of AWS provided the elastic infrastructure necessary to support Netflix's global expansion and handle varying loads with ease

- **Commitment to automation and continuous integration/continuous deployment (CI/CD)**: Automating its deployment processes, Netflix's CI/CD pipeline facilitated frequent and reliable updates, vital for managing multiple deployments daily

- **Containerization with Kubernetes**: Adopting Kubernetes for container orchestration, Netflix streamlined service deployment and scaling, enhancing operational efficiency

- **Focus on resilience and reliability**: Through chaos engineering, Netflix ensured its platform could withstand disruptions, maintaining **high availability** (**HA**) and a consistent user experience

Through these strategic moves, Netflix not only overcame its initial challenges but also set a new standard in cloud-native platform engineering, demonstrating how such an approach can lead to unprecedented scalability and operational agility.

The rise of immutable infrastructure and its implications

Immutable infrastructure is redefining the landscape of cloud-native environments by introducing an approach where once deployed, components remain unchanged; alterations require the deployment of new instances. This shift toward immutability offers several significant benefits:

- **Consistency and reliability**: This approach ensures that the infrastructure remains consistent across different environments, from development to production. It effectively addresses the common challenge of discrepancies between environments, often summed up as the "it works on my machine" problem. Immutable infrastructure achieves uniformity that is particularly beneficial in multi-cloud and complex distributed setups.

- **Enhanced security**: Immutable infrastructure naturally prevents configuration drift – the gradual deviation of system configurations over time. Locking down the state of components once deployed reduces the risk of unauthorized changes, thus enhancing the overall security posture.

- **Streamlined management and operations**: Managing updates and changes becomes more straightforward with immutable infrastructure. Since new changes require deploying new versions rather than modifying existing ones, this approach simplifies version control and reduces the complexities associated with traditional configuration management.

Having outlined the overarching advantages of immutable infrastructure, we will now examine Spotify's strategic implementation of this paradigm, illustrating the tangible impacts such an approach has on operational resilience and service delivery.

Spotify's immutable infrastructure strategy

Spotify's approach to immutable infrastructure, utilizing Docker and **Google Cloud Platform** (**GCP**), showcases the benefits of this model. In an immutable setup, instead of modifying existing servers for updates or changes, new containerized instances are deployed. This strategy minimizes deployment errors and system downtime. Each update results in a new container deployment, ensuring consistency and reliability in the environment. Old containers can be easily rolled back if needed, enhancing operational stability. This method also contributes to a better user experience, as it reduces the likelihood of service disruptions due to deployment issues. Spotify's case exemplifies how immutable infrastructure can lead to improved efficiency and reliability in digital services.

Advanced orchestration in multi-cloud landscapes

In the realm of multi-cloud strategies, advanced orchestration is not merely a requirement but a necessity. It's about orchestrating an entire ecosystem of services, applications, and infrastructure across diverse cloud environments. This orchestration transcends resource management; it involves automating deployment, scaling, and application management in a manner that is both efficient and resilient. It demands a profound understanding of each cloud environment's intricacies and the ability to weave these into a unified, functional system. Such orchestration is pivotal in harnessing the full potential of multi-cloud strategies, enabling businesses to leverage the strengths of each cloud service while maintaining overarching control and visibility.

Building on the foundation of advanced orchestration, let's turn our focus to Adobe, a company that exemplifies orchestration excellence in its deployment across multi-cloud platforms, leveraging a blend of AWS and Azure to drive innovation and operational efficiency.

Adobe's orchestration mastery

Adobe's orchestration mastery in its Creative Cloud services is a prime example of advanced orchestration in a multi-cloud environment. By leveraging both AWS and Microsoft Azure, Adobe employs sophisticated orchestration tools to manage its wide array of services seamlessly across these platforms. This approach is instrumental in ensuring HA, enabling smooth and uninterrupted updates, and maintaining consistent performance regardless of the cloud provider. The advanced orchestration tools used by Adobe facilitate efficient resource management, automate deployment processes, and optimize load balancing, demonstrating the effectiveness of sophisticated orchestration in managing complex, multi-cloud infrastructures.

Looking forward, the trajectory of cloud-native platforms is unmistakably toward more integrated, automated, and secure environments. The evolution of platform engineering, the shift toward immutable infrastructure, and the imperative of advanced orchestration in multi-cloud scenarios are not mere technological trends. They represent a fundamental shift in our approach to IT strategy and business innovation, heralding a new era of efficiency, agility, and security in the cloud-native landscape.

Introduction to AI and ML in cloud-native evolution

AI and ML significantly enhances the cloud-native ecosystem. AI brings smart automation, advanced data analytics, and new capabilities for handling complex tasks, fostering smarter decision-making and operational efficiency. ML algorithms analyze vast cloud datasets to predict trends, automate responses, and personalize user experiences. Together, they enable more resilient, self-optimizing cloud services that can preemptively address issues, optimize resources, and evolve with user demands, driving the evolution of cloud-native solutions toward more intelligent, adaptive, and autonomous systems. Recent **generative AI (GenAI)**, in particular, has the potential to revolutionize aspects such as database management, UI design, and complex architectural decisions, truly embodying the innovative spirit of cloud-native evolution. With that said, next, we will explore an interesting topic on the futuristic possibilities of application modernization. Application modernization is all about how you transform your legacy application into a modern cloud-native application.

Modernizing applications with GenAI

The integration of GenAI into cloud-native development will revolutionize application modernization. Currently, it is achieved by having a mix of tools, frameworks, and best practices (such as manually following the cloud-native patterns and principles – 12-15 factors covered in *Chapter 2, Building the Backbone of Cloud-Native Applications*, of this book). This process involved manual code refactoring, transitioning from monolithic structures to microservices, and manual deployment and scaling, all of which were time-intensive and complex.

As we move forward, GenAI transforms this landscape by automating code refactoring, streamlining the transition to microservices, enabling AI-driven deployment and scaling, and enhancing monitoring and maintenance. This evolution significantly simplifies the modernization process, reducing technical overhead and introducing more efficient methods for updating applications. Let's delve into how this could be handled in green- and brownfield environments when it comes to application modernization.

Streamlining application modernization – brownfield

In transforming existing applications (so-called brownfield) with the support of AI to meet modern demands, key steps include harnessing automated code refactoring and embracing the shift to microservices, all facilitated by the power of GenAI. Let's explore these transformative processes next:

- **Automated code refactoring**: One of the most significant ways GenAI simplifies application modernization is through automated code refactoring. AI tools can analyze legacy code bases and suggest or even implement improvements and modernization strategies. This includes optimizing code for cloud-native environments, ensuring compatibility with modern APIs, and enhancing scalability and performance.

- **Migration to microservices**: GenAI aids in the decomposition of monolithic applications into microservices. By analyzing the existing application structure, AI can suggest the most efficient way to break down the application into smaller, independently deployable services, a key aspect of cloud-native architectures.

Example – Modernizing a legacy e-commerce application

To illustrate the transformative power of GenAI in modernizing legacy systems, let's consider the case of a legacy e-commerce platform. The following example will showcase the step-by-step process of automated code refactoring, highlighting how each phase contributes to enhancing the application's performance and preparing it for a seamless transition to a cloud-native architecture:

- **Automated code refactoring with GenAI**:

  - **Initial analysis**: Leveraging GenAI in application modernization begins by analyzing the entire code base of the e-commerce application. It identifies areas where the code can be optimized for a cloud-native environment. For instance, it might find that certain parts of the code are causing performance bottlenecks.

  - **Suggesting refactoring**: For example, it might recommend altering the way database queries are handled to improve efficiency or adopting asynchronous processing for handling user requests.

  - **Implementing changes**: Once the refactorings are approved by the development team, the AI tool can assist or even automate the process of rewriting parts of the code. This process is done iteratively and in alignment with the best practices of cloud-native development.

- **Migration to microservices**:

    - **Service identification**: GenAI models can help analyze the monolithic architecture to identify logical service boundaries. For instance, it might suggest separating user account management, product catalog management, and order processing into distinct services.

    - **Microservices design**: For each identified service, the AI tool proposes a design that includes how the service will communicate with others, its database schema, and its deployment requirements. It ensures that each service is loosely coupled and independently deployable.

    - **Assisting in deployment**: Once we have all the details, with the help of a GenAI model, it becomes easier to generate containerization scripts and Kubernetes manifests for each microservice. It also suggests an incremental deployment strategy, where services are deployed one at a time to minimize disruption.

- **Outcome**:

    The legacy e-commerce application is successfully transformed to a cloud-native application and into a set of microservices. Each service can be scaled independently, making the application more resilient and easier to manage. The application now efficiently utilizes cloud resources, and new features can be deployed faster and more safely.

This example demonstrates how GenAI can significantly simplify the process of modernizing legacy applications. By automating code refactoring and aiding in the migration to a microservices architecture, GenAI enables businesses to leverage the full potential of cloud-native technologies, leading to applications that are more scalable, maintainable, and aligned with modern development practices.

Revolutionizing the development life cycle – greenfield

In the greenfield approach, GenAI is a game-changer at every step of the development life cycle, from conception to coding. Here's how it's making a difference:

- **Conceptualization and design**: GenAI is already changing the initial stages of application development. For instance, when designing a new application, developers can now use AI to generate initial design concepts or UI mockups based on specified criteria. This capability accelerates the design process and offers a range of creative options that might not have been considered otherwise.

- **Code generation and optimization**: In the coding phase, AI tools can write boilerplate code, suggest optimizations, and even refactor existing code to improve efficiency and performance. For example, a developer working on a cloud-based analytics tool can use AI assistants such as Microsoft Copilot, Google Duet AI, and Amazon Q to generate initial code for data processing algorithms, significantly speeding up the development process.

- **Automated deployment**: GenAI can also assist in the deployment phase. It can analyze the application requirements and automatically generate deployment scripts for various cloud environments, ensuring optimal configuration and resource allocation. For instance, an AI tool could generate Kubernetes manifests for deploying a microservices-based application, ensuring that each service is properly configured and ready for deployment. We will delve deep into how cloud-native platforms have become a foundational pillar for GenAI.

- **Ongoing maintenance and updates**: In the maintenance phase, AI can continuously monitor the application, suggest performance improvements, and even predict potential issues before they occur. This proactive approach to maintenance helps keep the application running smoothly and efficiently. We will be covering this in the upcoming **AI for IT Operations** (**AIOps**) topic in detail.

- **Co-piloting application development**: GenAI will become the co-pilot in application development, especially when modernizing existing applications. It can suggest code improvements, troubleshoot issues, and propose alternative methodologies, thereby enhancing the development process. This collaboration can significantly reduce development time and improve the quality of the final product.

- **Balancing AI contributions with developer expertise**: While GenAI can accelerate development, it's essential to balance its contributions with human expertise. Developers need to critically evaluate AI-generated suggestions and ensure they align with the application's goals and technical requirements. This balance ensures that the final application is not only innovative but also functional, reliable, and aligned with business objectives.

Example – Developing a new social media platform

Imagine the inception of a new social media platform designed to provide innovative interaction methods with a focus on privacy and user-generated content. This greenfield project leverages GenAI to streamline the development process, ensuring a modern, scalable, and feature-rich application built from the ground up:

- **Conception and initial design aided by GenAI:**

  - **Idea generation**: GenAI begins by assisting in brainstorming sessions and providing creative concepts for the social media platform based on current market trends and user preference.

  - **Design mockups**: Utilizing AI-driven design tools, the team quickly creates a series of UI mockups, which are iteratively refined to ensure an intuitive user experience.

  - **Feature planning**: The AI system suggests a list of potential features and functionalities that could give the platform a competitive edge, such as advanced content recommendation engines or privacy-preserving algorithms

- **Automated code generation and optimization:**

  - **Code prototyping**: The AI tool rapidly prototypes the foundational code for the platform, adhering to cloud-native principles and ensuring readiness for a microservices architecture

- **Code review and optimization**: As the prototype takes shape, the AI continuously analyzes and refactors the code to enhance performance, maintainability, and scalability

- **Optimization for deployment**: GenAI aligns the code base with deployment best practices, preparing for containerization and orchestration within a Kubernetes environment

- **Building and deployment**:

  - **Microservices architecture**: The AI system suggests an optimal microservices breakdown, such as separating user profile management, content delivery, and messaging functionalities

  - **Deployment strategy**: For each microservice, GenAI generates deployment manifests and suggests a phased rollout plan to ensure a smooth launch with minimal risk

- **Outcome**:

  The result is a modern social media application, architected with a microservices design that enables scalability and rapid feature development. The platform is cloud-native from the onset, with each component designed to operate independently, ensuring HA and a robust user experience. The social media platform launches successfully, with the ability to quickly adapt to user feedback and market changes, underpinned by the flexible and scalable infrastructure that GenAI helped create.

This greenfield example showcases the potential of GenAI to not only facilitate the creation of innovative applications but also to establish a solid foundation for future growth and adaptability in the cloud-native era.

The cloud-native platform becomes a foundational pillar for GenAI

In the preceding topics, we covered how AI will accelerate developers; now, let's shift our focus to platform engineers. To start with, it's becoming increasingly clear that cloud-native technologies, particularly Kubernetes, are becoming the foundational infrastructure for hosting and managing GenAI models. This synergy is poised to redefine how AI models are developed, deployed, and scaled, offering unprecedented efficiency and flexibility. In this section, we will explore how Kubernetes optimally supports the demands of GenAI and examine new tools that enhance GenAI within the cloud. Then, we will shift gears to investigate the role of AI in managing complex cloud architectures and its impact on cloud-native innovation.

Kubernetes – the preferred environment for GenAI

Today, Kubernetes has emerged as the go-to environment for GenAI models. Its ability to handle complex, scalable, and distributed systems makes it ideal for the demands of GenAI. Major players in the AI field, such as Hugging Face, OpenAI, and Google, are already leveraging Kubernetes-powered cloud-native infrastructures to deliver robust and scalable AI platforms.

Advantages of Kubernetes

The use of Kubernetes offers numerous benefits for GenAI applications, including improved resource management, scalability, and the ability to handle the high computational demands of AI model training and inference. This environment also provides the resilience and reliability needed for critical AI applications. Let's look into some of the advantages:

- **Enhanced resource management**: Kubernetes efficiently allocates resources to meet the intensive computational demands of AI model training and inference

- **Scalability**: It allows GenAI applications to scale resources up or down as needed, providing flexibility to handle variable workloads

- **High computational handling**: Kubernetes is adept at managing the heavy computational loads associated with GenAI applications, ensuring smooth operations

- **Resilience and reliability**: The platform is designed for HA, offering robust failover capabilities essential for mission-critical AI applications

- **Automated rollouts and rollbacks**: Kubernetes can automate the deployment process, implementing updates and changes without downtime

Emerging tools and platforms in the cloud-native ecosystem

Here, we will learn about some tools and platforms to enhance GenAI within the cloud:

- **Innovative tools for GenAI**: Today, tools such as Hugging Face's *Text Generation Inference*, AnyScale's *Ray Serve*, and *vLLM* are at the forefront of running model inference within containerized environments. These tools are designed to optimize the performance of AI models while ensuring they can be easily deployed and managed within a cloud-native infrastructure.

- **Maturation of frameworks and platforms**: In the coming years, we can anticipate a significant maturation in the frameworks, tools, and platforms designed for Kubernetes, specifically tailored for managing the life cycle of foundation models in GenAI. This development will enable users to pre-train, fine-tune, deploy, and scale generative models with unprecedented efficiency.

Navigating advanced architectures with AI assistance

Let's understand how GenAI can help in advanced architecture:

- **Exploring serverless computing**: GenAI is also making strides in guiding both developers and platform engineers through more advanced cloud-native concepts such as serverless computing. It provides insights and code suggestions for building serverless applications, enabling developers to explore this efficient and scalable architecture. This guidance is particularly valuable for anyone who is transitioning from traditional server-based architectures to serverless models. We will be touching on the details of serverless in the next topic of this chapter, so stay tuned.

- **Adapting to technical capabilities**: While AI can suggest cutting-edge solutions, it's important to align these suggestions with the technical capabilities and understanding of the development team. For instance, a team new to cloud-native concepts might find it more practical to start with managed databases and application servers before progressing to serverless architectures.

Futuristic outlook of GenAI in cloud-native development

Looking ahead, the role of GenAI in cloud-native development is poised to become even more significant. We can anticipate the following:

- **Reference architectures and best practices**: Key players in the cloud-native ecosystem will likely introduce reference architectures, best practices, and optimizations specifically for running GenAI on cloud-native infrastructure. This guidance will be crucial for organizations looking to harness the power of GenAI within their cloud-native environments.

- **Extension of Large Language Model Operations (LLMOps)**: LLMOps, which focuses on the operational aspects of **large language models** (**LLMs**), will evolve to support integrated cloud-native workflows. This evolution will encompass the entire spectrum of model life-cycle management, from development to deployment, ensuring that GenAI models are not only powerful but also seamlessly integrated into the cloud-native ecosystem.

- **Advanced predictive capabilities**: Future GenAI tools will offer advanced predictive capabilities, not only in terms of code generation but also in predicting market trends and user preferences. This will enable developers to create applications that are not only technically sound but also closely aligned with user needs and market demands.

- **Seamless integration across development phases**: GenAI will become more seamlessly integrated into all phases of the development life cycle, from initial design to deployment and maintenance. This integration will ensure a more cohesive and efficient development process.

- **Enhanced collaboration between AI and developers**: The future will see a more enhanced collaboration between GenAI and human developers. AI will not only assist in technical aspects but also in creative processes, bringing a new level of innovation to application development.

The integration of GenAI into cloud-native development is setting the stage for a new era in application development. With its ability to enhance every phase of the development life cycle, GenAI is not just a tool but a transformative force, driving efficiency, innovation, and creativity in the cloud-native ecosystem. As we look to the future, it's clear that GenAI will play a pivotal role in shaping the next generation of cloud-native applications, making them more adaptive, efficient, and aligned with evolving business and user needs.

As GenAI redefines the landscape of cloud-native application development, it seamlessly paves the way for the integration of ML, another transformative technology. This integration marks a natural progression from AI-driven innovation to ML-powered management and optimization. Let's get into the details next.

ML – a pivotal tool in advanced cloud-native application management

ML will become an indispensable tool in the management of next-generation cloud-native applications. Its role extends far beyond mere responsiveness to immediate changes; it can delve into the realms of predictive analytics and proactive system adaptation. In the diverse and complex world of multi-cloud environments, the predictive prowess of ML is proving to be invaluable.

Predictive analytics and proactive adaptation

Let's understand how ML can be used for predictive and proactive approaches:

- **Anticipating future demands**: In multi-cloud environments, where resource demands can fluctuate unpredictably, ML's ability to forecast future needs is crucial. By analyzing historical data and current trends, ML algorithms can predict upcoming demands, allowing systems to adjust resources proactively. This foresight ensures that applications maintain optimal performance, even under varying load conditions.

- **Adapting to user behavior**: ML algorithms excel at detecting and adapting to changes in user behavior. By continuously analyzing user interaction patterns, these algorithms can optimize application performance and resource allocation in real time, ensuring a seamless user experience.

Efficiency and resource optimization

Now, let's see how ML can be used for efficiency and resource optimization:

- **Forecasting resource requirements**: One of the key strengths of ML in cloud-native management is its ability to forecast resource requirements accurately. This capability allows for more efficient use of cloud resources, reducing waste and cost. For instance, an ML algorithm can predict peak usage times for an application and scale resources accordingly, ensuring that the application runs efficiently without over-provisioning.

- **Maintaining operational efficiency**: ML algorithms play a critical role in maintaining the efficiency of cloud-native applications. They can identify inefficiencies in the system, such as underutilized resources or bottlenecks, and suggest adjustments to improve overall performance.

ML in multi-cloud infrastructure management

ML plays a pivotal role in taming the complexities and enhancing the agility of multi-cloud infrastructure, enabling smarter management and dynamic allocation of resources. Let's understand this further:

- **Complexity management**: The management of multi-cloud infrastructures is inherently complex, with each cloud environment having its own set of characteristics and challenges. ML algorithms can analyze data from these varied environments to provide a unified view of the infrastructure, simplifying management and decision-making.

- **Dynamic resource allocation**: In multi-cloud environments, dynamic resource allocation becomes essential. ML algorithms can automate this process, continuously analyzing workload and performance data to allocate resources where they are most needed.

The following table sheds light on some of the key distinctions between AI and ML:

Aspect	AI	ML
Data requirements	Diverse data volumes	Large quantities of data points
Expected outputs	Ranges from insights and advice to decisions	Quantitative outputs such as scores or labels
Operational mechanism	Designed to emulate human reasoning with precision	Relies on statistical models that learn and infer from patterns in data
Management needs	Requires human supervision for optimal functionality	Directed by data experts to refine and interpret model findings

Table 10.1 – AI versus ML

As we witness the transformative impact of GenAI in enhancing the development life cycle of cloud-native applications, and ML streamlining multi-cloud infrastructure management, we are led to the next evolutionary juncture in cloud computing. This progression naturally culminates in the integration of predictive analytics with AIOps, a synergy that signifies a major advancement in the management and optimization of cloud resources. This integration not only complements the capabilities brought forth by GenAI and ML but also elevates the operational intelligence of cloud systems to new heights.

Predictive analytics and AIOps – redefining cloud resource management

The integration of predictive analytics with **AIOps** is the transformation of cloud management. By utilizing AI, cloud-native systems gain the capability to not just react to current issues but also foresee and address future problems. This shift empowers cloud environments to become more resilient, efficient, and self-managing, significantly enhancing operational intelligence. Predictive analytics enables the anticipation of system needs and optimization of resources, while AIOps evolves into more than just a maintenance tool – it becomes an active agent in continually improving system performance and stability, ushering in a new era of advanced and proactive cloud management.

To have a comprehensive image of AIOps, let's have a look at the following diagram:

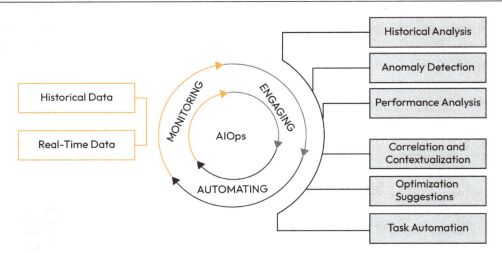

Figure 10.1 – Components of AIOps

Understanding the data life cycle and its pivotal role in AIOps is crucial for optimizing cloud management strategies. Let's examine the key stages, from data collection to actionable insights:

1. **Historical and real-time data analysis**: This is data that has been collected from the IT infrastructure over time. AIOps tools can use historical and real-time data to identify patterns and trends and to make predictions about future events.

2. **Anomaly detection**: After analyzing the data, the AI algorithm is able to identify unusual events or deviations from the established norms, indicating potential issues.

3. **Performance analysis**: This involves evaluating various metrics to assess the system's efficiency and identify areas for improvement.

4. **Correlation and contextualization**: Identify the main cause of issues and provide context for insights.

5. **Optimization suggestions**: Based on the analysis, the system recommends actions to improve system performance and prevent future problems.

6. **Task automation**: Closing the cycle, automation is the ability of AIOps to automate routine tasks, such as provisioning resources, resolving minor issues, and deploying updates.

Now, let's get into predictions on AI and ML and how they may influence cloud-native development in the coming years.

Predictions for AI and ML in cloud-native development

As we stand on the precipice of technological evolution, it's pivotal to forecast the profound influences AI and ML are poised to imprint on cloud-native development. This contemplation is not merely speculative; it's a foresight grounded in the rapid advancement we're witnessing today:

- **Automated code generation**: The dawn of AI in coding heralds a new epoch where the creation of code transcends human speed and accuracy, streamlining deployment cycles and diminishing the margin for error

- **Advanced security postures**: In the ceaseless battle against cyber threats, AI and ML emerge as sentinels, offering unprecedented real-time vigilance that will bolster the fortifications of cloud-native landscapes

- **Personalized user experiences**: AI's proficiency in distilling insights from user behavior promises to revolutionize the user experience, curating interactions that are as unique as the individual at the keyboard

- **Resource usage optimization**: ML stands as the steward of efficiency, ensuring resources are wielded with prudence that translates into tangible economic and operational benefits

- **Proactive system maintenance**: With predictive intelligence, AI is set to transform maintenance from a reactive to a proactive stance, ensuring the smoothest of sails in the often-turbulent digital seas

Strategic recommendations for embracing AI and ML in cloud-native development

The integration of AI and ML within the cloud-native paradigm isn't merely a technical upgrade–it's a strategic revolution. To navigate this transition, businesses must adopt a multifaceted strategy that interweaves technical acumen with visionary foresight. The recommendations are set out here:

- **Cultivate specialized AI talent**: Develop a robust talent pipeline by recruiting and nurturing a dedicated team of AI specialists, including data scientists, ML engineers, and AI architects. Prioritize continuous learning and development to stay ahead of the AI curve.

- **Data as a strategic keystone**: Elevate data to a core strategic asset by enhancing its quality, accessibility, and governance. Implement robust data management practices that enable seamless data flow and analytics, paving the way for informed decision-making and innovative AI applications.

- **Pilot with high-impact use cases**: Begin with targeted AI initiatives that promise a high **return on investment** (**ROI**). Focus on specific, measurable goals to demonstrate value and build momentum for wider AI adoption across the enterprise.

- **Foster an AI-inclusive culture**: Encourage an organizational culture that embraces AI, promoting cross-functional collaboration and proactive engagement with AI tools and methodologies.

- **Invest in scalable AI infrastructure**: Ensure that the technical infrastructure—computational power, storage, and networking—is scalable and flexible to support the growing demands of AI algorithms and large datasets.

- **Adopt AI-driven development practices**: Integrate AI into the **software development life cycle** (**SDLC**), from automated testing and code generation to deployment and monitoring, to enhance efficiency and reduce **time-to-market** (**TTM**).

- **Ensure ethical AI adoption**: Establish clear guidelines and ethical frameworks to guide the responsible use of AI, ensuring that AI systems are transparent, fair, and accountable.

By adhering to these strategic recommendations, organizations can forge a path toward a future where cloud-native development is synonymous with intelligent, adaptive, and highly responsive systems. The aim is not just to deploy AI but to embed it into the very fabric of the organization's cloud-native architecture, creating systems that are not only technologically advanced but also aligned with the broader business vision.

The emergence of serverless architecture and EDA

In this section, let's explore the genesis and growth of **Function as a Service** (**FaaS**) as a cornerstone of this shift, charting its impact on the cloud-native ecosystem and its symbiotic relationship with the latest advances in AI and ML.

The evolution and future of FaaS in cloud-native ecosystems

FaaS, a cornerstone of serverless computing, marks a pivotal shift in cloud-native ecosystems. It simplifies cloud architecture by abstracting server and infrastructure management, empowering developers to concentrate on discrete functions within their applications. This evolution signifies a move toward greater agility and scalability in application development. By enabling on-demand resource utilization, FaaS offers a more cost-effective model, only incurring costs for the actual execution time of functions. As the future unfolds, FaaS is expected to streamline cloud application development further, fostering innovations in how software is constructed, deployed, and scaled in cloud environments.

FaaS revolves around a series of principles to leverage its agility and cost-effectiveness. FaaS goes hand in hand with the microservices architecture, benefiting from its distributed and granular nature, allowing cloud-native applications to become decentralized processing units. FaaS is event-driven, an architecture we explored in detail in *Chapter 3, Designing for Diversity with Multi-Cloud Application Strategies*, meaning that functions can be triggered upon defined computer events. FaaS is then, by nature, cost-effective, as most FaaS providers facilitate pay-per-use billing systems, instantly removing the risk of over-provisioning cloud resources.

The future outlook

Looking ahead, FaaS is poised to become more integrated with AI and ML, enabling even more dynamic and intelligent cloud-native applications. We can anticipate advancements in FaaS that will further reduce latency, enhance performance, and offer more granular scalability options.

Real-time processing and IoT integration in multi-cloud environments

The combination of serverless architectures and the **Internet of Things** (**IoT**) in multi-cloud environments is revolutionizing how data is processed and analyzed. In this setup, serverless computing allows for flexible, on-demand processing of IoT-generated data. This means that data can be processed closer to where it's generated (at the edge), facilitating real-time analytics and responses. Such an approach is particularly beneficial for IoT applications requiring rapid decision-making, such as in smart city infrastructure or real-time monitoring systems. This integration represents a significant advancement in cloud computing, offering efficient, scalable, and timely data processing solutions.

Example

A notable example is the use of AWS Lambda for processing data from IoT sensors in real time. This setup allows for immediate data analysis and response, crucial in scenarios such as smart city infrastructure management, where real-time data processing is essential for traffic control, environmental monitoring, and emergency response.

Case studies of serverless architectures in large-scale applications

Serverless architectures benefit from the provision of ready-to-use servers by cloud providers who guarantee the maintenance and scalability of the underlying infrastructure. Developers can then containerize their applications and ship them to the cloud provider. Serverless architectures have been successfully implemented in large-scale applications, showcasing their scalability and efficiency.

Let's delve into real-world applications and explore how serverless architectures are not just theoretical concepts but practical solutions driving efficiency and innovation in well-known enterprises.

Example 1 – Netflix's serverless video encoding system

Netflix's video encoding system is a prime example of serverless architecture in action. By leveraging AWS Lambda, Netflix efficiently manages the encoding of thousands of hours of content, scaling resources up or down based on demand. This approach not only optimizes resource utilization but also accelerates the content delivery process.

References

Blog post: Scaling video encoding with serverless functions on AWS: `https://dashbird.io/blog/serverless-case-study-netflix/`

White paper: Building a highly scalable video encoding infrastructure at Netflix: `https://netflixtechblog.com/tagged/video-encoding`

Example 2 – Coca-Cola's serverless vending machine solutions

Coca-Cola implemented serverless technology to manage its vending machines' operations. Using Google Cloud's serverless platform, it can monitor and analyze data from machines worldwide in real time, optimizing restocking and maintenance operations.

The emergence of serverless architecture and EDA is revolutionizing cloud-native and multi-cloud environments. From the evolution of FaaS to the integration of real-time processing with IoT and the implementation in large-scale applications, these architectures are setting new standards for efficiency, scalability, and innovation in the cloud computing landscape. As we continue to explore these technologies, we are not just witnessing an evolution; we are part of a transformative movement that is reshaping the future of cloud computing.

References

Google Cloud Functions overview: `https://cloud.google.com/functions`

Case study: Coca-Cola optimizes operations with Google Cloud Functions: `https://dashbird.io/blog/serverless-case-study-coca-cola/`

Advanced security paradigms for cloud-native applications

In an era where boundaries are no longer defined by physical infrastructures, the paradigm of security is undergoing a radical transformation. Enter Zero Trust architecture – a model that fundamentally disrupts conventional security frameworks and fortifies the resilience of cloud-native and multi-cloud environments.

Reimagining security – the advent of Zero Trust in multi-cloud environments

The adoption of **Zero Trust** architectures in cloud-native and multi-cloud environments is revolutionizing security measures. This approach, grounded in the principle of "*never trust, always verify*," represents a significant shift from traditional perimeter-centric security models. Zero Trust emphasizes continuous verification of identity and privileges within a network rather than relying on static defenses. It requires robust **identity and access management** (**IAM**), real-time monitoring, and granular control over access to resources. This model is particularly relevant in multi-cloud environments where the traditional network perimeter is no longer applicable, making security a more dynamic and adaptive process.

If we observe closely the following diagram about Zero Trust architecture, we will see that it combines many of the concepts discussed throughout the book. The Zero Trust architecture is a multi-layered security approach for access control. The first layer is composed of **policy-**, **role-**, or **attribute-based access control** (**PBAC**, **RBAC**, and **ABAC**, respectively), examined in detail in *Chapter 5*, *Managing Security, Data, and Compliance on Multi-Cloud*, After that, IAM systems ensure authentication through **multi-factor authentication** (**MFA**) and grant access to the authorized segment of data, services, or other assets:

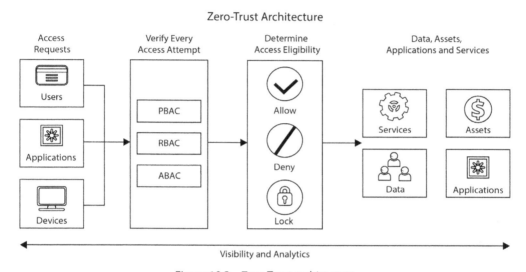

Figure 10.2 – Zero-Trust architecture

Innovative implementation – Zero Trust in a diverse cloud ecosystem

Imagine a scenario where an organization operates across AWS, Azure, and Google Cloud. In this diverse ecosystem, Zero Trust architecture becomes not just a choice but a necessity. Every access request, irrespective of its origin, undergoes rigorous authentication and authorization. Encryption is omnipresent, ensuring data integrity and confidentiality. This meticulous approach to security is particularly crucial in a multi-cloud setup, where the complexity and diversity of environments can otherwise lead to inconsistent security postures.

Harnessing AI and ML – the vanguard of cloud-native cybersecurity

The integration of AI and ML into cloud-native cybersecurity is not just an enhancement; it's a game-changer. These technologies bring forth an unprecedented ability to analyze, learn, and predict from vast datasets, offering a proactive shield against emerging cyber threats.

Let's illustrate the transformative impact of AI and ML in cybersecurity with a practical scenario that showcases how these technologies enhance **threat intelligence** (**TI**) and response across cloud-native platforms.

Case in point – AI-powered TI and response

Envision a cloud-native application that spans multiple cloud platforms. Here, AI-driven systems tirelessly monitor network traffic and user activities. They are adept at discerning patterns, identifying anomalies that signal potential threats, and initiating swift, automated responses. This could range from isolating a suspicious network segment to real-time alerts to security teams, thereby nipping cyber threats in the bud.

Navigating future security frontiers in cloud-native ecosystems

As we peer into the horizon of cloud-native security, several key focus areas emerge, each presenting its unique set of challenges and opportunities:

- **Robust data privacy mechanisms**: In an era where data is the new oil, ensuring its privacy becomes paramount. Future cloud-native applications will need to embed more robust data protection mechanisms, aligning with evolving global data privacy norms.

- **Automated compliance frameworks**: The complexity of cloud-native ecosystems necessitates automated solutions for maintaining compliance with an ever-expanding tapestry of security standards and regulations.

- **Quantum-resistant cryptography**: The dawn of QC heralds new threats to current cryptographic standards. Future security paradigms must evolve to include quantum-resistant algorithms, ensuring long-term data protection.

- **Unified security orchestration**: Managing security across a multi-cloud landscape demands a unified approach. Future solutions will likely converge toward integrated security management platforms, offering comprehensive visibility and control.

- **Securing the edge**: As cloud-native architectures increasingly intertwine with edge computing, securing these distributed nodes becomes a critical imperative.

In essence, the future of cloud-native application security is not just about fortifying defenses but about rethinking and reshaping these defenses to be more intelligent, adaptive, and integrated. As we venture into this future, we are not just responding to threats; we are preemptively architecting a more secure digital world.

With this comprehensive exploration of advanced security paradigms, we now turn our gaze to the next section. Stay tuned as we unravel how this nascent yet powerful technology is set to redefine the cloud computing ecosystem.

Quantum computing (QC) and its impact on cloud technologies

As we stand at the vanguard of technological innovation, QC emerges as a trailblazer with the potential to redefine the cloud computing landscape. This section will delve into how QC is poised to bring a paradigm shift in data processing, offering unprecedented computational power and the promise of solving complex problems that are currently beyond our grasp.

QC – revolutionizing the cloud landscape

The advent of QC will revolutionize the cloud computing landscape, representing a monumental leap forward from classical computing. QC introduces principles of quantum mechanics into computing, enabling the handling of complex problems at unprecedented speeds. This technology has the potential to vastly enhance data processing capabilities in the cloud, offering novel solutions to challenges that are currently insurmountable for classical computers. As QC continues to evolve, it's poised to redefine the future of cloud technology, opening new horizons for innovation and advanced problem-solving in various fields. Let's explore these groundbreaking advancements and what QC brings to the cloud ecosystem:

- **The quantum cloud – unleashing unprecedented power**

  Picture a cloud environment supercharged with QC capabilities. This quantum cloud will be capable of tackling problems of immense complexity, far beyond the reach of traditional computing methods. From optimizing global supply chains to unlocking mysteries in quantum physics, the quantum cloud will open doors to new realms of possibilities.

- **Quantum encryption – reinventing security in the cloud**

  Quantum encryption, rooted in quantum physics, is set to dramatically redefine security in the cloud. It leverages quantum mechanics, particularly the concept of **quantum key distribution (QKD)**, to create encryption systems that are theoretically immune to traditional hacking methods. Unlike classical encryption, which can potentially be cracked with enough computational power, quantum encryption's security is based on the fundamental laws of physics, making it exceptionally robust. This paradigm shift in encryption technology could provide unparalleled data protection in cloud environments, ensuring secure communication and data storage even against emerging sophisticated cyber threats.

- **QKD – a new era of security**

  Imagine a cloud-native application that employs QKD. In this scenario, encryption keys are transmitted using quantum states, which are inherently secure due to the laws of quantum mechanics. Any attempt at interception changes these states, making eavesdropping detectable. This quantum-enhanced security isn't just an improvement; it's a game-changer in protecting sensitive data in the cloud.

Example of QC

Let us take an example. Consider the field of pharmaceutical research. Traditionally, simulating the interaction of a new drug with various proteins requires vast amounts of computational power, often running for days or weeks on classical computers. QC, with its ability to process complex calculations at incredible speeds, can significantly reduce this time. This acceleration allows for quicker iterative testing, potentially bringing life-saving drugs to market much faster.

Yet, QC isn't always the go-to. For tasks such as web hosting or routine data analysis, classical cloud services are more cost-effective and accessible. QC's current high costs and specialized nature reserve its use for high-stakes scenarios where its speed can be game-changing. This demonstrates a clear example where QC's unique capabilities are leveraged for maximum impact, while traditional computing resources continue to handle the bulk of everyday processing tasks.

Navigating the quantum future in cloud computing

As we edge closer to integrating QC into cloud technologies, it's crucial to prepare for this transformative shift. This preparation involves several key strategies:

- **Building quantum-ready infrastructure**: Cloud providers need to start laying the groundwork for QC by developing infrastructure that can integrate with quantum technologies as they mature.

- **Cultivating quantum expertise**: The rise of QC will demand a workforce skilled in quantum technologies. Educational initiatives and training programs will be essential in cultivating this new talent pool.

- **Developing quantum-resistant cryptography**: With QC's potential to crack current cryptographic methods, there's an urgent need for quantum-resistant algorithms to protect data against future quantum threats.

- **Fostering collaborations**: The complexity of quantum technologies calls for partnerships between cloud providers, QC firms, and academia to drive innovation and practical applications.

- **Addressing ethical and regulatory issues**: QC introduces new challenges in data privacy and security. It's vital to establish ethical guidelines and regulatory frameworks to navigate these issues responsibly.

Strategic recommendations

As we stand on the brink of a quantum leap in cloud computing, it is imperative to chart a strategic course that will harness this emerging power effectively. Here, we outline a set of strategic recommendations designed to position organizations at the forefront of this technological revolution:

- **Initiate quantum-ready algorithms**: Organizations should begin experimenting with quantum-inspired algorithms to gain early insights into the quantum advantage, setting the stage for seamless integration when quantum supremacy becomes a practical reality.

- **Quantum-resilient cybersecurity**: It's critical to proactively evolve cybersecurity measures with quantum-resistant encryption methods, ensuring that data remains protected against the unprecedented computational abilities of quantum machines.

- **Cultivate quantum synergies**: Building robust collaborations between established **cloud service providers** (CSPs) and innovative QC start-ups through strategic partnerships and venture capital investments will be essential. This will create a fertile ground for quantum innovations to flourish within cloud ecosystems.

In essence, the fusion of QC with cloud technology is poised to revolutionize how we process information, secure data, and solve complex problems. This convergence is not just a mere addition to the cloud arsenal but a transformative force that will expand the horizons of what's achievable, ushering in a new epoch of computing that is profoundly capable, inherently secure, and brimming with untapped potential. As we move toward this quantum-inclusive future, we do so with the understanding that we are on the precipice of a computational renaissance.

Sustainable cloud computing – a new era

As we forge ahead into a future where technology intersects with ecological responsibility, *sustainable cloud computing – a new era* is emerging as a guiding principle. This pivotal movement goes beyond mere efficiency–it's about integrating sustainability into the very fabric of cloud computing. This section will shed light on how green computing is taking center stage in cloud-native development, embodying an innovative fusion of technological advancement with environmental ethics.

Green computing – the heart of future cloud-native development

In the evolving landscape of cloud computing, **green computing** has transitioned from a niche concern to a fundamental element in cloud-native development. This shift underscores the increasing recognition of technology's environmental impact and a resolute commitment to minimizing it. Green computing in cloud-native development involves strategies such as optimizing server efficiency, using renewable energy sources, designing energy-efficient software, and implementing environmentally conscious policies. This approach not only addresses environmental concerns but also aligns with a broader shift toward sustainable and responsible technology use, showcasing the tech industry's role in fostering a sustainable future.

The eco-friendly cloud – balancing technology with sustainability

Envision a future where cloud-native applications are not only efficient and scalable but also environmentally friendly. In this era, developers and companies prioritize eco-friendly practices, such as optimizing resource usage and reducing waste. Green computing becomes an integral part of the development life cycle, from design to deployment, ensuring that cloud-native applications contribute positively to environmental sustainability.

Energy-efficient strategies in multi-cloud infrastructures

In multi-cloud infrastructures, energy efficiency emerges as a pivotal aspect of sustainable cloud computing. As organizations utilize services from various cloud providers, the challenge is to harmonize energy consumption across these platforms. This involves strategies such as using energy-efficient hardware, optimizing data transfer and storage processes, and implementing software solutions that minimize resource waste. Cloud providers are increasingly focusing on renewable energy sources and more efficient data center designs to reduce the overall carbon footprint. For businesses, this shift toward energy efficiency in multi-cloud environments not only supports sustainability goals but also often leads to cost savings and enhanced system performance.

Innovative approaches to energy efficiency

Innovative approaches to energy efficiency in cloud computing include leveraging AI and ML to optimize resource allocation and reduce power consumption. By analyzing usage patterns and predicting demand, these systems can dynamically adjust the infrastructure, such as powering down unnecessary servers during low-usage periods. Additionally, implementing more energy-efficient hardware and transitioning to renewable energy sources helps minimize the carbon footprint. The combination of smart software and sustainable hardware represents a powerful strategy for achieving eco-friendly and cost-effective cloud operations.

Imagine multi-cloud infrastructures where AI and advanced analytics are used to monitor and optimize energy consumption. These systems can intelligently distribute workloads across different cloud environments based on energy efficiency, reducing the overall carbon footprint. Energy-efficient cloud computing is not just about reducing costs; it's about responsible resource utilization.

Remember – achieving carbon neutrality involves balancing emitted carbon with actions that remove an equivalent amount of carbon from the atmosphere. It's quantified by assessing emissions from all sources related to cloud infrastructure and operations. Then, it involves investing in renewable energy, efficiency technologies, or purchasing carbon credits to offset these emissions. In architecture, it drives decisions toward greener technologies and energy sourcing, affecting both the operational footprint and the end design of cloud services. It's a measurable commitment to sustainability, beyond monetary donations, impacting every architectural choice to favor eco-friendly alternatives.

Case studies of sustainable practices in cloud computing

The journey toward sustainable cloud computing is already underway, with several companies leading the charge through innovative practices.

Let's examine the real-world embodiment of sustainable principles in the cloud sector, highlighting trailblazing initiatives by industry leaders that exemplify commitment to eco-friendly technology and operations.

Case study – Microsoft's sustainability initiatives

Microsoft, for instance, has made significant strides in sustainable cloud computing. It has committed to being carbon-negative by 2030 and is investing in renewable energy sources to power its data centers. Microsoft's Azure cloud platform incorporates sustainability in its operations, demonstrating that environmental responsibility can go hand in hand with technological advancement.

For more details, you can check the following links:

- **Environmental Sustainability Report**: `https://www.microsoft.com/en-us/corporate-responsibility/sustainability/report`
- **Microsoft sustainability blog**: `https://www.microsoft.com/en-us/industry/blog/sustainability/`
- **Microsoft Cloud for Sustainability**: `https://www.microsoft.com/en-us/sustainability/cloud`

Case study – Google Cloud's carbon-neutral operations

Google Cloud has achieved carbon-neutral status for its global operations. By improving energy efficiency in its data centers and investing in renewable energy, Google Cloud sets a benchmark for sustainable cloud computing. Its commitment extends to helping customers track their carbon footprint, making sustainability a shared goal.

For more details, you can check the following links:

- **Environmental Report**: `https://sustainability.google/reports/`
- **Google Sustainability website**: `https://sustainability.google/`
- **Google Cloud sustainability**: `https://cloud.google.com/sustainability`

Strategic imperatives for a green cloud horizon

Organizations poised to pioneer in the era of green cloud computing must embrace a holistic strategy that not only signals their environmental commitment but actively advances it. Here's how they can achieve this:

- **Establish clear environmental objectives**: Set ambitious yet achievable targets for carbon emission reduction and renewable energy integration, creating a roadmap for the organization's sustainable transformation

- **Benchmark carbon efficiency**: Integrate carbon efficiency metrics into the core performance indicators for cloud infrastructure and design, ensuring that every system iteration contributes to the overall sustainability agenda

- **Pursue sustainability credentials**: Secure recognized sustainability certifications, underscoring the organization's dedication to **environmental, social, and governance (ESG)** excellence, reinforcing trust and transparency with stakeholders

These tailored recommendations aim to guide organizations in aligning their cloud computing practices with an environmentally conscious ethos that benefits not only the planet but also their operational and corporate identity.

Embracing a sustainable future in cloud computing

As we move forward, sustainable cloud computing will become increasingly important. Green computing, energy-efficient strategies, and a commitment to reducing environmental impact will be key drivers in the evolution of cloud-native and multi-cloud technologies. This shift toward sustainability is not just an ethical imperative; it's a strategic and operational advantage. By embracing sustainable practices, cloud computing can continue to grow and innovate in a way that is harmonious with our planet's health.

Next, we will explore the convergence of edge computing with cloud-native, examining how this integration is shaping the future of cloud computing and contributing to the development of more efficient, responsive, and sustainable cloud architectures.

The convergence of telco and edge computing with cloud-native

The integration of telecommunications and edge computing within cloud-native architectures is spearheading a technological revolution. This nexus is unleashing a new paradigm where the advanced capabilities of 5G networks are synergizing with edge computing to drive substantial gains in computing efficiency and application performance in cloud-native environments.

5G as a game-changer for edge-enhanced cloud applications

As we venture further into the future of cloud-native technologies, the convergence of telecommunications, particularly 5G and beyond, with edge computing stands out as a transformative trend. This synergy is poised to significantly enhance the capabilities of cloud-native applications, offering unprecedented speed, reduced latency, and enhanced connectivity.

Imagine a world where 5G networks provide the backbone for edge computing, enabling cloud-native applications to process data closer to the source. This integration allows for real-time data processing and decision-making, essential in scenarios such as autonomous vehicles, smart cities, and IoT-driven industries. The ultra-low latency and high bandwidth of 5G networks make it possible to leverage the full potential of edge computing, leading to more responsive and efficient cloud-native applications.

Managing distributed data in multi-cloud and edge environments

In a landscape where cloud-native applications span across multi-cloud and edge environments, managing distributed data becomes a critical challenge. The key lies in ensuring data consistency, availability, and security across these dispersed environments.

Strategies for seamless data management

The following are some strategies for seamless data management:

- **Implement distributed databases**: Use databases designed for distributed systems to ensure data integrity and accessibility across cloud and edge computing environments

- **Synchronize data across environments**: Employ advanced synchronization mechanisms that facilitate real-time data consistency across all nodes

- **Robust data governance**: Develop and enforce stringent data governance policies that define data ownership, access controls, and quality standards

- **Strong encryption protocols**: Apply strong encryption methods to safeguard data in transit and at rest, ensuring that even if data is intercepted, it remains secure

- **IAM**: Integrate comprehensive **identity management** (**IdM**) protocols to control who has access to what data, ensuring that only authorized entities can access sensitive information

- **Automated backup and recovery**: Establish automated backup processes and clear DR protocols to protect against data loss and ensure quick restoration of services

- **Monitoring and compliance tools**: Utilize tools for continuous monitoring of data and compliance with regulatory requirements, ensuring that data management practices meet legal and policy standards

Future trends in edge and cloud-native integrations

The integration of edge computing with cloud-native technologies is just beginning. Looking ahead, several trends are likely to shape this integration further:

- **AI-driven edge computing**: The future will see more AI and ML models being deployed at the edge, enabling smarter, context-aware applications that can process and analyze data locally.

- **Autonomous edge management**: As edge computing becomes more prevalent, there will be a shift toward autonomous management of edge devices and applications, leveraging AI for self-healing and self-optimizing systems.

- **Interoperability and standardization**: Ensuring interoperability between different cloud providers and edge devices will be crucial. This may lead to the development of new standards and protocols for edge computing.

- **Sustainable edge computing**: With the growing focus on sustainability, future edge computing solutions will prioritize energy efficiency and reduce environmental impact.

- **Edge as a Service (EaaS)**: The concept of EaaS will gain traction, where edge computing capabilities are offered as a scalable service by cloud providers, much as with SaaS, PaaS, and IaaS today.

The convergence of telco, particularly 5G and beyond, with edge computing marks a significant evolution in the cloud-native landscape. This convergence is set to unlock new capabilities, enhance application performance, and drive innovation in various sectors. As we embrace these advancements, the future of cloud-native applications looks more distributed, intelligent, and efficient than ever before.

Next, we will understand the integration of blockchain with cloud-native development. Get ready to explore how these two powerhouse technologies are merging to unlock unprecedented opportunities.

Blockchain integration with cloud-native development

Welcome to an insightful exploration of integrating blockchain technology with cloud-native development. This combination opens new frontiers in building secure, efficient, and transparent applications. Let's delve into how this integration enhances cloud-native ecosystems and the challenges it presents.

Understanding blockchain in a cloud-native context

Blockchain, essentially a digital ledger distributed across a vast network, offers unique benefits when integrated with cloud-native technologies. Each block in the blockchain contains a batch of transactions linked to form a chain, ensuring data integrity and traceability. Let's see some benefits of integrating blockchain with cloud-native.

Key benefits of blockchain integration

Some benefits include the following:

- **Enhanced data security and privacy**: Blockchain's cryptographic security mechanisms add a crucial layer of protection in cloud-native environments, safeguarding sensitive data against unauthorized access and breaches

- **Distributed and resilient architecture**: The decentralized nature of blockchain complements cloud-native architectures, enhancing **fault tolerance** (**FT**) and reducing **single points of failure** (**SPOFs**), crucial for uninterrupted services

- **Improved traceability and compliance**: Blockchain's immutable ledger is invaluable for tracking transactions and data changes, aiding in regulatory compliance and ensuring data integrity

- **Smart contract automation**: Blockchain's smart contracts automate processes in cloud-native ecosystems, from resource management to business logic execution, enhancing efficiency and consistency

- **Interoperability and standardization**: Blockchain fosters interoperability between different cloud platforms, using standardized protocols for seamless interactions across diverse environments

Practical use cases and examples

Now, it is time you understand the use of blockchain technology with some examples and practical use cases:

- **Supply chain management (SCM) in cloud-native systems**: In a cloud-native environment, SCM applications can leverage blockchain for enhanced traceability and security.

  For instance, a cloud-native application for pharmaceutical SCM can use blockchain to securely record and track each step of a medicine's journey. This ensures data integrity and transparency across the supply chain, which is particularly important in distributed cloud environments where data and services are spread across multiple locations.

- **IAM in cloud-native applications**: Blockchain can be integrated into cloud-native IAM solutions to provide a more secure and decentralized approach to identity verification.

  In cloud-native banking applications, blockchain can be used to create a tamper-proof, decentralized ledger of customer identities. This enhances security and privacy, as blockchain's immutable nature makes it extremely difficult for identity data to be altered or stolen.

- **Decentralized finance (DeFi) and cloud-native platforms**: DeFi applications, built on blockchain, align well with cloud-native principles such as scalability, resilience, and continuous delivery.

  Cloud-native development allows DeFi applications to be scalable and highly available, catering to a global user base. The decentralized nature of blockchain complements this by providing a secure, transparent foundation for financial transactions without central intermediaries.

Addressing challenges and considerations

In navigating the complexities of integrating blockchain with cloud-native architectures, we must address several pivotal challenges and considerations. Let's dissect these key areas to ensure successful and efficient use cases:

- **Technical complexity**: Integrating blockchain with cloud-native architectures demands expertise in both domains, ensuring effective interaction between blockchain networks, microservices, and cloud-native tools such as Kubernetes.

- **Scalability and performance**: Balancing cloud-native scalability with blockchain's transaction processing speed is challenging, especially in public blockchains. Decisions on on-chain versus off-chain data processing significantly impact performance and costs.

- **Regulatory and legal aspects**: Navigating the evolving regulatory landscape, especially concerning data privacy and blockchain's immutable, decentralized nature, is crucial for compliance.

By understanding these benefits, use cases, and challenges, we can appreciate the transformative potential of blockchain integration in cloud-native development, paving the way for more secure, efficient, and innovative digital solutions.

The future outlook

As blockchain and cloud-native development continue to mature, their integration will become increasingly commonplace, fostering a new era of trust, transparency, and innovation in various industries. By staying informed about the latest advancements and overcoming existing challenges, we can unlock the full potential of this powerful combination.

Up next, we delve into the rise of LC/NC (Low-code and No-code) platforms for cloud-native development. Discover how these intuitive platforms are revolutionizing application developments.

The rise of LC/NC platforms

LC/NC platforms are innovative software development tools designed to simplify and accelerate the application development process. These platforms are revolutionizing the field of software engineering by enabling individuals, even those with minimal or no coding experience, to build and deploy applications efficiently. In this evolving landscape of cloud-native development, LC/NC platforms are emerging as game-changers.

LC/NC platforms in modern application developments

LC/NC platforms are increasingly playing a pivotal role in cloud-native development, offering a suite of tools and capabilities that significantly enhance the development process in a cloud environment. Here are some of their benefits:

- **Empowering citizen developers in the cloud**: LC/NC platforms empower citizen developers – those with limited or no coding experience – to create and deploy cloud-based applications. These platforms provide user-friendly, visual interfaces with drag-and-drop tools and pre-built components, making it feasible for a broader range of users to contribute to cloud application development. This democratization of development aligns perfectly with the cloud's accessibility and scalability.

- **Accelerating cloud-native development speed**: The pre-built modules and automation capabilities of LC/NC platforms drastically reduce development time, a crucial advantage in the fast-paced cloud-native ecosystem. These platforms enable rapid prototyping and deployment, allowing businesses to swiftly adapt and respond to market demands and technological advancements in the cloud.

- **Fostering collaboration and agile development**: Holistically, LC/NC platforms enhance collaboration between technical and non-technical teams, breaking down traditional barriers. This collaborative environment fosters agile development practices, encouraging faster iteration cycles and continuous improvement – principles at the heart of cloud-native development.

- **Cost-efficiency in cloud-native projects**: By reducing reliance on extensive developer resources and complex code bases, LC/NC platforms offer a cost-effective solution for application developers. This aspect is particularly beneficial for organizations looking to leverage the cloud's capabilities without incurring substantial development and operational costs.

Challenges and considerations

The integration of LC/NC platforms in cloud-native development brings unique challenges and considerations that need to be carefully addressed:

- **Security and control in a cloud environment**: In cloud-native development, security concerns are paramount. While LC/NC platforms can expedite development, it's crucial to thoroughly assess their security features, especially when dealing with sensitive data in the cloud. Questions about data encryption, user access control, and compliance with cloud security standards become vital. Additionally, understanding the vendor's track record in handling security in a cloud context is essential to ensure enterprise-grade protection.

- **Scalability and customization limitations**: Cloud-native applications often require scalability to handle varying workloads. While LC/NC platforms provide a level of scalability, they may not always match the granular control and flexibility offered by traditional coding, particularly for complex, large-scale cloud applications. Balancing the ease of use of LC/NC platforms with the need for advanced customization and scalability is a critical consideration in cloud-native development.

- **Integration with cloud ecosystems and existing systems**: Seamless integration with existing cloud services and legacy systems is another crucial factor. LC/NC platforms should be compatible with the organization's current cloud infrastructure, including various cloud services, APIs, and microservices architectures. Ensuring that these platforms can easily connect with existing databases, authentication systems, and other enterprise tools is essential for creating a cohesive cloud-native ecosystem.

- **Vendor lock-in and flexibility**: Choosing an LC/NC platform often ties an organization to a specific vendor's ecosystem. This can lead to challenges in migrating to different platforms in the future. Evaluating the flexibility of these platforms, including the ability to export and import workflows and data, is important to avoid vendor lock-in, especially in a cloud-native environment that values agility and adaptability.

Addressing these challenges and considerations is key to successfully leveraging LC/NC platforms in cloud-native development, ensuring that they not only simplify the development process but also align with the broader goals of cloud-native strategies.

The future outlook

LC/NC platforms are poised to become essential in streamlining the creation of modern softwares.

Also, the combination of generative AI and LC/NC platforms represents a significant leap forward in democratizing technology and the cloud-native ecosystem. As these platforms become more sophisticated, they will enable businesses of all sizes to harness the power of AI, creating more intelligent, responsive, and efficient applications with ease. This synergy not only simplifies the development process but also opens up new possibilities for innovation, making advanced technology accessible to a broader audience.

As we embrace the simplicity and efficiency of LC/NC platforms, we also turn our attention to cloud-native governance and compliance in the future. This next section will explore how evolving regulatory landscapes and technological advancements are shaping governance and compliance strategies in the dynamic world of cloud-native and multi-cloud environments.

Cloud-native governance and compliance in the future

As we advance, the lattice of governance and compliance will become increasingly intricate. This section is poised to dissect forthcoming challenges and opportunities as we stride into an era where regulatory landscapes are not just changing but converging with advanced technologies. We will delve into the transformative strategies that organizations must embrace to stay compliant in a world where data privacy laws, such as the **General Data Protection Regulation** (**GDPR**) and the **California Consumer Privacy Act** (**CCPA**), dictate a new order of operational conduct and where AI and ML become instrumental in navigating the complex currents of compliance management.

Navigating evolving regulatory landscapes

In the future, we can expect these regulations to become more complex and far-reaching, impacting how cloud-native applications are developed, deployed, and managed. The key challenge will be to stay agile and compliant amid these ever-changing regulatory demands.

Adapting to global data privacy laws

Consider the implications of global data privacy laws such as the GDPR in Europe or the CCPA in California. Cloud-native applications will need to be designed with privacy and data protection at their core, ensuring compliance across different jurisdictions. This will involve not just technical measures but also a deep understanding of various legal frameworks and their implications on data handling and processing.

Automated compliance and governance tools

To manage the complexities of compliance in cloud-native environments, the future will see a greater reliance on automated tools. These tools will use AI and ML to monitor, analyze, and ensure compliance across various aspects of cloud-native applications.

AI-driven compliance management

Imagine a scenario where an AI-driven tool continuously scans cloud-native environments for compliance with various standards and regulations. It automatically adjusts configurations, updates policies, and even generates compliance reports, significantly reducing the manual effort and complexity involved in maintaining compliance.

Best practices for maintaining compliance in dynamic environments

Maintaining compliance in dynamic cloud-native environments will require a set of best practices that are adaptable, scalable, and efficient, as follows:

- **Continuous compliance monitoring**: Implementing continuous monitoring mechanisms to ensure ongoing compliance with regulatory requirements. This involves real-time scanning and auditing of cloud-native environments.

- **Policy-as-code (PaC)**: Adopting a PaC approach, where compliance policies are codified and automatically enforced across the cloud-native ecosystem. This ensures consistency and reduces the risk of human error.

- **Collaboration between development and compliance teams**: Encouraging closer collaboration between developers and compliance teams to ensure that compliance is integrated into the development process rather than being an afterthought.

- **Regular training and awareness**: Conducting regular training sessions and awareness programs for all stakeholders involved in cloud-native development and deployment to keep them updated on the latest regulatory requirements and best practices.

- **Leveraging cloud provider expertise**: Utilizing the expertise and tools provided by CSPs to enhance compliance efforts. Many providers offer specialized services and tools designed to help with regulatory compliance.

Remember – as cloud-native technologies advance, governance and compliance will remain critical components. The future of cloud-native governance and compliance lies in leveraging automated tools, adopting best practices, and staying adaptable to the evolving regulatory landscape. By doing so, organizations can ensure that their cloud-native applications are not only innovative and efficient but also secure and compliant.

With our exploration of cloud-native governance and compliance complete, we now turn our attention to the next section. This section will summarize potential advancements and challenges and inspire a forward-looking mindset among cloud professionals.

Conclusion – preparing for a cloud-native future

As we reach the zenith of our exploration into the evolving universe of cloud-native and multi-cloud technologies, it's time to distill our insights, confront challenges on the horizon, and gear up for a future that is as exhilarating as it is transformative.

Envisioning the future – a tapestry of advancements and challenges

Our journey has unveiled a future where advancements in cloud-native technologies are not just incremental improvements but paradigm-shifting innovations. The integration of AI and ML promises to endow cloud-native applications with unprecedented intelligence and autonomy. QC's entry into cloud environments heralds a new epoch of computational power, capable of solving complex problems in moments. Serverless architectures and EDAs are poised to redefine efficiency and scalability, while the ethos of sustainable cloud computing ensures that our technological strides are in harmony with environmental stewardship.

Yet, these advancements bring forth a constellation of challenges. The intricacies of multi-cloud management, the imperative of robust security and compliance across diverse ecosystems, and the relentless pace of technological evolution call for unwavering vigilance and proactive strategies. Navigating this landscape will demand more than technical acumen; it will require a holistic understanding of the broader implications of these technologies.

The imperative of continuous learning and adaptation

In this ever-shifting terrain, the ability to continuously learn and adapt is not just an asset; it's a necessity. For cloud professionals, this means embracing a culture of perpetual growth and intellectual curiosity.

The following table explores the possibilities of how AI redefines key aspects of resource management, infrastructure maintenance, and application development, leading to smarter, more efficient, and cost-effective cloud solutions:

Cloud computing aspect	AI's transformative impact	Example
Resource management	Enables dynamic resource allocation, optimizing cloud performance and cost-efficiency.	An AI system dynamically scales server resources for an e-commerce site during high-traffic events such as Black Friday, ensuring smooth performance without overspending.
Infrastructure maintenance	Predictive AI algorithms reduce downtime by proactively scheduling maintenance and anticipating failures.	AI can analyze server health data to predict and prevent a critical database server failure, scheduling maintenance before it impacts users.
Application development	Accelerates app development, reducing time and errors through code generation and automated security updates.	An AI tool can automatically generate secure, efficient backend code for a new mobile app, significantly speeding up the development process.
Data analysis	Advanced AI analytics unlock deep insights from cloud data, driving smarter business decisions.	Processing customer data from a cloud-based CRM to identify emerging market trends, helping a company tailor its marketing strategy.
Security and compliance	Enhances cloud security and compliance monitoring, proactively identifying and addressing risks.	An AI-powered security system detects unusual network patterns indicative of a cyber attack and automatically initiates protective measures.
Serverless computing	Optimizes serverless architectures for efficient resource use and performance scaling.	AI can manage a serverless cloud function, automatically adjusting its resources based on real-time user demand during a marketing campaign.

Cloud computing aspect	AI's transformative impact	Example
DevOps practices	Automates DevOps processes, from testing to CI/CD, ensuring faster and more reliable software delivery.	Integrating an AI system into a CI/CD pipeline automatically tests new code commits, identifies bugs, and suggests optimizations before deployment.
Multi-cloud management	Simplifies managing workloads across multiple cloud environments, enhancing operational efficiency.	Intelligently distributes workloads between AWS and Azure, optimizing for cost and performance based on real-time cloud service metrics.
User experience	Personalizes cloud services and interfaces, improving user engagement and satisfaction.	An AI-driven cloud service customizes its UI for each user, adapting to their preferences and usage patterns for a better experience.
Cost optimization	Provides strategic recommendations for cost savings, making cloud expenses more manageable.	AI can be leveraged to analyze and predict usage patterns automatically across cloud services to recommend cost-saving measures, such as downscaling underutilized resources or choosing more cost-effective options.

Table 10.2 – AI transformation in key aspects of cloud computing

Championing lifelong learning

The future belongs to those who are prepared to continually expand their knowledge and skills, staying abreast of emerging technologies and methodologies. This commitment to lifelong learning can take many forms – from formal education and certifications to self-directed study, participation in professional communities, and hands-on experimentation.

Useful learning resources include the following:

- **Cloud-Native Computing Foundation (CNCF) training**

  - **Website**: `https://www.cncf.io/training/courses/`
  - **CNCF Kubernetes certification (CKA)**: `https://www.cncf.io/training/certification/cka/`

- **Free training courses**: `https://training.linuxfoundation.org/`

  - **Examples**:

  - **Introduction to Kubernetes**: `https://kubernetes.io/docs/tutorials/kubernetes-basics/`

  - **Cloud-native service mesh fundamentals**: `https://training.linuxfoundation.org/training/cloud-native-logging-with-fluentd-lfs242/`

- AWS training courses

  - **Website**: `https://aws.amazon.com/training/`

  - **AWS Certified Solutions Architect – Professional**: `https://aws.amazon.com/certification/certified-solutions-architect-professional/`

  - **AWS Certified Developer – Associate**: `https://aws.amazon.com/certification/certified-developer-associate/`

  - **AWS Certified DevOps Engineer – Professional**: `https://aws.amazon.com/certification/certified-devops-engineer-professional/`

  - **AWS Certified Solutions Architect – Associate**: `https://aws.amazon.com/certification/certified-solutions-architect-associate/`

  - **Free courses**: `https://aws.amazon.com/free/`

    - **AWS Certified Solutions Architect – Associate**: `https://aws.amazon.com/certification/certified-solutions-architect-associate/`

    - **AWS Cloud Practitioner Essentials**: `https://aws.amazon.com/training/classroom/aws-cloud-practitioner-essentials/`

- Microsoft Azure certifications

  - **Website**: `https://learn.microsoft.com/en-us/credentials/`

  - **Azure Solutions Architect Expert**: `https://learn.microsoft.com/en-us/credentials/certifications/azure-solutions-architect/`

  - **Azure Developer Associate**: `https://learn.microsoft.com/en-us/credentials/certifications/azure-developer/`

  - **Azure DevOps Engineer Expert**: `https://learn.microsoft.com/en-us/credentials/certifications/devops-engineer/`

- **Azure Cloud Engineer Associate**: `https://learn.microsoft.com/en-us/credentials/`

- **Free courses**: `https://learn.microsoft.com/en-us/training/topics/universities`

- **Examples**:

  - **AZ-104 Azure Administrator Associate**: `https://learn.microsoft.com/en-us/training/career-paths/administrator`

  - **AZ-900 Azure Fundamentals**: `https://learn.microsoft.com/en-us/training/paths/microsoft-azure-fundamentals-describe-cloud-concepts/`

- **Google Cloud certification program**

  - **Website**: `https://cloud.google.com/learn/training/`

  - **Professional Cloud Architect**: `https://cloud.google.com/learn/certification/cloud-architect`

  - **Professional Cloud Developer**: `https://cloud.google.com/learn/certification/cloud-developer`

  - **Professional Cloud DevOps Engineer**: `https://cloud.google.com/learn/certification/cloud-devops-engineer`

  - **Associate Cloud Engineer**: `https://cloud.google.com/learn/certification/cloud-engineer`

  - **Google Cloud Fundamentals**: `https://www.coursera.org/learn/gcp-fundamentals`

  - **Free courses**: `https://www.cloudskillsboost.google/`

    - **Examples**:

    - **Google Certified Cloud Architect**: `https://www.cloudskillsboost.google/paths/12`

    - **Google Cloud Fundamentals**: `https://www.coursera.org/learn/gcp-fundamentals`

- **General Cloud Development Courses and resources – Basic to Advance**

  - **For Beginners**:

    - **Udacity - Cloud Native Foundations Nanodegree**: `https://www.udacity.com/course/cloud-native-application-architecture-nanodegree--nd064`

- **Coursera - Developing Cloud Native Applications**: `https://www.coursera.org/learn/getting-started-app-development`

- **Linux Foundation - Introduction to Kubernetes (CNF)**: `https://www.edx.org/learn/kubernetes/the-linux-foundation-introduction-to-kubernetes`

- **For Intermediate Learners**:

  - **A Cloud Guru - Certified Kubernetes Application Developer (CKAD)**: `https://learn.acloud.guru/course/certified-kubernetes-application-developer/overview`

  - **Pivotal - Modernizing Applications for Cloud Native Delivery**: `https://www.pluralsight.com/courses/cloud-foundry-developer-1dot7-pivotal`

  - **Kubernetes Academy - Certified Kubernetes Security Specialist (CKS)**: `https://kube.academy/`

- **Additional Resources**:

  - **CNCF Learning Resources**: `https://www.cncf.io/`

  - **The Serverless Ledger**: `https://aws.amazon.com/qldb/`

  - **Microservices.io**: `https://microservices.io/patterns/`

- **Developing and Deploying Containerized Applications**: `https://www.pluralsight.com/courses/deploying-containerized-applications`

- **Serverless Computing for Developers**: `https://training.serverlessguru.com/`

- **Cloud Native Security Foundation**: `https://www.cncf.io/training/courses/`

- **Cloud Native Continuous Integration and Delivery**: `https://www.cloudbees.com/capabilities/continuous-integration`

Remember – these are just starting points. Consider your specific learning goals and experience level when choosing courses and certifications.

Cultivating a forward-looking mindset

As we stand on the brink of this new era, fostering a forward-looking mindset among cloud professionals is paramount. This mindset is characterized by an eagerness to explore uncharted territories, a readiness to rethink conventional paradigms, and a resilience to adapt to the unexpected.

Innovation as a guiding star

The future of cloud computing will be shaped by those who dare to innovate, who are not afraid to challenge the status quo, and who view every problem as an opportunity for creative solutions. Encouraging such a culture of innovation will be crucial in harnessing the transformative potential of cloud-native technologies.

Bracing for the unforeseen

Perhaps the most defining aspect of preparing for a cloud-native future is developing the agility to navigate the unknown. It's about building a professional ethos that is as flexible as it is robust, capable of responding to emerging challenges and seizing new opportunities.

Summary

In summing up, the journey into the future of cloud-native and multi-cloud technologies is one of extraordinary possibilities and significant challenges. As we embark on this path, our success will hinge on our ability to continually learn, to innovate with purpose, and to foster a mindset that looks beyond the horizon. This journey is not just about keeping pace with change; it's about leading it and shaping the future of cloud computing with vision, expertise, and an unwavering commitment to excellence.

With this comprehensive and forward-looking conclusion, we close our exploration of the future outlook for cloud-native and multi-cloud technologies. This chapter has not only illuminated the path ahead but also equipped you with insights, strategies, and the mindset to navigate and influence this dynamic and exciting future.

Index

Other Books You May Enjoy

If you enjoyed this book, you may be interested in these other books by Packt:

Technology Operating Models for Cloud and Edge

Ahilan Ponnusamy, Andreas Spanner, Mirco Hering, Vincent Caldeira, Neetan Chopra

ISBN: 978-1-83763-139-1

- Get a holistic view of technology operating models and linked organization goals, strategy, and teams
- Overcome challenges of extending tech operating models to distributed cloud and edge environments
- Discover key architectural considerations in building operating models
- Explore the benefits of using enterprise-ready open-source products
- Understand how open hybrid cloud and modern dev and ops practices improve outcomes

Azure for Developers

Kamil Mrzygłód

ISBN: 978-1-80324-009-1

- Identify the Azure services that can help you get the results you need

- Implement PaaS components – Azure App Service, Azure SQL, Traffic Manager, CDN, Notification Hubs, and Azure Cognitive Search

- Work with serverless components

- Integrate applications with storage

- Put together messaging components (Event Hubs, Service Bus, and Azure Queue Storage)

- Use Application Insights to create complete monitoring solutions

- Secure solutions using Azure RBAC and manage identities

- Develop fast and scalable cloud applications

Packt is searching for authors like you

If you're interested in becoming an author for Packt, please visit `authors.packtpub.com` and apply today. We have worked with thousands of developers and tech professionals, just like you, to help them share their insight with the global tech community. You can make a general application, apply for a specific hot topic that we are recruiting an author for, or submit your own idea.

Share Your Thoughts

Now you've finished *Multi-Cloud Handbook for Developers*, we'd love to hear your thoughts! Scan the QR code below to go straight to the Amazon review page for this book and share your feedback or leave a review on the site that you purchased it from.

`https://packt.link/r/1-804-61870-5`

Your review is important to us and the tech community and will help us make sure we're delivering excellent quality content.

Download a free PDF copy of this book

Thanks for purchasing this book!

Do you like to read on the go but are unable to carry your print books everywhere?

Is your eBook purchase not compatible with the device of your choice?

Don't worry, now with every Packt book you get a DRM-free PDF version of that book at no cost.

Read anywhere, any place, on any device. Search, copy, and paste code from your favorite technical books directly into your application.

The perks don't stop there, you can get exclusive access to discounts, newsletters, and great free content in your inbox daily

Follow these simple steps to get the benefits:

1. Scan the QR code or visit the link below

https://packt.link/free-ebook/978-1-80461-870-7

2. Submit your proof of purchase
3. That's it! We'll send your free PDF and other benefits to your email directly

www.ingramcontent.com/pod-product-compliance
Lightning Source LLC
Chambersburg PA
CBHW080629060326
40690CB00021B/4870